MARRIAGE AND FAMILY THERAPY:
A SOCIOCOGNITIVE APPROACH

Nathan Hurvitz, PhD, MSW
Roger A. Straus, PhD

SOME ADVANCE REVIEWS

"This book has been in the works for a long time and represents the most fully developed sociological approach to marriage and family therapy. I highly recommend it to both the student of marital and family therapy, as well as to the advanced practitioner interested in integrating new concepts into his or her work."

Ronald F. Levant, EdD
Associate Professor
Program in Counseling Development
Rutgers University
New Brunswick, New Jersey

"The brain-child of Nathan Hurvitz would have died with him had not Dr. Straus taken care of its survival. Thanks to his patient dedication, we have a milestone in family therapy. Hurvitz's work with families, within their larger sociocultural systems, here faithfully presented, has much to teach all of us who are concerned about effective family therapy. I wonder if good family therapy can be less than what Hurvitz, thanks to Dr. Straus, models for us in this refreshing book."

Daniel L. Araoz, EdD
Professor of Mental Health Counseling
CW Post Center
Long Island University
Brookville, New York

Marriage and Family Therapy
A Sociocognitive Approach

Marriage and Family Therapy
A Sociocognitive Approach

Nathan Hurvitz, PhD
Roger A. Straus, PhD

The Haworth Press
New York • London • Sydney

The Haworth Press, Inc., 10 Alice Street, Binghamton, NY 13904-1580
EUROSPAN/Haworth, 3 Henrietta Street, London WC2E 8LU England
ASTAM/Haworth, 162-168 Parramatta Road, Stanmore (Sydney), N.S.W. 2048 Australia

Library of Congress Cataloging-in-Publication Data

Marriage and family therapy : a sociocognitive approach / Nathan Hurvitz, Roger A. Straus.
       p.   cm.
   Includes bibliographical references and index.
   ISBN 1-56024-060-1 (acid free paper). — ISBN 1-56024-061-X (pbk.)
   1. Marital psychotherapy. 2. Family psychotherapy. I. Straus, Roger A. (Roger Austin),
1948- . II. Title.
RC488.5.H87 1991
616.89′156 — dc20   90-25788
                                                                              CIP

Dedicated to Faye Hurvitz

CONTENTS

ABOUT THE AUTHORS

Nathan Hurvitz (1915-1986), PhD, MSW, held California licenses as a psychologist, marriage and family counselor, and clinical social worker. The author of over 40 articles in scholarly and professional journals, he was widely recognized not only for his sociocognitive approach to marriage and family therapy, but also as a pioneer in the field of peer self-help groups and for his contributions to radical psychotherapy. Dr. Hurvitz received his doctorate in sociology from the University of Southern California, specializing in marriage and family counseling.

Roger A. Straus, PhD, is an internationally renowned clinical sociologist and co-founder of the Sociological Practice Association. He taught for several years at Alfred University, and since 1986 has been conducting applied research as a senior study director with the National Analysts Division of Booz•Allen & Hamilton. He is the author of more than a dozen articles in professional journals, the textbook *Using Sociology: An Introduction From the Clinical Perspective* (General-Hall, 1985), the best selling *Strategic Self-Hypnosis* (Prentice-Hall Press, Rev. Ed., 1988), and most recently, *Creative Self-Hypnosis* (Prentice-Hall Press, 1989), which is currently being translated into Japanese. Dr. Straus received his doctorate in sociology from the University of California at Davis.

Senior Editor's Comments

When I first received the prospectus for this book from Roger A. Straus I was frankly unsure if it could be "pulled off." After all, writing a book about the clinical work of another person is a very difficult task. Except for some notable exceptions, such as Jay Haley's *Uncommon Therapy*, I have found these third person style books either overly cumbersome to read, or sickeningly aggrandizing, almost hero-worshipping.

I decided to go with the book, despite my reservations, for what I considered to be some very important reasons. First, Nathan Hurvitz, although quite well known in the field of clinical sociology, is a relatively obscure name to the vast majority of family clinicians. This is an unfortunate situation stemming from professionals' tendency to read from a narrow band within their own discipline, rather than sample the breadth of knowledge from related fields. It is too bad, also, because during his 35 years of practice Nathan Hurvitz became known among clinical sociologists as one of the masters of marital and family therapy.

Another reason I wanted this book to be part of *HAWORTH Marriage and the Family* is that it is immensely practical. It offers a step-by-step method of assessment and change for couples and families. These methods have been especially useful when dealing with working-class and underprivileged groups. Hurvitz's cognitive-social behavioral approach is a fascinating marriage of modern sociological theory with contemporary psychological concepts. The result is a model which takes into account the societal origins of clients' problems and aggressively intervenes for change.

A third reason I decided to include this book in our program is that, frankly, the early chapters that I read were so well written, so engaging, that I could not put them down. Roger Straus, himself an internationally renowned clinical sociologist, is also a fine writer who can make even theoretical material interesting and exciting to read. Dr. Straus is the author of numerous articles in professional journals; the textbook *Using Sociology: An Introduction* (General-Hall, 1985); the best-selling book, *Strategic Self-Hypnosis* (Prentice-Hall, 1982, revised edition in press); and the forthcoming *Creative Self-Hypnosis* (Prentice-Hall, in press).

When the final manuscript arrived, I was more than pleased to see that I had made the right decision. The book is great! Dr. Straus presented the work of Nathan Hurvitz in a way that was extremely readable, and more important useful. It is wonderfully written, well organized, and filled with fascinating clinical examples. And family clinicians unfamiliar with the clinical sociological approach to family therapy are in for a treat, as this approach to conceptualizing and treating families is unique and highly usable.

I hope you enjoy *Marriage and Family Therapy: A Sociocognitive Approach* as much as I did. I would appreciate any comments about this or other books in our program, along with the types of books you would like to see published in the future.

Terry S. Trepper, PhD
Senior Editor
HAWORTH Marriage and the Family

Foreword

For some time I have followed Nathan Hurvitz's efforts to apply symbolic interaction concepts to clinical practice. I have read his articles in sociological and psychological journals and have found them to be very perceptive statements, showing a discriminating and thoughtful application of the point of view we call symbolic interactionism. I have also been impressed with his ability to compress the complexity of the symbolic interactionist scheme into a short account without sacrificing its essential features.

I am therefore pleased that Dr. Hurvitz has written this book about marital and family therapy. It integrates concepts, principles, and practices derived from symbolic interaction and is based on his many years of clinical experience. This book is thus one of a growing number of publications which report on the application of symbolic interactionism to social practice.

As Dr. Hurvitz correctly notes, George Herbert Mead may be considered the "father of American cognitive psychology." However, Mead's social behaviorism is an even more dynamic cognitive approach than those employed by most cognitive psychologists. In Mead's view, cognitions do not necessarily lead to particular actions but rather become the elements that an individual examines, analyzes, and evaluates, and from which he or she "chooses" before taking a particular action. Cognitions, attitudes, attributions, personal psychologies or perceptions do not determine an individual's behavior but all of these play a part in the definition of the situation within which his or her behavior, cognitions and affect are demonstrated.

Although I cannot evaluate the clinical judgments and practices

---

Note: This Foreword was written by Herbert Blumer to appear in this book's original version (before Nathan Hurvitz's death).

reported by Dr. Hurvitz, I regard his work as a significant beginning application of Mead's social behaviorism to clinical practice. I
trust others will utilize and build upon this pioneering effort.

Herbert Blumer
Professor Emeritus
University of California, Berkeley

Preface

It is a rare pleasure to greet the publication of this book on family therapy by Nate Hurvitz and Roger Straus. Hurvitz occupies an honorable place in the field of family and marriage therapy and this book well expresses his particular, significant contribution. I am particularly grateful to Roger Straus for "midwifing," to use his term, the well-deserved appearance of this work. His editing, updating, and additions to the text have added greatly to its value.

The publication of this book has a special meaning, not only because of its valuable technical content, but also because of the unusual qualities of Nate Hurvitz as a professional and as a human being. Nate was an original and independent person, who farmed his own patch. He was not a member of the academic inner circles or the conference/workshop world that developed around family and marriage therapy. Yet Nate's work has been very influential in largely unacknowledged ways. Without an academic appointment or career, he published a series of important papers in professional journals; papers which were and continue to be widely read, cited, and used in professional educational programs. For more than thirty years through his full-time private practice, he engaged on the front lines of daily work with troubled people. For a good part of those years, he worked mostly with Jewish and black clients and their families. Working in a depressed area of Los Angeles, he maintained his commitment to be of service to people in need. He did this, continuing his heavy work and writing schedules, in the face of a serious and long-standing heart condition. Nate considered himself a radical therapist concerned with understanding his clients in broad socioeconomic contexts. This understanding recognized the need for extensive social reform which led him to formulate the "radical therapy" component of his sociocognitive approach and to help move people in that social reform direction.

These qualities in Nate's work stimulated me to contact him and to correspond with him over a good number of years. We only met a few times, yet I retain a vivid picture of him as a very real, open, warm, modest person; a devoted family man; a brilliant, dedicated helper; and a man of great moral and intellectual integrity.

Nate was an innovative, creative thinker and practitioner, a rare blend of theoretician and practical performer. The types of people and problems he was asked to help with called for imaginative, inventive responses. The realistic and sound theoretic framework for his work was shaped and tempered by his extensive practice experience with lower-class black, and Hispanic clients. He developed new methods and procedures that were suitable and effective for his clientele, yet had an evident universal applicability. For example, interactive, terminal, and instrumental hypotheses and their use in helping spouses develop a common definition of their situation is a particularly interesting and fertile way of helping resolve conflicting expectations and interpretations in marital and family relationships. This procedure expresses a sociocognitive approach that is as valid as those of cognitive and rational emotive therapies developed at a later time. As is evident in the many case excerpts given in this book, Nate had an exceptional gift for articulating these ideas in simple, clear terms that made sense to clients and evoked their acceptance. He was also flexible in taking on special challenges and formulating new approaches, as in working with one spouse about a marital conflict.

Nate avoided categorization. He was a dedicated social worker who also identified himself as a clinical sociologist, clinical psychologist, and social psychologist. He had a special interest in folklore, which he collected, spoke, and wrote about. He was not a charismatic person and did not present himself as a guru or founder of a new, world-shaking school of therapy. Nor did he collect disciples. There was a scholarly frankness about the sources of his ideas and innovations; he did not attempt to hype up his contributions or to categorize his own approach as a heaven-sent answer to all problems. He was responsive and encouraging to his admirers but without any effort to pull them into his own orbit.

It is of interest that Nate audiotaped a great many of his interviews with clients (with their consent), studied them, and made suitable excerpts available to others. I made very effective use of some of his interview tapes in my teaching of marriage and family therapy. They were fascinating and helpful to students. Some of this material is included in the many case illustrations given in this book. Nate carried on exemplary clinical research, delving into his own immediate experiences and discussions with clients, as well as into the clinical literature which he studied intensively. He applied ideas from symbolic interactionism and cognitive behaviorism as well as from other sources, integrating them into his own practice paradigm. He sought to identify and make manifest the theoretical structure that informed his work and the procedures that could be most helpful.

A very distinctive characteristic of Nate's work is that his theoretical formulations (for example, about limitations and predicaments) were developed for direct practice use. Rather than articulating them in arcane professional jargon for communication with other professionals, he used clear and simple terms. They could be easily conveyed to clients, making his explanations and suggestions appear to be self-evident and common sense. This theoretical framework and the implementive technical procedures which flow from it, remain a singularly helpful contribution to the practice of marriage and family therapy.

Nate was an excellent teacher with clients, never didactic or authoritarian, yet persuasive and influential by virtue of his expertise and his empathic and warm relationships. His therapeutic style was genuinely collaborative with clients. He was reasonable and accepting in his reactions; very open and direct in sharing his observations, thinking, and feelings. He confronted behavior and beliefs rather than the person. The reflections and analyses of this practice experience gave a special lucidity, vividness, humanity, and truth to his papers and to this book. His work's illustrations and explanations demonstrate an extraordinary insight and understanding of the therapeutic process. His mastery of psychodynamics and family/

group dynamics made for illuminating discussions with clients and appears in this book. He was a very competent practitioner who knew what he was doing, for what reasons, and to what ends. This book is one that students and practitioners can well learn from.

Max Siporin, DSW
Professor Emeritus
School of Social Welfare
State University of New York at Albany

Introduction

This volume presents the theory and method of sociocognitive marriage and family therapy—a humanist alternative to conventional behavioral, psychodynamic, and family systems approaches that was developed over some 35 years of practice by the late Nathan Hurvitz. The first two chapters present the theoretical frame of the approach. The third chapter introduces the assessment and change concepts central to sociocognitive practice. The remaining four chapters show how these principles are applied through the opening, change-producing, and termination phases of marriage and family therapy. Our emphasis is practical, showing how sociocognitive principles and techniques can be used with families of all social classes and cultural backgrounds. While forming a systematic approach in and of themselves, these concepts and methods are easily adapted to and integrated within more conventional cognitive-behavioral or family systems therapy.

Trained as a social worker, Hurvitz turned to the social behavioral tradition of symbolic interactionism for his practice theory. He was a humanist who recognized that the problems of spouses and family members were intimately linked to larger societal problems. He identified with the radical therapy movement and argued that a commitment to progressive social change was a necessary part of the therapist's role. His own practice became a test of both his theories and his convictions as the Los Angeles neighborhoods he served changed from a middle-class Jewish population to mostly poor and working-class blacks. Rather than flee to a more affluent community, Hurvitz chose to stay and work with those who were most negatively impacted by the problems and injustices of contemporary American society. As a result, he developed an approach that enables the therapist to cross social, cultural, and racial boundaries to work with families with very different social characteristics than his or her own. This includes inner-city blacks who are among the least well served by conventional therapeutic approaches, as case examples drawn from Hurvitz's practice will illustrate.

My introduction to Hurvitz came in 1978, when he contributed an article to a special issue of *American Behavioral Scientist* I was editing on clinical sociology. I immediately fell in love with his work which, I was amazed to find, closely paralleled the approach I was developing in my own practice (Straus, 1977). During our few meetings we discovered that, while a generation apart in age, we shared humanist values, a symbolic interactionist perspective, progressive politics, and an interest in hypnosis and suggestion.

Hurvitz told me he was writing a marriage and family text that would bring together the material scattered throughout his many articles and professional presentations — what had been summarized in the paper he had written for me. I waited eagerly for the volume, but it never appeared. He had contracted with a major publisher who announced publication but then dropped the project in 1981. At the time of his death in 1986, Hurvitz was working on a revision of the "Projook," as he termed the manuscript.

A sociological colleague, Jerrald Krause, then picked up the project, but was unable to complete it due to competing commitments. Through John Glass, the same mutual friend who had placed us in contact a decade earlier, I then contacted Hurvitz's widow and offered to "midwife" the book. I found myself with nearly nine hundred pages of partially revised manuscript, including some chapters existing only in outline form. Terry S. Trepper, Senior Editor, *HAWORTH* Marriage and the Family, expressed an interest in publishing the book and you hold the result in your hand.

This volume is a labor of love in two acts. The original manuscript represented years of continual effort on Hurvitz's part; it was truly his life's work. Having talked and written extensively about his ideas for over ten years, I felt honored to be entrusted with this project and obliged to ensure that the book would be a fitting memorial to Nate. I have lived with this project for over a year now and, as I trust will be evident, I have done far more than the simple job of editing I had originally envisioned.

The final product is a true, albeit posthumous, coauthorship. I have not only pared, reorganized, and otherwise edited Hurvitz's original, but updated and fleshed out a number of areas. A considerable amount of my own new material has been added in the process (especially in Chapters One, Two, Three and Seven). My objective has been to tease out the essence of the sociocognitive approach and to keep Nate's authorial voice as much intact as possible.

Where I have added to the original, I have attempted to remain true to Nate's intentions and values. Not a few times I have written several paragraphs or pages of new material only to find that Nate had brought up the identical ideas, concepts, or methods later in his manuscript — often in virtually identical terms to my own. By now, I could not easily say where Nate's words or ideas leave off and my own begin. I would like to think that by the time you complete your own exploration of this material, you too will find that it has become a part of your thinking and your practice.

Roger A. Straus, PhD
Philadelphia, PA
February 1990

Chapter One

The Sociological Foundations
of Family Therapy

Caring and effective therapy demands mastery of conceptual tools even more than familiarity with technique (which, after all, comes from experience). Therefore, we begin our examination of the principles and practice of sociocognitive family therapy with a discussion of its theoretical foundations.

We use the rubric *family therapy* inclusively, to refer to working with both couples (married or unmarried) and whole families (traditional dual-parent heterosexual marriages with children or nontraditional alternatives, such as single-parent households). The same concepts and methods used to understand and change marital interactions are used to change family interactions and relationships.

THE SOCIOCOGNITIVE APPROACH

We prefer to typify the approach presented in this volume as *sociocognitive therapy* since it draws upon concepts from sociology as well as techniques from cognitive psychology. This approach begins with the recognition that the therapist is dealing with troubled relationships among social actors who participate in a real world. The ultimate causes of marriage and family problems are found in the real world experiences of family members—their spousal and family member interactions, their everyday activities, and their specific location in a particular historical society. Therapy itself is concerned with helping clients change unsatisfactory and ineffective personal relationships within the context of their real world situation.

In so doing, the therapist recognizes that human beings are crea-

4

tive social actors who respond to events in terms of the meanings those experiences hold for them and not to the raw stimuli themselves (Lofland, 1976; Sarbin, 1977). These meanings do not originate within the conscious or unconscious mind, although they are undoubtedly filtered and tinged by such individual factors. Rather, they are forged through interactions with others and reflect the nature and structure of the social relations in which they originate. The family therapist who practices according to these insights seeks to help family members overcome personal and interpersonal troubles by establishing common meanings. These factors facilitate positive interactions and effective responses to real world situations. Levant has characterized this perspective as interactional-situational, experiential, and phenomenologically oriented (1984).

Humanist and Humanistic Orientations

The sociocognitive approach is also characterized by its explicitly humanist value orientation (Lee, 1988). The sociocognitive therapist does not presume to manipulate family members for their own good or to be the repository of esoteric knowledge too arcane for clients to understand and apply. Rather, therapist and clients are participants in a joint effort to provide family members with the knowledge and tools to help themselves. Our model and preferred metaphor is one of empowering rather than healing, fixing, or reprogramming dysfunctioning families or family members.

Our approach is also humanistic in the Maslovian sense, but differs principally from Maslow's original vision (1970) in our extension of the holistic concept not only to include but to emphasize the social dimension. We share Maslow's belief that human beings are generally trying to do their best and that their problems more often stem from misconceptions or personal limitations than from psychopathology. While our approach recognizes that cognitions, feelings, and subjective experiences are important, it does not share the belief of many humanistic psychologists that these are the ultimate keys to changing social behavior. Rather, the sociocognitive therapist is interested in what occurs within individuals only when it enables us to understand and explain behavior, meanings and feelings *as manifested in social interaction*. Individuals and their significant others then can be helped to change what occurs between them.

Relationship to Family Systems Therapy

By using the label *family therapy*, we not only intend to convey the concept of *doing therapy with families* but also to assert our affiliation with the family therapy movement. The movement abandoned "the traditional psychotherapeutic emphasis on individual history and biography" for interventions directed at the family system itself (Voelkl & Colburn, 1984). As this citation suggests, the mainstream family therapy movement has been dominated by an alternative paradigm focusing on the family group as a more or less integrated *system*. That is, they view the family as an interconnected network of relationships forming a whole that is greater than, and different from, the sum of its parts.

Family Systems Therapy

While there is wide variation in how these concepts are defined and translated into practice, family systems therapists treat the problems of individual family members as problems of the system. They shift the focus of therapy away from what goes on within individuals toward understanding and changing the system of family relationships to help the individual members (Bowen, 1976; Duhl, 1983; Fisch, Weakland & Segal, 1982; Haley, 1981; Minuchin, 1974; Satir, 1972). Whether employing the original biological system metaphor or the more recent cybernetic metaphor introduced by Bateson (1972), systems therapists focus on homeostatic processes by which the system maintains its pattern and downplay the autonomous role of the individual family member (Krause, 1986).

Contextualism

While essentially sympathetic to the notion of the family as an integrated whole, Hurvitz rejected the family systems paradigm because it did not adequately grasp the unique qualities of human conduct and was ultimately asocial. As a humanist, he felt that the underlying model of an organic or cybernetic system was neither adequate nor appropriate. Hurvitz believed that we can better grasp the character of family situations as a joint production or improvisation by the individuals involved. The improvisation emerges from interactions yet serves as the context framing subsequent lines of action—a world view known as *contextualism* (Pepper, 1942; Sarbin, 1977; Straus, 1981).

Social-Ecological Orientation

Hurvitz also believed that a systems paradigm distorts the nature of interpersonal situations by promoting a type of tunnel vision in which the family is artificially sundered from its social context. The field biologist seeks to understand animal behavior by observing them in the context of their natural habitat. They are seen as participants in a larger ecology. Hurvitz shared this naturalistic approach; only the natural habitat of the human being is society. He argued that one cannot artificially separate the family and its troubles from the social ecology within which family members interact and learn their behaviors, meanings, and feelings.

This emphasis on the social ecology is not entirely consistent with Hurvitz's contextualist social psychology. A strong case can be made that our approach should be properly categorized as an expanded, humanist paradigm that integrates contextualism with a systems orientation (Straus, 1989b). Sociocognitive therapy might be thought of as a hybrid between strict contextualism and the ecological systems perspective (Siporin, 1980a) in which practitioners emphasize "a concern with the life situation of clients, in extended family, work, neighborhood, and social networks, and with institutional organizations and cultural arrangements" (Siporin, 1980b; see also Freedman & Rosenfeld, 1983).

MACROSOCIOLOGICAL FACTORS

However labelled, our perspective revolves around what C. Wright Mills (1959) identifies as the *sociological imagination*: making sense of the personal and interpersonal problems of society members in the context of the larger societal environment and its problems. This macrosociological approach means that we focus upon and seek explanations at the level of the entire society, even for the personal problems and predicaments of individuals and their groups, such as the family. The remainder of this chapter will be devoted to exploring the macrosociological foundations of sociocognitive therapy.

Rationale for a Microsociological Approach

The viability of this approach to family problems depends on establishing that these are not idiosyncratic situations that can be explained in terms of the particular individuals involved. We can only apply a macrosociological analysis to specific problems or cases if they are, in fact, substantive instances of generic situations occurring throughout the society. Recognizing this logical demand, Mills presented the basic argument for the relevance of the sociological imagination to family therapy some thirty years ago:

> Inside a marriage a man and a woman may experience personal troubles, but when the divorce rate during the first four years of marriage is 250 out of every 1,000 attempts, this is an indication of a structural issue having to do with the institutions of marriage and the family and other institutions that bear upon them. (1959: 9)

While the numbers may have changed (alas, not for the better), the argument remains compelling that marriage and family problems happen to ordinary people. These problems are not the result of something unique or wrong about those who experience them but are a consequence of factors affecting marriages and families throughout the American society.

The Sociological Imagination

The sociological imagination is one of the central principles underlying sociocognitive family therapy. It cannot be emphasized too strongly or too often that marital problems and conflicts are a normal consequence of lives affected by the social and economic institutions of our American society and culture. In the overwhelming number of instances, marital and family conflicts, disorganization, and destruction are no less tied to the realities of organized social life than is unemployment.

Hurvitz considered it unthinkable for the family therapist *not* to be outraged by the deleterious effects of the social structure upon the family. He identified this perspective with *radical therapy*. The radical therapist, as Hurvitz saw it, helps people function more effectively while simultaneously assisting them to understand the societal sources of their personal and interpersonal problems. The therapist may also engage in more direct efforts to help change what is perceived to be a pathogenic system. In addition to many important causes such as peace, amnesty, civil liberties, minority rights, and labor, the radical therapist fights for the rights of hospitalized mental patients, prisoners and other institutionalized members of society. The therapist also supports alternate treatment facilities and programs, supports peer review and community review bodies and procedures of all psychotherapy activities. These activities are associated with the radical therapist's vision of and work for a nonexploitative society that fosters humanist and life-affirming relationships between people (Hurvitz, 1977c).

Social Structure and Its Consequences

The macrosociological approach focuses on the more or less stable social arrangements observable within a society. These form the *social structure*. In characterizing the social structure of an entire society, we generally emphasize institutions or systems of interrelated institutions through which the work of society is actually carried out (Parsons, 1951). For example, the production and allocation of goods and services are carried out by the institutions of the economic system.

Every historical society institutionalizes inequality in the form of a *social stratification* system which ranks families and individuals into a hierarchy of layers or groups with more or less power, prestige, wealth, and privilege. Different societies at different times have institutionalized a variety of social stratification systems. These include the caste system of ancient India and the feudal systems of Medieval Europe and Japan. Each system of stratification is related to the organization of economic production in that society.

In feudalism, for example, the majority of the population are serfs or peasants who engage in agricultural production on land owned by a hereditary nobility, originally chieftains and warlords.

Capitalism and the Class System

Conservative and radical social analysts alike consider the central feature of our American society to be its capitalist socioeconomic system. In capitalism, resources are allocated according to success in economic competition and other market factors. Although it is not something Americans are comfortable talking or thinking about, like any capitalist society, ours is characterized by a class system. People are divided among a hierarchy of social classes separated by economic position. Perhaps nothing has a more pervasive influence on family life than the social realities imposed by our capitalist system (Zaretsky, 1976).

Lower class individuals and families have less access to resources of all types (e.g., goods, services, education, health care services) and tend to experience more mental and physical illness, crime, and family instability than do others. Social class is essentially an ascribed status conferred as a result of the family one is born into and perpetuated by the differences in opportunity and resources available to different social classes. While it is always theoretically possible for one to work into a higher class, research suggests that few people move very far up or down the system (Coleman & Rainwater, 1978).

Today's American society displays more extreme class inequalities than other industrialized democracies (Gilbert & Kahl, 1982). For example, the top one-fifth of the adult population owns three-fourths of the nation's wealth, not including income (Rice, 1985). There is, in fact, a disquieting trend toward a more rigid class structure in the U.S. Ever more wealth is becoming concentrated in the hands of a small proportion of the population while a rapidly growing inner-city and rural underclass dominated by minorities is largely excluded from participation in the general economy and hence are dependent on public assistance (Wilson, 1987).

Social Location

Social class is only one of the dimensions along which families and individuals are ranked in American society. It may be the single most important dimension of social location because, in capitalist societies, class determines access to economic resources. However, modern societies present a complex stratification system in which an individual's or family's position is determined by several factors or vital features (Glassner & Freedman, 1979).

Location within this system often determines family members' access to resources and opportunities, roles attributed to or open to families and family members, and how individuals are treated and regarded by others and themselves. Thus, it is crucial that the therapist be able to recognize and appreciate the significance of the vital features of a family member's social location as discussed in this chapter.

Social Status

Social scientists use the term *status* to denote any particular position in the social system, and also in the sense of denoting the measure of a person's social worth. Max Weber, one of the founding parents of 20th century sociology, was among the first to stress the multidimensional nature of social stratification. He argued, for example, that social status — the relative prestige accorded a person or group — was of similar importance to social class (Gerth & Mills, 1946). As such, status is a more immediate determinant than class of how others judge and treat an individual. Social scientists often combine these two concepts and describe individuals' or families' socioeconomic status.

Status is perhaps most directly reflected in lifestyle with members of a "status group" generally sharing a common way of life (Gerth & Mills, 1946). Members of a status group or category often display an attitude of derogation toward those whose lifestyles imply lower status and emulation or envy toward those whose lifestyles convey higher status. Discrepancies in social status among family members, between family members and non-family groups or others, and between what family members and others perceive their social status to be, are all important sources of family troubles seen by the therapist.

Ethnicity and Race

Ethnicity refers to one's hereditary membership in a distinct group with a historically based subculture of its own and a sense of ethnic or racial identity. Each subgroup possesses a unique subculture based on its historic experience, with its own set of values, symbols and beliefs (Glassner & Freedman, 1979). Sometimes this is tied up with religion, as in the case of the Jews. At other times it is associated more with racial identity, as in the case of American blacks.

Social structures that perpetuate inequality commonly define a racial boundary between ethnic or status groups and institutionalize social arrangements relegating those on one side of that boundary to the status of a minority group.

> We may define a minority as a group of people who, because of their physical and cultural characteristics, are singled out from others in the society in which they live for differential and unequal treatment and who therefore regard themselves as objects of collective discrimination. (Wirth, 1945, p. 347)

Although the preponderance of marriage within one's group tends to foster phenotypic differences among ethnic groups, the distinction between the races is actually social and not biological. The rhetoric of race masks the reality of a more general process in which more powerful groups in the society institutionalize their dominant position.

Just as it is unfashionable to think of the American society as possessing a class structure, it has become unfashionable to accept that racial discrimination and prejudice remain entrenched in the American society. Such racism continues to foster intergroup conflict and family discord while also continuing to relegate certain minorities — notably blacks and Hispanics — to a generally lower socioeconomic status than whites of equivalent competency, education, and age. "Whether one is assessing income differences between the races among the highly educated or lowly educated a similar gap is found that is associated with their racial characteristics" (Willie, 1989, p. 174).

While ethnicity and race can imply negative consequences due to the stigmatization and discrimination directed against members of minority groups, *ethnic consciousness* can be a source of pride, strength, and self-esteem for family members. Particularly when ethnic group values foster behavior commensurate with the American Dream (such as the work-and-education ethic of both Jewish and Asian immigrant groups), ethnicity can have socially valued consequences. Similarly, many black and Hispanic Americans are looking to their own "roots" as a source of pride. However, defining oneself as belonging to a particular group in opposition to all others can become a barrier to interaction with the larger society and help perpetuate ethnic stereotypes, discrimination, and poverty.

Age and Life Stage

Age is another vital feature to which the therapist needs to be sensitive (Glassner & Freedman, 1979). It is important to recognize that age is not so much a biological or objective fact as a social fact. An individual, for example, passes through a sequence of socially recognized *life stages*: childhood, adolescence, youth or young adulthood, midlife, and old age. Each of these represent a social category rather than a function of biological development; for instance, youth and midlife are social inventions that have emerged relatively late in this century.

New institutions, role expectations, and even laws have emerged around each of these life stages. For example, the enfranchisement of 18-year olds to vote and the nearly simultaneous establishment of new laws setting the drinking age at 21 years of age effactually defined the limits of a post-adolescent youth phase with limited adult rights and responsibilities. Currently, with the aging of the U.S. population, we are also experiencing a redefinition of the meaning of later stages of life; we no longer refer to 40-year olds as middle aged or those in their 60s as elderly and required to act the part.

There are similar stages in family life, such as dating, marriage, having and raising young children, having adolescent children, having children leave the house and then experiencing an "empty nest syndrome" (LaRossa, 1984). Each of these involves a set of roles and expectations. As with life stages, these stages of the family life cycle are organized in relation to macrosociological changes in both the family and other institutions of the American society. For example, there is a widely reported trend in which young adult children (and, often, their spouses) are moving back in with their parents because of the increasingly prohibitive cost of purchasing or renting their own homes. These changes clearly have ramifications for family members that are often seen by the therapist.

Sex and Gender Roles

While commonly confused, sex and gender are different concepts. *Sex* is a biological matter. With extremely rare exceptions, human beings are either biologically male or biologically female. *Gender* is another matter entirely; it refers to the roles and expectations associated with biological sex by culture and social structure. Although there appear to be innate psychobiological differences between the sexes, human beings are not naturally masculine or feminine in thought, feeling, or behavior. Rather, we learn how to be boys and girls, men and women, as our particular society, culture, and social group define these things at a specific time in history (Handel & Elkin, 1988).

Not only do we learn a set of expectations for our gender, but we also learn the complementary expectations for the other gender. That is, we learn a *role set* enabling us to interact on the basis of *role reciprocity.* By role reciprocity, we mean that men and women act according to the behavioral expectations of the role sets they have learned by living in American society (Merton, 1968).

Experience tells us that a person's image of the opposite sex tends to be highly stereotyped. While "male" and "female" are social roles, we tend to attribute them to the nature of the human organism. They become defining elements of who we are to ourselves and to others. The institutions of society foster and perpetuate the resulting gender roles. In fact gender roles are so pervasive that it is difficult to accept the idea that they are *not* innate. Nevertheless, many of the apparently psychobiological differences between men and women—such as their characteristically different attitudes and responses toward intimacy—appear related to societal relegation of infant care-taking and "mothering" almost exclusively to women (Rubin, 1984).

Power and Manipulation

Many sociologists feel that power is directly related to sex and gender. Power may be formally defined as

> The process wherein individuals or groups gain or maintain the capacity to impose their will upon others, to have their way recurrently, despite implicit or explicit opposition, through invoking or threatening punishment, as well as offering or withholding rewards. (Lipman-Blumen, 1984)

We have already commented on power and powerlessness in a general way, suggesting that family members' feelings of powerlessness are often a key factor in their thoughts, feelings, and behavior. These tend to be related to their position in the social structure.

Lipman-Blumen (1984) offers an insightful set of concepts relating gender roles to power. Arguing that "the uncertainty of life is the basis of the human need for power and control," she suggests that these needs underlie the historic sexual division of labor between the genders and, in particular, the subordination of women to men. However, power and control are always two-way relationships:

> The differentiation of sex and gender roles symbolizes a power relationship in which each group labors repeatedly to exert its will over the other. The more powerful group assets its demands; the less powerful group seeks ways to circumvent or subvert the more powerful group's wishes. When the dominant group controls the major institutions of a society, it relies on *macromanipulation* through law, social policy, and military might, when necessary, to impose its will and ensure its role. The less powerful become adept at *micromanipulation*, using intelligence, canniness, intuition, interpersonal skill,

charm, sexuality, deception, and avoidance to offset the control of the powerful. (1984, p.8)

Lipman-Blumen further suggests that both the powerful and the powerless take the social structure for granted, attributing their condition to innate abilities and predispositions. The power relationship between men and women has become the paradigm for all power relationships in human societies (e.g., between the races, between bosses and employees, and even between parents and children).

The concepts of macromanipulation and micromanipulation can be fruitfully applied to understanding both the roles individuals play in their families or the outside world and the "games" family members often play. It is widely recognized that the traditional relationship between husband/father and wife/mother in the American family institutionalizes the pattern of male dominance and female economic dependence.

The entrance of women into the labor market and the assumption of responsibilities outside the home have contributed to a change in the traditional role relationship between middle-class husbands and wives. Some of these changes have challenged the dominance of men who have often tried to defend their position through strategies of macromanipulation. These defenses range from the withholding of financial resources to arguments and even physical violence. In some cases, for a woman to seek a therapist's help is defined as a threat. For example, one of Straus's clients was a diabetic woman who sought help because uncontrolled eating of sweets led her to experience blackouts, sometimes when driving with her children. When her husband learned that she had initiated therapy, he took away her checkbook and credit cards.

Women have sought to counter or neutralize these threats by the range of tactics cited by Lipman-Blumen, above. While constructive ways to deal with these relationships will eventually be worked out, the changing roles of men and women in the family have prompted a power struggle that has caused many marital and family problems. Until then, many of the stories brought to the therapist's attention will continue to reflect the unresolved strains and tensions associated with the power relationships of men and women.

Effects of Social Change

The changing roles of men and women in American society represents one of the ways in which social change affects family members and contributes to their troubles. In the last decade of the 20th century, three additional features of American social structure are emerging as critical influences on our lives and relationships. Each involves basic structural changes that cause enormous strains and dislocations throughout the society, the effects of which can certainly be seen by the family counselor.

The first feature is the transition from an industrial system emphasizing production and consumption of goods to a service-based economy emphasizing electronic information technology (e.g., computers). The second is the coming of age of a "mass society." Companies and institutions are growing larger and more impersonal while services directed at ever-larger audiences are becoming more standardized and are offering new possibilities for covert manipulation of popular tastes and opinion (Mills, 1956). The third is progressive inflation of costs and expectations, so that it becomes increasingly difficult for consumers to keep up economically and virtually mandatory for both spouses to work in order to support their family.

Social change may have a variety of other direct and indirect consequences for family members. One consequence is that individuals may feel threatened by what is perceived to be a surfeit of change. They may become disturbed by changing values, beliefs, rules, roles, and norms. Some come to feel alienated, cut off from the society around them and relegated to the status of objects. In other cases, individuals react to the stress of change by adopting a reactionary or traditionalist attitude, seeking to assert the "old verities" by adherence to old-fashioned standards, politics, or religion. This may take the form of returning to childhood roots or joining fundamentalist religious or social movements that offer expressive or symbolic relief (e.g., in the form of "charismatic" religious ecstasy). They may seek comforting rituals or direct action to combat what they perceive as unacceptable social or cultural changes (e.g., anti-abortion activists who blockade clinics in order to "rescue the unborn").

Another immediate consequence of social change is the shifting status of families and family members affected by changes in the larger structure of opportunity in the American society. Some families experience relatively dramatic and sudden upward mobility, so that those who were once at the bottom margins of acceptable society may join the moneyed elite. A presumably larger proportion of families, however, experience downward mobility as their economic fortunes decline. Newman (1988) shows that fear of downward mobility has become an important source of strain in the American middle- and upper-middle-classes.

Such effects are closely related to the disparity between rising expectations and reality. Many have accepted the values of the *American Dream* but do not have the economic resources to have a lifestyle commensurate with those goals and values. For example, although owning one's own house has become an integral part of Americans' expectations, inflated real estate costs prohibit an increasing proportion of Americans from achieving that goal. In fact, rental costs are escalating to the point where we now have a shockingly large homeless population.

Culture and the American Dream

Culture, as the term is used by social scientists, refers to the shared beliefs, assumptions, values, understandings, images, and symbols (including language) that guide people's thinking, feeling, and behaving. Phenomenologically-oriented social scientists emphasize how culture shapes or even determines the ways we think and feel and the reality that we experience and take for granted (Berger & Luckmann, 1966). Structurally-oriented sociologists emphasize that culture is a basic means by which individuals' motivations and efforts are aligned and coordinated so as to permit social groups and entire societies to function (Parsons, 1951). The therapist needs to be aware of the close correspondence between social structure (the dominant values and ideologies of a society) and what members of that society think, feel, and believe. Each appears to reflect, support, and shape the other.

Hurvitz ironically characterizes the dominant values and ideology of our late 20th century society as the *American Dream*. One must understand the cultural facts of life in order to understand the family problems that our clients bring to us (Wirth, 1931). At the broadest level, we are convinced that the cultural themes identified with the American Dream not only form and guide the behavior, meanings, and feelings of Americans, but represent one of the key underlying causes of family members' problems and conflicts.

Values and Ideologies of the American Dream

"Success" is the Holy Grail, the ultimate object of attainment in the American Dream. The tokens of success are money, things, and power (the ability to control the lives of others). To be truly successful, a person would have to attain the maximum of all three. Entrenched in and supported by the institutions of our society, this success orientation is perhaps the central source of both conflict and motivation in American society. As Merton (1968) suggests:

> The family, the school and the workplace—the major agencies shaping the personality structure and goal formation of Americans—join to provide the intensive disciplining required if an individual is to retain intact a goal that remains elusively beyond reach, if he is to be motivated by the promise of a gratification that is not redeemed. . . . That the American Dream can be realized if one has the requisite abilities. (pp. 136-137)

However, there is an implicit contradiction in the American Dream. Lying at the heart of our historical society are two mutually contradictory ideologies forming the double helix (as it were) of our cultural heritage. Individually and together they support and perpetuate the success ethic. Positively, the tension between them is doubtlessly responsible for some of the historic dynamism and avoidance of extremes that characterize American society. Negatively, however, they place us in a kind of cultural double bind (Bateson, 1972).

We most often associate the first ideology with capitalism and the secularized culture once typified by the big city. It consists of what have often been called the "modern values" of *competition, individualism* (Williams, 1970), and *personal responsibility* for all life chances (Rice, 1985). As Rice puts it:

> The individual and not the group is seen as the center of social life; all our institutions, social arrangements, and public policies revolve around the individual pursuit of the "inalienable rights" of life, liberty and the acquisition of property . . . Credit and blame are placed on the individual, regardless of the objective reasons for particular outcomes. (p. 159)

The second ideology is often identified with rural and small town or country life. This is the reservoir of the traditional, mom-and-apple-pie values championed by conservatives: *hard work, conformity* to community norms, and *respect for authority.* One might also include *religiosity.* These, too, are viewed as means to the end of success and can, indeed, serve in that capacity. However, their function in the social order appears to be social control. These values instill the "disciplining" and "motivation" to which Merton (1968) refers. Additionally, the traditional values are treated as our culture's sacred values. They are characteristically invoked by those with money or power when seeking to support their policies and defend the status quo, whether at the level of the government, the school, or the family.

Untoward Consequences of the American Dream

Clearly not all can succeed, but all compete against each other. Competition encourages aggression, for each must think of himself or herself first to win. In many settings, winning is the only thing. Competition also fosters cheating, exploitation and oppression of others with the corresponding concern that others will cheat, exploit, and oppress us. Cheating and concern about being cheated create an atmosphere of anxiety, fear, hostility, and violence for many people.

Another consequence of the extreme value placed on individual success is inappropriate self-devaluation. Most Americans tend to feel powerless and to blame themselves for their personal and social problems. Their prevailing mood is depression and anxiety and they are beset by psychosomatic complaints. When these people have family difficulties, they cannot perform their tasks at work; when they have difficulties at work they cannot fulfill their family responsibilities. This creates a cycle of increasing disability at both the personal and interpersonal levels.

Socialized to explain situations in terms of individualism, these Americans do not recognize the societal causes of their personal limitations, interpersonal predicaments, and conflicts. They do not have the personal resources to examine and change their lives; therefore they live with constant stress. They blame themselves when things go wrong and function under the burden of a generalized feeling of guilt. Such people have learned to be helpless and dependent on others. They have become resigned to accept, as their due, whatever treatment they receive from those more powerful or successful than they are. Alternatively, one might speculate that some try to overcome that hopelessness, despondency, and sense of powerlessness by changing their brain chemistry through prescription medications, alcohol, narcotics, or cocaine.

Institutional Sources of Family Troubles

Members of a society participate in a wide variety of social institutions. We have already referred to the economic, social stratification, political, religious, educational, and family institutions. Each institution (or, for that matter, subordinate social group) assigns a somewhat different set of expectations for behavior, or social role to each participant depending on his or her position within the institution. Consequently, individuals have as many different social roles as institutions (and social groups of all types) with which they interact. Thus, every individual plays multiple roles inside and outside the family such as mother, wife, neighbor, Sunday School teacher, administrator, employee and PTA member.

Family members are forced to juggle sets of conflicting demands and to enact sometimes incompatible roles (e.g., loving husband and inflexibly demanding boss). Furthermore, the demands made by one institution may constitute barriers to fulfillment of demands made by another. For example, very commonly the workplace demands overtime or leaves one so exhausted that family roles, such as spending quality time with the children, are neglected.

The institutions of a society tend to embody and support the dominant culture. This can be seen very clearly in our economic institutions, which simultaneously reward and reinforce the paradoxical values of the American Dream (e.g., both competitive individualism and conformity). Such contradictions within the institution create strain at the organizational, interpersonal, and intrapersonal levels. All of these can affect the performance of family members.

Manifest and Latent Functions

Systems theory is a relative newcomer on the social science scene. There is a far older approach employed by sociologists and anthropologists known as *functionalism* that similarly views any social entity as more than the sum of its parts. This perspective likens society (or any social group) to a living organism whose primary goal or mandate is survival. Functionalists contend that any social arrangement persists because it serves that goal in some way. To understand the parts, then, one must look at how they serve the whole—what their functions are. For example, we have looked at the family, the schools, and the mass media as institutions with the function of socialization (Parsons, 1951; Turner, 1986).

Hurvitz found Merton's (1968) distinction between manifest and latent functions to be particularly useful in family therapy. *Manifest functions* are what a social arrangement or a behavior is intended to do. They are known and explicit; for example, the manifest function of school tracking systems is to enable children to progress at their own level of competency. The manifest function of compulsory attendance laws is to ensure that all children get at least a minimally adequate education.

Latent functions are the unintended, implicit, or covert functions that an arrangement or behavior serves. These may be nothing more than unanticipated long term consequences of immediate behaviors. Cigarette smokers do not intend to give themselves cancer and drug addicts do not share needles in order to acquire AIDS. Latent functions may also serve a purpose; The chronic invalid may use his or her condition to gain sympathy or maintain leverage over other family members. Very often, social arrangements with a noble manifest function serve less savory purposes in the social structure as latent functions.

Untoward Effects of Socializing Institutions

The latent functions of social institutions are a prime example of this concept. Some institutions have the explicit function of transmitting and reinforcing cultural values (Merton, 1968). These include the family, the school, organized religion, and the mass media. Such institutions are the primary means through which our society socializes its members and brings them to internalize (among other things) the values, goals, and role expectations appropriate to their place. While this is not, of course, their sole function, these institutions are the primary vectors of the American Dream. They are the instrumentalities by which ideologies and values are transmitted from one generation to the next and from one social group to another.

In addition to the manifest function of transmitting the official values of the society, the latent function of these institutions is to perpetuate oppressive aspects of social stratification. It is now widely accepted that schools have contributed to the continuation of racial injustice and poverty through segregation. Even tracking systems, ostensibly designed to provide appropriate learning experiences for children of different levels of ability and achievement, characteristically shunt culturally disadvantaged children into the lower, non-college-bound tracks.

Studies have also shown a latent relationship between compulsory school attendance, juvenile delinquency, and school crime (Hall, 1985). For example, researchers have found that school districts with compulsory attendance laws requiring teenagers to remain in secondary school until age 18 have higher rates of school crime compared to districts where students are allowed to drop out at an earlier age (Toby, 1983).

The mass media, among which television has become increasingly dominant, are also important sources of problems affecting family life. In addition to the suspected relationship between the amount of killing and other violence shown on television and the increasing rates of violent crime there are other, perhaps even more insidious, relationships between what is communicated by mass media and problems encountered by the family therapist. Prominent among these is *false consciousness* — a view and interpretation of the world that is not in the best interests of those adopting that perspective.

There are many forms of false consciousness promulgated by the mass media and other socializing institutions. These include sexism, racism, chronic feelings of inadequacy or low self-esteem, and obsessive self-involvement prompting individuals to seek self-gratification to the exclusion of concern for the welfare of others. One of the most insidious forms of false consciousness is the elevation of individualism to a global, all-purpose explanatory scheme or perspective; i.e., the way social problems are explained or interpreted on an individual level that is consonant with the American Dream. The media tend to slight the societal causes and processes that cause personal distress and tragedies and, instead, blame the victim (Mills, 1963; Ryan, 1971). For example, the burgeoning rate of teen pregnancy is attributed to individuals' lack of self-discipline or immorality; the crack cocaine epidemic to lack of the moral fiber to "just say no."

The cumulative effect of these continual media lessons is that individuals come to see the world in terms of personal responsibility for everything that happens. They blame their personal troubles on themselves and not on the societal factors that cause those problems. Thus, the same social dynamics that victimize individuals also prompt them to blame themselves. One implication of this is that any actions taken to overcome their problems are likely to be misdirected and to complicate rather than resolve those problems.

The Family as a Social Institution

The family, and not the individual, is the principal structural unit of most societies, including our own. For example, individuals are assigned social status largely in accordance with their family's status, and with its economic position in particular. The family's economic position affects or determines its relationship (and that of its members) to virtually all other institutions of the society; from the kind and amount of health care and education they receive, to their experiences with the legal, justice, and penal system. All the institutions of our society declare the importance of the family, even as they pull its members in different directions and weaken the family unit whose strength and stability they claim to prize (Kenniston, 1977).

Strains and conflicts within the family echo and reflect those within the larger social order. Among the central issues affecting the family is the increasingly precarious role of the family itself as a social institution. While the family's overall social status generally continues to be contingent on the husband/father's occupation, both spouses typically serve as breadwinners to pay the bills and maintain their lifestyle. These many conflicting roles, demands, and expectations place great strain on the family's breadwinners. In turn, this strain may diminish their capacity for maintaining desired relationships within the family.

As agencies of child socialization and acculturation, families transmit the parents' values and those of the larger society to their children. At the same time, like any other social group, any specific family tends to develop its own culture. This represents a twist on the larger culture in that only certain values, goals, beliefs, and expectations are emphasized. Thus the individual family might be considered a kind of filter or lens through which the dominant culture and values are tinted or distorted in the process of transmission. This is a source of many family problems.

For example, many parents give their children material things because work leaves them too stressed or exhausted to give the children time and affection, because they simply do not know how to share these things, or because they equate sharing the fruits of their economic success with love. Conflict may result between spouses or between parents and children (who may later accuse their parents of having bribed them with material things to buy their unearned love). Failure to live up to these expectations may create a sense of guilt and failure on the part of less economically successful parents (who cannot afford expensive clothes or other things for their children) and deprivation and resentment on the part of children (who cannot have the things valued by their peers).

The Macrosociological Perspective and Family Therapy

The sociological imagination enables us to see that marriage and family problems must be understood in relation to both their overall incidence and their social context. Being in the same boat, so to speak, with tens of thousands or even millions of other Americans, clients who seek our help with such problems should not have to suffer under the burden of personal guilt, blame, or shame for their difficulties. Helping family members enmeshed in dissatisfying and ineffective relationships to understand and, perhaps, take active responsibility for the societal causes of their difficulties is part of the therapeutic enterprise. In addition, concepts derived from the macrosociological perspective help the therapist develop effective interventions.

However, the therapist's more immediate task is to help troubled family members create desired change in their interpersonal situations. Toward this end, a macrosocial perspective can provide crucial insights into family members' interactions and behavior. We believe that it is necessary for the therapist to acquire a working familiarity with the nature and implications of the social structure, particularly with respect to the vital features of social location discussed earlier.

Chapter Two

Sociocognitive Therapy
and Symbolic Interactionism

Ultimately, therapy comes down to helping our clients deal with their troubles. In the present chapter, we switch our focus from the macrosocial context to the microsocial level of the family members who are our actual clients.

MICROSOCIOLOGY

Microsociology focuses on individual social actors as they act and interact, creating the more or less stable patterns of social relationships described in Chapter One. The central assumption of a microsocial perspective is that human beings are literally social creatures. Unlike the social psychology with which most readers are probably familiar, such an approach retains the sociological imagination and keeps in sight the myriad threads connecting family members to the larger social fabric.

Social Behaviorism

While he is little known today outside of academic sociology and sociological social psychology, the early 20th century social philosopher George Herbert Mead might be considered the father of American cognitive psychology. Emphasizing the primacy of society, Mead views the individual as literally a social creature:

> Social psychology studies the activity or behavior of the indi-
> vidual as it lies within the social process; the behavior of the
> individual can be understood only in terms of the behavior of
> the whole social group of which he is a member. . . . For
> social psychology, the whole (society) is prior to the part (the
> individual), not the part to the whole; and the part is explained
> in terms of the whole, not the whole in terms of the part or
> parts. (Mead, 1934, pp. 6-7)

Hence, as discussed in Chapter One, understanding the individual
requires understanding the real world within which he or she lives.

Mead formulated the paradigm of social behaviorism. Unlike the
"scientific" behaviorism of Skinner and his predecessors, this approach accounts for the externally observable aspect of activity as
well as "the parts of the act which do not come to external observation, and it emphasizes the act of the human individual in its natural
social situation" (Mead, 1934, p. 8).

According to Mead, the key to understanding human behavior —
and the necessary condition for social cooperation — is our ability to
represent and express attitudes and intentions through language and
other symbol systems. We engage in cooperative action by orient-
ing and adapting our behavior through the exchange of meaningful
gestures, including speech acts:

> Just as in fencing the parry is an interpretation of the thrust,
> so, in the social act, the adjustive response of one organism to
> the gesture of another is the interpretation of that gesture by
> that organism — it is the meaning of that gesture. (Mead, 1934,
> p. 78)

Conduct versus Behavior

This leads to a subtle but ultimately radical difference between
our social behaviorism, the empiricist or scientific behaviorism
championed by Skinner (1965), and more recent cognitive behavioral approaches (Bandura, 1986). Following Mead, we recognize
that human beings do not merely emit behaviors, but engage in
conduct. That is, human beings act with reference to their social
context. While scientific behaviorists view the mind as a black box

(or dispense with it entirely), Meadians view it as a process in which our lines of action are worked out within an ongoing internal dialogue *as if with another person*.

That imaginary other is the *self*, our conception of what the pronoun "me" refers to, who we are in the social world. In his famous analysis of child socialization, Mead contends that our initial self-concept is based primarily on how our family members behave toward us. However, it then incorporates our experiences with a wider range of *significant others* such as peer group members. Thus, we develop a repertoire of alternative social selves reflecting our various social relationships. Eventually, we synthesize a global conceptualization of how the world-as-a-whole views us (the *generalized other*); this is what one normally refers to when speaking of "me" or "oneself" (Mead, 1934).

Symbolic Interactionism

The social behavioral analysis of mind, self, and society was further developed by Mead's student, Herbert Blumer, who labeled his approach symbolic interactionism:

> Symbolic interactionism rests . . . on three simple premises. The first premise is that human beings act toward things on the basis of the meanings that the things have for them. Such things include everything that the human being may note in his world . . . The second premise is that the meaning of such things is derived from, or arises out of, the symbolic interaction that one has with one's fellows. The third premise is that these meanings are handled in, and modified through, an interpretative process used by the person in dealing with the things he encounters. (1969: p. 2)

In his elaboration of these concepts, Blumer employs a "root image" of human beings as creative, acting organisms who construct shared meanings and build up lines of action, rather than respond to internal or external forces and events. As this emphasis on meaning demonstrates, symbolic interactionism offers a life-affirming alternative to the mechanistic image so often identified with the social and behavioral sciences (Sarbin, 1977; Straus, 1981).

In addition to meaning, Blumer stresses the role of imagination in symbolic interaction. For him, the explanation of how social cooperation is possible lies in the process of taking the role of the other. Each party to an interaction literally imagines him- or herself in the place of another so as to gain insight into the other's perspective and anticipate the other's responses. Moreover, as parties interact, each asserts and acts upon their own meanings and adapts to the meanings expressed by the others.

Other Theoretical Influences

Contemporary symbolic interactionists have also been influenced by other sociological social psychologists working in this general tradition. Two of these influences are particularly relevant for sociocognitive therapy.

Thomas's definition of the situation. W. I. Thomas, roughly a contemporary of Mead, was an early clinical sociologist who worked in the child guidance clinics of his time (Wirth, 1931). Thomas contributed the famous phenomenological principle of the definition of the situation: if people "define situations as real, they are real in their consequences" (Thomas & Thomas, 1928). This principle was adopted by Blumer, but Thomas's phenomenological approach has also had a direct influence on contemporary thinking and practice.

Thomas's principle was subsequently elaborated by Merton (1968) into the well-known concept of the *self-fulfilling prophecy*. This concept states that people will tend to transform accepted definitions of the situation into actuality by behaving as if they were true. We see this in families when one child is defined as the smart one and consequently encouraged or even coerced to excel in school while another is defined as less able and therefore not provided with the same opportunities or encouragement. The result is that the second child's academic performance is inferior to that of the first — and is taken as proof of lower ability.

Goffman's dramaturgical analysis. A more recent influence on symbolic interactionists has been Goffman's *dramaturgical perspective*. Goffman employs the metaphor of theater, analyzing human conduct as the performances of social actors managing their personal and interpersonal situations to achieve their purposes. For example, Goffman (1959) calls attention to the way social actors manage the impression they make by conveying an appropriate *presentation of self* to their audience.

In effect, Goffman operationalizes the concepts of Mead, Blumer, and Thomas. Thus, the dramaturgical analyst considers a situation to be defined by the acts of the participants (Sarbin, 1984). This is meant literally, implying that what they do *is* the operational reality. In other words, "you are your act" (Straus, 1982, 1989). According to the dramaturgical perspective, life is improvisational theater in which we are both the actors and one another's audience. While some therapists have applied an explicitly dramaturgical perspective to family therapy (Church, 1985), Hurvitz drew his social psychological approach primarily from Blumer.

Contemporary Integrations

Many contemporary interactionists have returned to a more pragmatic (in both the philosophic and colloquial senses) conceptualization of social actors than those suggested by either Blumer or Goffman. They emphasize the importance of self, role, and identity as factors in the individual's construction of action. They also argue that people act in accordance with their self-images — even if that requires them to adjust their self-definitions to fit. Such an approach emphasizes connections between one's self and the identities imputed by other group members and society-at-large based on one's roles and statuses. That is, contemporary integrations focus on the dialectic between *self-interaction* (one's thoughts, feelings and other cognitions) and *hetero-interaction* (transactions with other social actors):

> The self . . . is composed of various identities (or role-identities; McCall and Simmons, 1978) and is lodged in roles, relationships, and statuses that develop as the self reflects upon itself as an object (Stone, 1962). These identities are organized in a salience hierarchy according to individual's commitment to them (Kornhauser, 1962), their likelihood of being involved in various situations (Stryker, 1968, 1980), and their degree of "merging" with individuals' "real selves" (Turner,

1976, 1978). They arise as individuals form different sets of structured relationships with others, and are modified by persons' greater or lesser resistance to changes in the face of changing circumstances (Stryker, 1980). (Adler & Alder, 1989, p. 299)

The Adlers themselves highlight:

> the integrating role of the reference group in influencing evolution or modification of the self-concept. Whereas theories of social comparison, social evaluation, and self-attribution tend to set *individuals'* ongoing self-concept formation against the background of the reference group, this research supports the normative and associative principles that lodge individuals and their sense of self *within their conception of the group*. (1989, p. 309; emphasis added)

These insights closely parallel Hurvitz's thinking—both his understanding of the emergence of family members' problems and the process of sociocognitive therapy as he developed it.

THERAPEUTIC APPLICATIONS OF SYMBOLIC INTERACTIONISM

The preceding discussion has introduced some of the principles of symbolic interactionist social psychology (see also Charon, 1989; Horner, 1979; Stone & Farberman, 1981; Stryker, 1980). Now we turn to consideration of specific concepts and methods linking these general microsociological notions to sociocognitive family therapy.

The Social Act as an Organizing Concept

The atomic unit in the sociocognitive perspective is the social act. A social act occurs when interactants take their own and the other's subjective meanings into account and adjust to one another's behavior, meanings, or feelings. One person acts and the other responds to that act as he or she understands it. The first person then interprets and responds to that response. As Cohen graphically summarizes it (1985):

$$Action < - > Reaction = Interaction$$

Participants test their own definitions of the situation until a common meaning is established thereby making joint action possible and continuing interaction predictable. This does not necessarily mean that they will cooperate and have positive feelings toward one another. For example, the intent of one may be to inform the other that their hitherto intimate relationship has ended. While one has feelings of satisfaction and relief, the other may feel disappointment and depression or even rage and hatred for betraying trust or affection.

Most social acts, however, are repetitive events associated with the participant's everyday routine activities. They vary in generally predictable patterns from hour to hour, weekday to weekend, and month to month. Special events such as birthdays, anniversaries, and holidays punctuate these repetitive rounds but usually according to the individual's and family's accustomed patterns and rituals. Catastrophic, one-time events (ranging from death or divorce to a job loss or children leaving home) disrupt these rounds and require the negotiation of new, largely unprecedented meanings. The result is strained common definitions of the situation and stress among those involved.

Analyzing Social Acts

Analysis of the social act reveals situational definitions that participants share as well as those they do not, which consequently, become sources of conflict and misunderstanding. Wirth (1951) points out that the *most* important information we need about any person or group are these definitions that are taken for granted and of which we are not consciously aware. These subconscious definitions are nevertheless manifested in social acts and can, therefore be teased out by careful analysis of interactions and accounts.

The sociocognitive therapist examines social acts to gain a practical understanding of family members' conscious and subconscious definitions. The therapist shares that understanding with family members to facilitate a positive redefinition of their mutual situation. The sociocognitive therapist gains access to the social acts of family members in order to accomplish this task. The first tactic is to establish a context in which family members can be observed interacting with one another as well as with the therapist. This is accomplished by setting up both one-on-one and conjoint sessions in which the therapist meets with all or several family members together. The second tactic is the examination of family members' accounts as revealed privately to the therapist and in the presence of other family members.

Role of Therapeutic Discussion

The sociocognitive therapist's basic method for accessing family members' meanings is *therapeutic discussion*. Through discussion, the therapist enters into the interaction and relationships of the family to understand and facilitate change according to family members' expressed desires. The sociocognitive approach employs three forms of discussion: reflective, analytic, and directed.

Reflective Discussion

Reflective discussion is thoughtful. It encourages contemplative, deliberate, and careful consideration of the elements that enter into each individual's definition of the situation. It focuses on the identification and evaluation of issues, alternative actions, and their possible outcomes. Reflective discussion requires the therapist to listen carefully and summarize or reflect family members' questions and statements. This must be done in such a way as to facilitate their expression of feelings, enhance their understanding, and perhaps enable them to engage in problem-solving discourse regarding issues and actions.

Analytic Discussion

Analytic discussion examines the separate elements or aspects that enter into each family member's definition of the situation. Analytical discussion considers the action of particular individuals in relation to the actions of others. It breaks up or resolves issues and actions into a simpler form in order to facilitate evaluation. It reviews pertinent issues and actions to distinguish internal structure and dynamics, similarities and differences. Thus enabling family members to devise satisfying and effective coping strategies.

Directed discussion

Directed discussion is instrumental and aimed at specific ends (for example, securing information or making a decision about family members' relationships, the onset of their differences, or the preferred resolution). Directed discussion focuses attention and encourages observation and examination of issues, actions, and possible outcomes. It steers interaction in a particular direction to pursue a specific subject. It also serves as instruction, guidance, and education in that it extends to the therapist's explanations and interpretations regarding subjects and issues.

Facilitating Therapeutic Discussion

In the therapy setting, discussion is a change producing activity. During the process of discussion, the therapist continually identifies family members' ability to change as real. She supports their hope for change and helps them overcome the anxiety and demoralization that has accompanied them to the therapist.

There is also a tactical element to therapeutic discussion. The therapist assists each family member by asking questions and making statements or comments that help to define and achieve goals for therapy. This does not involve use of some checklist or systematic program of asking the "right" questions, rather the therapist:

1. Asks open-ended questions that are sufficiently structured to facilitate family members' discussion of marital or family problems and conflicts.
2. Employs probe questions that help family members focus on problems and conflicts when they have difficulty with open-ended questions.
3. Requests specific examples when family members report differences or difficulties in vague and general terms.
4. Involves family members in discussion among themselves.
5. Attempts to get family members to discuss their problems in

such a way that each assumes some responsibility for their difficulties.

6. Prompts family members to discuss their bargaining, decision making, and problem solving activities to evaluate the relative effectiveness of each family member's conduct.

7. Leads family members' discussion and evaluation of individual and joint actions that can be taken to resolve their problems and difficulties.

8. Assists family members to consider available alternatives and to decide which they would prefer as the most desirable.

In this process, the therapist attempts to secure certain types of information about family members' meanings or definitions. General discussion will usually provide insight into family members' overall perspectives and definitions. More focused reflective, analytic, and directed discussion can enable the therapist to learn specifically:

1. How each family member perceives himself or herself.

2. How each family member perceives every other family member and how they perceive each other's perceptions of themselves.

3. How each family member and the family as a group perceives and defines their family, their relationships, and the world around them.

Other information obtained by discussion relates more directly to the way family members communicate, such as:

1. How they communicate with language, symbols and metaphors, body language, pacing and tone of voice.

2. How responsive family members are to each other's communication.

3. How carefully and effectively family member's listen to and "read" one another.

Two-Way Discussion

We will consider these types of information at greater depth in the remainder of this chapter. Before we leave the subject of reflective, analytical, and directed discussion, we should note that more is involved than just the therapist's questions and the family members' replies. Family members also ask questions to which the therapist replies.

In fact, when the therapist completes a series of questions or concludes a session with one or more family members, she should give them an opportunity to ask her questions. She might say, "I've asked you a lot of questions—some that you expected me to ask and some that you very likely didn't expect me to ask. Are there any things we talked about that we ought to discuss further? Are there any subjects that we didn't talk about that you want to tell me about? Are there any questions you want to ask me about the subjects we talked about?"

Useful Concepts

Several microsociological concepts are particularly useful in analyzing and evaluating the family members' discussion. These concepts give the sociocognitive therapist a handle by which to grasp the information presented by the family members as they talk and interact with the therapist and with one another (Cohen, 1986).

Accounts

It is essential for the therapist to treat family members' responses to questions like these as *accounts*, not merely answers. This concept is central to yet another modern variant of symbolic interactionism, ethnomethodology. Ethnomethodologists focus on how people organize the realities of daily life, particularly how they make sense or make things make sense (Garfinkle, 1967; Handel, 1982). We go through our lives without thinking about it very much. We attribute the ways we navigate the minutiae of daily life to common sense. Ethnomethodology takes a closer look at what "everybody knows" and finds that we actually follow a set of taken-for-granted, procedural rules in even the most routine aspects of our daily lives.

One of the first things such an inquiry reveals is that human beings read (or perhaps impose) order into (or onto) experiences and events. We do this through our accounts. An *account* is the narrative that social actors construct, perceive, and relate to organize the flow of experiences into an orderly story that makes sense (Handel, 1982). It is our attempt to map the territory we are traversing so that we can communicate about it to ourselves and to others. However, analysis of accounts suggests that our maps, as Korzybski has pointed out (1980), are literally *our* maps. They are sketches of reality from our own limited perspectives given our own needs, desires, interests, situation, and resources.

Consider, for example, the accounts related to the therapist by family members. The wife might explain:

> He came home after a fight with his boss, started drinking again and then he got mean and became violent and hit me.

The husband might, with equal conviction and sincerity, state:

> I had a hard day at work, came home and had a couple of drinks. She started in on me again and kept on nagging and putting me down until I couldn't take it any more and I lost my self-control.

Far from being unusual, contradictory accounts by participants in the same situation are the norm. This is well known to therapists, journalists, police investigators, and anyone who seeks to determine "the truth" about a situation from first-hand sources.

Features of Accounts

Our example illustrates several features of accounts which the therapist should be sensitive. First, it suggests the principle of relativity; that there is no single objectively true account of any situation. It is a natural temptation to ask which account is right, but that is a meaningless (or at least unanswerable) question. Every participant in a situation experiences it from his or her own viewpoint and takes from it a different account — in effect a different truth. This leads ethnomethodologists to suggest that, for all practical purposes, situations consist of accounts. The question is not which is true or false, but how and why participants construct the realities that they do.

A second, closely related insight is that all accounts exhibit the property of reflexiveness (Handel, 1982). In the process of making sense of experiences and events, we define situations in terms of their essential features. This appears to be straightforward, common sense, but the whole point of ethnomethodology is that common sense is anything but straightforward. The fact that the account itself identifies what is accountable implies that every account reflects (or projects onto the situation) the needs, wants, beliefs, and understandings of the account-maker. Reflexiveness cautions us that accounts tell us about the account-maker and the process of making things accountable as much as what they account for.

That example also illustrates the principle of indexicality which holds that accounts are situationally dependent (Handel, 1982). Like Chinese ideograms, their sense is largely determined by context. To decipher the mythological couple's stories, one must recognize that they are being related in the social situation of a therapy visit. They would probably be very different accounts if made in another setting, such as at home during a fight. Each account is a plea for the therapist to endorse the speaker's definition of the situation. At the same time, the account places a certain "spin" on the situation according to the principle of reflexiveness.

Motives

When social acts flow smoothly, interactants rarely concern themselves with motives. However, when their interaction becomes distressful or problematic, family members begin to scrutinize one another's motives. That is, they make sense out of the situation by reference to intentions, sometimes their own but most often the imagined or imputed intent of others. Family members question and form hypotheses about the others' motives, commonly identifying those motives as key causes of their interpersonal difficulties. Simultaneously, family members' own motives are used to justify or explain their actions, attitudes, and viewpoints in terms of reacting to others' expressed or implied intent.

Motives can be defined as accounts of the relationships among behavior, thoughts, and feelings prevailing in a certain social situation and particular historical period. In essence, a motive is an explanation of the connection between one or more persons' thoughts, feelings, and behaviors. However, such connections are hidden, implicit, unknown or at least unobservable; one can only infer motives.

Guesses about another's intents are rarely scientific in the sense of painstakingly building from observation of the other's behavior. Rather, family members rely on conventional wisdom ("everybody knows . . . ") and culturally acceptable explanations, interpretations, or metaphors about why people act as they do. Sociologists have demonstrated that there is, in fact, an entire vocabulary of motives associated with each historical society and its groups (Balch, 1979; Mills, 1940).

Problem-Solving Perspectives

The way family members frame accounts, including attributions of motive, reveals how they generally make sense of problematic situations. That is, they provide insight into the person's problem-solving perspective:

> People have a number of conventional and readily available alternative definitions for, and means of coping with, their problems . . . a perspective or rhetoric defining the nature and sources of problems in living and offering some program for their resolution. (Lofland & Stark, 1965, p. 167)

Among the perspectives most often presented to therapist are the:

1. *Psychiatric* — unconscious or other psychological and, more recently, psychobiological causes (e.g., brain chemistry).
2. *Religious* — traditional or nontraditional beliefs about God and the spiritual realm.
3. *Political* — negative effects of the social structure.
4. *Occult/Magical* — magical, supernatural, or paranormal phe-

nomena (an important contemporary variant of which might be termed "New Age").

5. *Common sensical* — conventional wisdom, inherent traits, or properties ("that's how things are") or fatalism.
6. *Individualist* — acceptance of American culture's ideology of individualism and the idea that one causes whatever occurs to him or her.
7. *Ethnic* — ethnic subcultures offer rich, often highly idiosyncratic, explanatory schemes and healing traditions.

Working with Problem-Solving Perspectives

In addition to revealing how family members organize their situational definitions, problem-solving perspectives may present the therapist with significant problems and opportunities. Perspectives to which Family members are deeply committed can become problematic because they not only prompt fixed and stereotypical interpretations but also create a cultural barrier between therapist and family member. For example, family members with an extreme fundamentalist Christian perspective may be unwilling or uable to accept accounts not framed in Scriptural terms and not explicitly invoking Jesus, God, or Satan.

At the same time, identification of commitment to a particular problem-solving perspective offers important therapeutic insights and opportunities. For example, unreflective application of all purpose accounts to problematic situations often presents a barrier to effective problem-solving action. Therefore, the therapist may endeavor to get family members to consider alternative explanations and courses of action.

The rule here is to go gently. Strongly held perspectives (which may seem absurd, ridiculous, counterproductive, or objectionable to an outsider) test the therapist's willingness to respect family members' goals, beliefs, and lifestyle. A frontal attack on the client's belief system is not only unwise (and ethically untenable), but is likely to cause a break with the client. The therapist can accomplish a great deal by learning and working within the client's metaphors and structuring therapeutic accounts compatibly with family members' own perspectives. Or the therapist may even consider utilizing elements of an alternative healing tradition within the therapy itself. For example, one might employ Scriptural analogies and metaphors with committed Christians and urge them to pray for calmness, strength, and divine guidance. Similarly, one might employ ethnic, psychiatric, or New Age analogies and metaphors, thus working with predispositions rather than against them. We should note that operating in this fashion does not preclude educating the family member about social and interactional realities. Rather, it calls for special sensitivity to "where they are coming from."

The therapist should also be aware that consistent or clearly inappropriate use of these problem-solving perspectives may indicate psychosis in one or more family members. Particularly when not supported by the family member's social milieu, constant reference to occult/magical phenomena, unchanging religious or philosophical principles, immutable natural laws, or oppressive social forces should prompt the therapist to investigate. It is good practice to secure appropriate guidance or consultation to determine whether the family member's treatment falls within one's sphere of professional (and legal) competency.

Interaction Hypotheses

Interaction hypotheses are attributions that reveal elements of one's definition of the situation including problem-solving perspectives. The concept of interaction hypotheses is central to sociocognitive therapy and is probably Hurvitz's most widely known contribution. We have already discussed one example, motives, a particular type of interaction hypothesis that emphasizes intent. In contrast, problem-solving perspectives are a more general type of account from which family members often draw their interaction hypotheses.

As with motives and problem-solving perspectives, interaction hypotheses are revealed whenever family members construct accounts of their own or others' actions, reactions, and interactions. They may do so spontaneously in the process of talking about their problems or personal and interpersonal situations or when explicitly prompted to reveal their accounts. For example, the therapist may ask, "How do you account for what happened?" or "Why do you feel that she does that?"

Interaction hypotheses are of two types: terminal and instrumental.

Terminal Hypotheses

Terminal hypotheses interpret behavior, meanings, or feelings as innate qualities—fixed and unchangeable conditions. They suggest that there is nothing that can be done to change the existing situation. Often, they select elements from family members' problem-solving perspectives and turn them into self-fulfilling prophecies. However well they appear to fit the facts, they offer no possible plans of action to change the family member's relationships or conditions. Common themes of terminal hypotheses include:

1. Psychodynamic interpretations ("He has an oral fixation").
2. Psychological name calling ("He's a latent homosexual").
3. Pseudoscientific explanations ("She's a Scorpio, and all Scorpios act like that").
4. References to unchanging religious or philosophical principles, immutable natural laws, oppressive social forces, and "what everybody knows" ("Everybody knows that if a man doesn't have sex regularly it builds up in him, so he just naturally looks for an outlet").
5. Attributions about innate personal or intellectual limitations and unchangeable traits ("He's got a jealous nature," "She's too dumb to know any better," "He was born without willpower, that's why he drinks the way he does").
6. Attributions about inability or refusal to change ("I don't think he'll ever change and there's no use in trying to change him").
7. Claims that unchangeable external factors cause family or personal problems ("He complains about the pressure at work and says that he has to do it and that's why he doesn't have time for the family").

Instrumental Hypotheses

Instrumental hypotheses explain behavior, meanings, or feelings in an open-ended, operational, processual and nonjudgmental way. In contrast to terminal hypotheses, they suggest that something can be done to change the family member's existing situation. Whether or not they are true, they fit the information available. They also offer a basis for plans of action that can change relationships and conditions. At the very least, they provide metaphors that suggest the possibility of change and improvement.

As a matter of course, the sociocognitive therapist encourages the spouses or family members to offer instrumental hypotheses. When offered by family members, they might explain problems caused by:

1. Communication difficulties ("She says it's because I don't listen to what she says, but I do—we just don't seem to understand each other").
2. Situationally related changes in relationships ("I think our troubles started when he got that new job—maybe it's the pressure or something").
3. Difficulty managing roles or situations ("He has no idea of what a little child can be expected to do—he expects too much—and then he's upset").
4. Longstanding habitual behavior, beliefs, and values ("His mother never taught him to pick up after himself and so when I ask him to pick up his clothes, he says I'm complaining").
5. Out-of-control feelings, cognitions, and responses ("I feel guilty about whatever goes wrong; even when I know that it's not my fault, I keep dwelling on it and blaming myself for allowing it to happen").

Therapeutic Hypotheses

The therapist evaluates family members' interaction hypotheses, both instrumental and terminal, in order to understand the family members' situation, meanings, perceptions, and problem-solving hypotheses. At the same time, the therapist forms and tests her own interaction hypotheses. Unlike the instrumental hypotheses that family members tend to spontaneously generate, these therapeutic hypotheses are deliberately formulated. They offer one or more family members a way to understand and change their own and/or others' behavior, thoughts, and feelings in a way that facilitates desired outcomes. Four general principles guide the therapist's formulation of interaction hypotheses and evaluation of family members' hypotheses:

1. *Parsimony* — hypotheses are based on the least complicated assumptions or inferences about people in general and about specific family members in particular.
2. *Reality* — hypotheses are based on the family members' real life experiences.
3. *Practicality* — for a hypothesis to be practical, it must focus on aspects of the family members' lives over which they have control and about which they can do something.
4. *Creative expediency* — one or more of these principles may be disregarded if the therapist's evaluation indicates that another hypothesis and associated activity, for which she has no theoretical justification at the moment, is a wiser, more effective course of action.

Eliciting Therapeutic Hypotheses

Throughout discussion with family members, the therapist probes for and invites hypotheses to explain their interactions, problems and situations. The therapist helps the family members to replace terminal hypotheses with instrumental hypotheses and unproductive instrumental hypotheses with therapeutic hypotheses. The therapist does this by:

1. Challenging terminal hypotheses;
2. Soliciting and helping devise practical instrumental hypotheses;
3. Informing family members about each other's hypotheses; and
4. Inviting explanations for why the family member perceives and interprets the other as indicated by their hypotheses.

In many cases, a family member's hypotheses offer insights and understandings that the person is unaware of communicating to the therapist. As suggested, they will generally reveal both the nature and intensity of commitment to the person's problem-solving hypothesis.

More concrete information is revealed as well. For example, consistent ascription of guilt feelings, insecurity, repressed hostility, fear of success or enjoyment of suffering and similar attributions of others' motivations, may tell the therapist more about the individual constructing the account than the family member being described.

Change Activities Using Interaction Hypotheses

Hypotheses are not used merely to provide information about family members, their perceptions, and interactions. Helping family members redefine their situation by upgrading interaction hypotheses to instrumental hypothesis is, in itself, a therapeutic activity.

Identifying the opening problem. The therapist also guides family members' generation of instrumental hypotheses. The purpose is to reveal problems or areas particularly amenable to change and to help family members identify a joint course of action to facilitate desired changes. Then, family members are encouraged to devise and to follow an action-plan based on this map:

> When you tell me he behaves like that because he's an only child, then I have to tell you that you're telling me that we can't change things—after all, he'll always be an only child. But when you tell me that maybe he behaves like that because you nag him—and you agree that you do—then we can try to control what you do that certainly plays a part in causing him to behave in the way you don't like. Also, you know that when you say, "I can't help myself," you're really saying, "I've always found it too hard to change in the past." But now the stakes are pretty high and both of you have agreed you want to improve your marriage. So you have to try harder now. What do you think you can do about your nagging to bring about the result you say you want?

As in this example, the therapist begins by helping family members to identify an *opening problem* based on their instrumental hypotheses. This is not generally the most important, severe, or troublesome problem, merely the one common to all situational definitions that appears most amenable to change. Working on the opening problem helps family members understand the principles by which the therapist works. It also shows that desired changes can be achieved by application of these principles. The joint action of solving the problem initiates the process of family members changing their meanings and interactions. At the same time, the success achieved by resolving this problem encourages the family members to exert further effort.

Testing goals. The therapist also investigates the family members' hypotheses in relation to their asserted goals. These goals may or may not have been explicitly formalized in a contract. She informs the family members that their continuing interaction should demonstrate that they are attempting to achieve a particular goal. If family members cannot see a connection between their activities and the goal, the therapist asks if they want to reconsider their goal or demonstrate greater commitment by formulating new hypotheses. These new hypotheses require them to initiate and participate in change activities directed toward that objective. When family members determine the actions needed to implement their hypotheses, the therapist helps each to elicit the behavior wanted in the other. With therapeutic support and guidance, each becomes a reciprocal stimulus for further encouragement and reinforcement of effective and satisfying interaction.

Organizing the change activity. Efforts directed at the most amenable problem may require family members to alter their definitions of the situation and make different assumptions about it. Sometimes the opening problem may be an issue that one or more family members has identified as what bothers them most about their relationship.

For example, Mrs. Jones may complain that her husband does not phone to let her know when he will come home from work. She expresses the belief that, if he did, they would not have any problems. Mr. Jones denies that this is the real problem and states that, even if he called as she desired, she would find something else to complain about. However, as this is something that is amenable to practical action, the therapist might identify it as a suitable opening problem.

The therapist would probably work with the husband in this regard. She would ask questions to help the husband understand that it is not the calls so much as what they represent to Mrs. Jones that are the issue here — respect, gentility, concern, or other similar qualities. Such a discussion might begin with the therapist asking:

> "Let's agree that what your wife says is upsetting her is not the real reason why she's upset. What do you think the real reason is?"
>
> When the husband suggests one or more hypotheses and these are evaluated, the therapist says, "You've offered a number of explanations of why your wife might be upset that fit the information we have better than the reason she gave. Why do you think she gave this reason?"
>
> The therapist then suggests that it may be helpful for Mr. Jones to call his wife as she desires for those reasons.

If the calls (and what they represent) are indeed the real problem, then following the suggestion will have solved it. That is, they will have agreed upon and effected a solution. As is virtually certain, if the calls do not solve their problem, then they are both guided to evaluate their situation and acknowledge other or more serious problems. They are encouraged to offer hypotheses which explain their interaction and to elicit further problems and possible solutions in accord with their expressed goals. Change activities are therefore iterative (repeated cyclically).

Overcoming Inability to Offer Hypotheses

Family members may be unwilling or unable to develop and offer therapeutic hypotheses. This may be the result of many factors, ranging from genuine pain and confusion, lack of security and trust in therapy. Or it may be an incapacitating psychological disturbance, a covert goal that is different from their asserted goal, fears of inadvertently revealing material that the person wants to keep concealed, or a belief that the situation is beyond help.

When one family member cannot offer instrumental hypotheses about another, the therapist suggests that each offer one which requires positive behavior or expression of positive feelings. This may be explained to one family member as a means of bringing about a desired change in another in accord with their expressed therapy goal. For instance, the therapist will suggest to Mr. Jones that he assume that Mrs. Jones wants him to behave so as to enhance her self-concept. If he behaves in this way his wife will probably respond so as to enhance his self-concept in return.

The principle here is generally useful. When the situation is ambiguous or a family member cannot offer instrumental hypotheses about another's behavior, its meaning, or associated feelings, the therapist suggests that each act or respond to make the other feel better about himself or herself. To motivate family members to follow this suggestion, the therapist explains that doing so will encourage behavior and feelings that will help them achieve their asserted goal.

Social Perceptions

Family members' accounts and interactions not only enable the therapist to understand their interaction hypotheses but provide insight into family members' *social perceptions*. This term means the way family members perceive themselves, one another and one another's perceptions of themselves (self-perception, other-perception and metaperception, respectively). These three types of social perceptions play an important role in the family interaction and relationships.

Each family member regards him- or herself in a particular way with respect to character, status, potential, accomplishments, moral worth, attractiveness, intelligence, and so forth. That person may want other family members to share these perceptions, but one or more of them may not. Alternatively, family members may want others to perceive them in a different way than they perceive themselves.

Implications of Social Perceptions

Because conduct is governed by the definition or the situation, discrepancies in self-perception, other-perception, and metaperception prompt discrepancies in how each family member wants or expects themselves or others to behave and their actual behavior. This can lead to unsatisfying interactions, perceptions that something is wrong with oneself or other family members, conflicts, and other troubles. On the other hand, when family members become more sensitive to how each perceives him- or herself, the others, and the others' self-perceptions, discussion can generate useful therapeutic hypotheses. These in turn can suggest changes that will assist family members in resolving their problems and conflicts.

The Four Questions Technique

For simplicity's sake, the therapist focuses on one *dyad* (set of two family members) at a time. She attempts to secure information from each dyad member concerning self-perception, other-perception, and two types of metaperception. These types of information are elicited by the Four Questions. Each of these questions is asked of one dyad member in regard to the second member and vice versa. Using the example of two spouses, Jack and Jill, the therapist asks:

Jack about:
1. his behavior, meanings, and feelings;
2. Jill's behavior, meanings, and feelings;
3. Jill's perception of Jack's behavior, meanings, and feelings;
4. Jill's perception of Jill's behavior, meanings, and feelings.

Jill about:
1. her behavior, meanings, and feelings;
2. Jack's behavior, meanings, and feelings;
3. Jack's perception of Jill's behavior, meanings, and feelings;
4. Jack's perception of Jack's behavior, meanings, and feelings;

The Four Questions are basic to sociocognitive therapy and will be employed in a variety of contexts throughout this volume. This technique makes the therapist aware of perceptions not ordinarily considered in the therapeutic situation or obtained by completing a checklist.

IMPLICATIONS
OF A MICROSOCIOLOGICAL PERSPECTIVE

Symbolic interactionism implies that we misattribute inevitability and necessity to the way things are, whereas the real world emerges from the ongoing negotiation of meaning in which each social actor participates. This suggests that the structure of interpersonal relationships and society is only fixed by our agreement to act as if it is so. Hence the structure is always contingent, always subject to renegotiation and change.

At the level of family issues, the sociocognitive therapist considers interpersonal problems to stem from the inability or refusal to negotiate and change joint meanings or poor communication between parties. This in turn implies that interpersonal difficulties can often be ameliorated by taking the role of the other.

The therapist acts on behalf of individual family members and the family members as a group. Marriage and family problems and conflicts arise among family members and can validly be represented as problems of the group or system. However, the distress caused by these troubles is not experienced by a relationship. It is experienced by the human beings who comprise and interact in a relationship. Similarly, the therapist cannot work with the relationship (or family system) directly. Rather, the therapist works with the individuals who comprise and participate in the relationship to bring about change at the level of that relationship.

The sociocognitive approach always proceeds on two parallel tracks. One track consists of working with the spouses as a couple or the family members as a group to understand and optimize their interpersonal processes and performances. The other track consists of working with one or more individual family members to help them understand and overcome their personal troubles and limitations.

The sociocognitive therapist is not concerned with which came first—the chicken of disruptive personal limitations or the egg of disturbed relationships. The therapist simultaneously makes efforts to change relationships and interactions, relieve the individual family members' distress, and overcome personal limitations that cause or intensify problems or conflicts in relationships.

Chapter Three

Working with Families
as Social Groups

In this chapter we move up a level of social interaction from individual family members to the family as a social group. We will then examine the types of family problems, conflicts, and crises that may arise and prompt family members to contact the therapist for help.

THE FAMILY AS A SOCIAL GROUP

As LaRossa points out, "the most important assumption in family sociology is that a family is a social group" (1984, p. 2). A social group is a plurality of persons who: (a) interact repeatedly; (b) exhibit a relatively stable pattern of interaction; (c) are structurally tied to each other; (d) share a set of goals, values, beliefs, and norms; and (e) think of themselves as a unit, identify with the unit, and draw a sense of support from it (LaRossa, 1984; Lofland, 1976). As we consider the premises and implications of this brief definition, we can begin to see the value of viewing the family as a social group.

Interaction and Group Structure

As a result of routine, day-to-day interaction, each family member acquires a status or position within the web of relationships that is the social structure of that group. A particular social role or set of behavioral expectations comes to be associated with each status within the group. Thus, the family social structure can be described by the roles and role relationships which emerge as family members come to hold mutual expectations for one another's conduct. In the traditional American middle-class family, the father has the greatest authority and is primarily responsible for the family's economic well-being. The mother holds authority over domestic matters and the children and is primarily responsible for child-rearing and physically maintaining the household.

Learning how to enact any role within the family group requires learning its relationship to every other role. Thus each family member must learn something of the role being taken by every other family member. For effective interaction, family members must learn not only their own role but the complementary roles forming the salient role set (Merton, 1968). For example, a child must not only learn his or her own role in the family but that of husband-and-father, wife-and-mother.

Focussing on Dyads

Except in the abstract, it is impractical to describe or work with the interactional structure of the family as a whole. The therapist reduces this complexity to a manageable level through the strategy of viewing the family as a unity of dyads. She then focusses on dyadic relationships within the family: between two individuals, an individual and a coalition of individuals, or two coalitions.

Every family member is involved in a dyadic relationship with every other family member, and every dyad in the family is attached to every other dyad. In this system-like relationship, whatever affects one dyad necessarily affects every other dyad (although some are affected more than others). For example, spousal conflict will more often affect the parent/child relationship than conflict between children will affect the spousal relationship.

Family Culture

Family members themselves come to recognize the formation of internal dyads and coalitions. Years afterward, they often characterize family relationships in such terms as "she was always her daddy's favorite." To the extent that these joint definitions become part of the family's discourse, they illustrate the concept of family culture. As with every group, families develop an entire cultural reality of their own through norms, values, goals, beliefs, symbols, and myths. This family culture defines how members perceive, conduct themselves within, and respond to, the real world.

Family Reality

The family culture also defines what that "real world" is for its members. In other words, as family members interact they construct jointly held meanings: understandings about themselves, their family, and the world outside the family. This illustrates the social construction of reality (Berger & Luckmann, 1966), or more specifically, of family reality (Reiss, 1981).

Group Boundaries

As with any social group, some manner of boundary always distinguishes family members from nonmembers and the family from the world outside the family. Such boundaries facilitate joint action and encourage members to identify themselves as a group and with their group. Boundaries are social facts; they have both symbolic (or cognitive) and interactional dimensions. They differentiate "us" from "them" and define regions of backstage interaction among one's intimates and of strategic interaction with outsiders (Goffman, 1959). Thus, family members act differently in the back-home environment than they do elsewhere — perhaps including the therapist's office.

Reference Groups

To the extent that we identify ourselves as members of a specific group, that group becomes a *reference group*. We adopt the culture or symbolic perspectives of our reference groups (Shibutani, 1955). And we conduct ourselves from the perspective of our reference groups. Thus, family boundaries ensure that the family serves as a reference group for its members, particularly children. Furthermore, those identifying with a group act as agents or members of that group to further its collective goals and purposes.

THE FAMILY AS A PRIMARY GROUP

According to the pioneering American sociologist Charles Horton Cooley, the family is the ideal of a specific type of social group, the *primary group* (1902). Defining characteristics of a primary group include:

a. relatively small size,
b. face-to-face interaction,
c. intense, emotionally involved relationships involving the whole person (rather than segmented roles such as teacher or checkout clerk), and
d. identification with the group so that membership becomes a central part of one's self-definition or identity.

The family is not merely a primary group, but *the* primary group. Not only is it the basic structural unit of virtually all societies (Goode, 1982), it is the first group we encounter and the one that initially socializes us. As readers will recall from the previous chapter, a person's self-concept develops in the context of symbolic interaction. While the same basic processes continue throughout adult life, it is universally recognized that we are to a considerable extent formed by childhood socialization (Elkin & Handel, 1988).

The Looking Glass Self

The child's initial socialization occurs within the family during a period in which humans depend entirely upon parents and other group members. Cooley (1902) observed that, beginning in early infancy, children learn to anticipate likely responses to their actions. They learn how to behave, in other words, by reading how others perceive them. Eventually, the child builds a concept of how others view her and respond to what they see. The child subsequently guides her own behavior by imagining others' responses and thoughts of her, a pattern that continues throughout life. Cooley labeled this process the looking glass self.

Significant Others

Not just anyone's actual or imagined responses have this effect, but those individuals whose judgments are important to one's self-image. Cooley terms these people *significant others* (1902). Clearly, in the earliest years of life, one's significant others are to be found within the family group. Eventually we find significant others outside our family: our peers, those we most respect, and characteristically, our spouses and members of the families we create. Throughout our lives, however, we find significant others within the context of our primary groups. Alternatively we enter into significant other status as we develop the intense, personal relationships that define a primary group.

In sociocognitive therapy, we focus on significant other relationships. For Jack to be a significant other to Jill, Jill must be a significant other to Jack. Significant others — those who hold such a relationship — display five characteristic features:

1. *Acting according to mutually-recognized role expectations*, so that each performs in accord with the other's role expectations for them;
2. *Sharing meanings held to be important*, so that the meanings held by each are or become important to the other;
3. *Having affective or expressive significance for and/or an affective relationship* with each other;
4. *Supporting the other's desired self-concept*, to engender or maintain positive self-esteem on the part of both self and other;
5. *Serving as models for one another through behavior, thoughts, and feelings*, so that each serves as a role model for the other and accepts the other as a model. (Hurvitz, 1979c)

DYNAMIC ASPECTS OF FAMILY RELATIONSHIPS

So far, we have looked at the family as a more or less static web of dyadic relationships. Now we turn to the dynamic aspects of interaction by which families maintain the qualities of a primary group. If something goes wrong, these can become sources of family troubles.

Exchanges and Reciprocity

The binding principle of any social group or institution is found in the social acts performed by members. In particular, the web of social relations is held together by *exchanges*. This term denotes a type of social act involving a transaction between members of a dyad. There is an implicit or explicit attempt to maintain reciprocity, a perceived balance between what each gives and gets (Blau, 1964; Cohen, 1986; Homans, 1961).

The concept of reciprocity has played an important part in the development of behaviorist family therapy (Ackerman, 1958; Lederer & Jackson, 1968; Nye, 1978; Stuart, 1969). Social learning theorists often reduce reciprocity to an arithmetic formula in which dyad members display similar rates of positive behaviors (Patterson & Reid, 1970). However, a mechanistic approach of this type fails to capture the essence of the phenomena (Gottman, 1979).

Constructed Reciprocity

Hurvitz proposes a model of constructed reciprocity. In this model, interactants construct and maintain a relationship such that each is perceived as an integral part of a whole. Such a relationship is termed complementary. The paradigm of a complementary relationship is spouses, whose roles, identities, and self-definitions are contingent on being dyad members. After all, one cannot be a spouse without a partner!

Role Reciprocity

To maintain their identities, spouses engage in reciprocal exchanges as well as joint action to maintain and further their marriage. In a healthy family relationship, then, complementarity is an explicitly accepted element of family roles. Consequently, role reciprocity becomes a normative goal toward which group members actively strive.

Those working with couples and families quickly become aware that reciprocity is not a mechanical balance of equal and opposite behaviors, costs or rewards. It is a jointly held meaning constructed by dyad members as they interact in specific situations. Because the flux of life presents continually changing and emerging situations, reciprocity is an ongoing, dynamic process. In this process, contradictions are resolved and their common meanings affirmed or modified. This serves as a basis for their continuing relationship. The maintenance of complementary relationships, then, depends on the continuous construction of jointly defined reciprocal exchanges.

Transformation

Hurvitz (1979c) identifies transformation as one of the processes by which significant others maintain constructed reciprocity. Therefore, it is an important element of family hardiness. Transformation is the restoration of constructed reciprocity through the offering of a surplus of some symbolic, expressive, or material currency in compensation for a "deficit" in prior exchanges. This can only occur if both parties define what is proffered as equivalent in value to the initial deficit in their exchange. Thus, symbolic transformation maintains constructed reciprocity.

This process not only maintains reciprocity but enables spouses and family members to complement one another. It creates a synergistic relationship in which interactants compensate for individual weaknesses through personal strengths. If one interactant fails the other in some way, this process is often called "making it up to him [or her]." For example, if the wife fails to fulfill the husband's role expectations for her, she may compensate by offering a "surplus" of affection or other conduct that enhances the husband's self-esteem. Thus, transformation enables family members to maintain effective and satisfying significant other relationships despite potential threats to reciprocity.

Disturbed Reciprocity

Complementarity and reciprocity cannot be taken for granted. Even stable patterns of constructed reciprocity are subject to disturbances originating from within or outside the social group. A vast assortment of events may disturb family reciprocity. These range from birth or death to acquisition or loss of jobs and rapid or dramatic changes in socioeconomic status or lifestyle. From experiences or events that bring fame, fortune, or notoriety to family members moving, from visits by friends or family members to loss of a pet, extramarital affairs, religious or political conversion of a family member—the list of possibilities is virtually infinite.

Disturbed reciprocity may have positive effects. Some families are able not only to forestall the potentially serious consequences but to turn the situation to their advantage. Others are unable to do so.

Family Hardiness

Those families who benefit and grow from the challenge of disturbed reciprocity share values and activities that foster and enhance group functioning. They have a family culture that is open to change and mutually supportive of its members. Family members share responsibility for making and implementing major decisions. Consensus and not coercion governs their actions. Such families have developed effective communication, joint action, and coping skills (such as bargaining, decision making, and problem solving). They also have come to accept that they have the will, the means, and the effort needed to cope with and overcome their disturbed reciprocity. In effect, on a joint level they demonstrate the properties identified by Kobasa (1981) as hardiness:

1. A positive orientation toward challenges and reasonable risk taking.
2. A positive commitment or sense of embracing the different aspects of their lives.
3. A belief that they have control over their own lives.

For such families, recognition and examination of a problem situation may catalyze joint action. Action leads not only to specific solutions but to changes in the interactional processes of the whole family group. In this way, members acquire skills that can be generalized and applied elsewhere. As a result, they become more capable or resourceful, and more committed to their values and goals. They devise more effective role relationships to meet specific objectives or overcome frustration of their general intentions.

Of course, hardiness is relative. Depending on the amount and kind of reciprocity disturbance, coping mechanisms of virtually any family can be strained to the breaking point. Clinical experience, however, shows that some families are less hardy than others and more readily succumb to detrimental effects of disturbed reciprocity. Their family culture and structure does not support the development of hardiness as described above. They also lack the skills and knowledge to construct and maintain reciprocity or complementary relations (e.g., through transformation).

Negative Consequences of Disturbed Reciprocity

When hardiness fails, the therapist sees an escalation of the family's inability to engage in effective and satisfying joint action. Individuals often begin to exhibit personal limitations that further disturb family reciprocity. Family members may stay away from home, engage in substance abuse, or become suspicious of other family members and anxious or depressed. They become increasingly unable to interact supportively as significant others. Communication breaks down and members share less and less of a common definition of the situation.

Under these conditions, egalitarian leadership and non-coercive authority may become authoritarian and coercive. Some investigators have suggested that reciprocity and coercion are in fact the alternative modes of response in any relationship (Patterson & Reid, 1970). Conflict may erupt within the family for two reasons. Either one or more dyads or coalitions already exist in a state of incipient conflict or the disturbance takes the form of conflict about a family or nonfamily person or issue. Expressing dissatisfaction with circumstances or relationships, may cause family members to become estranged. Changes in values and goals promote the appearance of personal limitations. The appearance of personal limitations changes values and goals in an escalating process of circular or reciprocal causation (Bateson, 1979).

Misattribution of Causes

When problems develop there is a tendency to lose sight of these growing differences in values and goals. Family members may not even realize that their meanings and expectations are changing and diverging. Rather, in accordance with the contemporary emphasis on feelings and psychological causes of behavior, they interpret all problems in terms of personal limitations (certainly the others' and perhaps one's own).

Not only does the family culture fragment, but solidarity as a social group breaks down. As problems become more severe, various combinations of family members form alliances to gain some advantage for themselves. This process commonly takes the form of scapegoating and adversarial coalitions.

Scapegoating

In scapegoating, family members designate one or more of their number (usually a child) as the problem or its source. They then behave commensurate with that label, typically constraining him or her to behave accordingly. This permits the family group to polarize itself at the expense of the negatively labelled member. The result is a sense of unity, solidarity, and cohesion in opposition to the scapegoat. Even though the family defines that individual as needing help, they often resist seeking help because scapegoating enables the family to develop an unfortunate but effective reciprocity.

Adversarial Coalitions

The family subgroup that forms in opposition to the scapegoat is but one example of adversarial coalition formation. Family members form subgroups which then compete to gain real or imagined advantage. The various dyads within the family may form coalitions or coalitions may form along other lines. In the absence of children, spouses may vie against one another, perhaps bringing their parents and relatives into the game. Parents may form coalitions against children, one sex may form a coalition against the other, or children may form coalitions against other children or adults. When divorced or widowed parents remarry, each spouse and their own children may form coalitions. This brings to mind the story of a remarried movie star who telephones her movie star husband, "Come quick, your children and my children are beating up our children!"

PROBLEMS, CONFLICTS AND CRISES

We now turn to a more formal consideration of the troubles that may occur within the family group. We will proceed to consider actual cases drawn from Hurvitz's practice that illustrate the types of family situations we have identified.

Problems

By definition, any trouble experienced by family members constitutes a *problem*. Technically defined, problems are unpleasant or perplexing situations or conditions which one or more family members believes require change, amelioration, or resolution. Problems subsume two broad types of situations or conditions, personal limitations and interpersonal predicaments.

Personal Limitations

When we say family members have limitations, we mean that they are limited in some way that affects family interaction and constitutes a problem for them. There are four general types of personal limitations:

1. biological deficits (e.g., in intelligence, appearance or health),
2. behavioral deficits (e.g., lack of social or work skills),
3. social deficits (e.g., belonging to a devalued, disprivileged or stigmatized social category), and
4. normative deficits (e.g., behavior, thoughts, or feelings considered illegal, immoral, or counter to values professed by significant others).

These limitations become problems only because family members define them as such. This may be due to disparities among their personal expectations or values, or because they prohibit members from functioning effectually in the outside society.

Interpersonal Predicaments

An interpersonal predicament exists when group members accuse one another of having a limitation which is a problem to them (typically while denying their own limitations) or when one admits a limitation while claiming that another is responsible. Because personal limitations are essentially definitions of the situation, predicaments reflect differing perceptions of physical, psychological, and social limitations or even values professed by other family members. Discovering and clarifying the specific elements of predicaments underlies the development of plans and means to resolve family problems and conflicts.

Interpersonal predicaments develop when one spouse or family member attempts to "help" another to overcome his or her personal limitations. The help that is offered as needed and appropriate may be perceived as superfluous, stupid, or demeaning. Thus, even an earnest and well-meant attempt to help may prompt resistance and become a source of conflict. On the other hand, the offer might reflect scapegoating, an attempt to deny one's own limitations, or a ploy to get "one up" in a pattern of conflict and negative interaction.

Interpersonal predicaments represent a genuine *bind* in which family members are unable to jointly resolve interactional difficulties, manage disturbed reciprocity, or effectively cope with the demands of the real world. Predicaments also represent the struggle of individuals or family subgroups to control the joint definition of the situation to advance either their own or the collective interests of the family. In either case, predicaments further disrupt reciprocity, strain coping resources and increase perceived significance of (or even engender new) personal limitations. This creates further predicaments and often leads to serious conflict.

Family Conflict

Conflict is often, but not necessarily, associated with family problems. To the sociologist, conflict denotes "direct and overt interaction between parties in which the actions of each party are directed at inhibiting their adversary's attainment of its goals" (Turner, 1986, p. 179).

As pointed out by Simmel (1964) and Coser (1956), conflict is ubiquitous in social life and can have positive functions for the family or other social group. For example, conflict tests and makes explicit shared definitions. Its resolution can enhance cohesiveness while expanding the group's repertoire of coping and problem solving skills. In fact,

> [A] positive use of conflict frequently seen in clinical practice is the release of tensions and, concurrently, the unspoken sources of these tensions. Some clinicians go so far as to recommend that married couples engage in periodic conflict in

order that tensions be released and emotional interactions initiated. The couples are encouraged to learn how to fight fairly. Simmel warns that within close primary groups such as families there is the tendency to deal with conflict by avoiding it. (Glassner & Freedman, 1979, p. 89)

Some degree of conflict is a condition of family life. It may be accepted as a continuing part of the family members' relationship and may be supported by the family culture. However, interpersonal conflict can also wreak havoc on the interactions and strain the family group to the breaking point.

Disruptive Conflict

Disruptive conflict can be defined as discord that is expressed behaviorally, verbally or nonverbally by one or more family members. Conflicts may be about their own or others' personal limitations or interpersonal predicaments that block or impede interaction as significant others and engagement in joint action. It is qualitatively different from what we might term the mundane conflicts that arise among family members. The family becomes an arena of overt conflict in which one or more members reject other family members because of real, exaggerated, imagined, or alleged limitations.

Disruptive conflict (or simply "conflict" as we will refer to it) follows when family members cease working to help one another overcome limitations by redefining the situation so as to re-establish reciprocity. Instead, they deny responsibility for their interpersonal predicaments. In a full-blown conflict situation, they assert to the therapist that there is almost constant strife between them. In such a situation, all family members generally agree that they have serious problems that are destroying their relationship.

Conflict occurs when one or more family members believe (or claim to believe) that others no longer interact with reciprocity, justice, equity, or fairness. This may be a result of acts of commission, when one family member says or does something to hurt or harm another. Or it may occur by omission when, by not acting, one family member causes another to suffer harm. Conflict can also occur through an intermediary, for example, when one family member harms another by doing or not doing something for or against a third party, often another family member. Conflict may be about a particular subject, process, or individual. Conflict can take many behavioral forms, from noisy verbal confrontations, beatings, or even murder threats to the silent treatment, withdrawal, and desertion.

Family members may try to suppress or deny all conflict as a means of maintaining reciprocity. Unresolved conflicts, interaction however, can trigger escalation in which reciprocity and interaction become increasingly disrupted. When this occurs, family members become disengaged or alienated from one another. They interact negatively as significant others and find themselves unable to engage in constructive joint action.

Family Crisis

A *crisis* exists when one or more family members threaten to leave or expel other members despite the group's wishes. The possibility of a crisis resulting in the dissolution of the marriage or family is a real one in every case that comes to the therapist. Although a crisis will sometimes resolve itself, other times someone outside of the family (such as the therapist), must exert extraordinary efforts on behalf of the family and its members. The family members that contact the therapist for help may not be willing or able to communicate a possible crisis. Consequently, the therapist approaches each new couple or family as though they are experiencing a crisis.

Types of Crises

Hurvitz identifies several types of crises as seen relatively often by the sociocognitive therapist. One is defection, in which a spouse decides unilaterally to leave the relationship. That spouse informs the other, behaviorally or verbally, that she or he wants to terminate the marriage. Family members may leave to pursue their own goals and values (e.g., another man or woman), or to prevent further diminishment of goals and values (e.g., due to physical or emotional abuse).

A variation of this is a youth or young adult leaving the family for a love relationship of which family members disapprove. In other cases, young adults may leave to join a social, religious, or political group or movement — commonly with a charismatic leader to whom the person transfers allegiance. In either situation, negative responses and attempts by family members to prevent the breaking away tend to exacerbate conflict and give the crisis the character of a defection.

Dissolution is a second type of crisis characterized by a mutual decision to break up the relationship. This may occur when a couple (including lesbian and gay couples) identifies their relationship as having failed and accepts the need to separate or divorce. The decision to call it quits may follow a precipitating event or series of events such as financial problems or discovery of an affair. It may include blame, resentment or other negative feelings directed toward the other as well as shame, guilt, and failure directed at oneself.

Ejection is a third type of crisis. It occurs when placement is sought for one or more family members that the family is unable to care for or to manage. This occurs when parents decide to place one or more children, due to severe illness, handicap, or behavior problems, in a foster home or other institution. It may also involve a decision to place an adult spouse or a spouse's parent in a nursing home or other institution due to age or disability. Or, increasingly common among impoverished inner city families, there may be abandonment of a child by an unwed (often teenaged or drug-addicted) mother to the care of the grandparents.

Regardless of type, the therapist's goal is optimal resolution of the crisis according to the values, goals, needs and self-images of the family members. This may mean accepting and facilitating a couple's decision to separate or a family's decision to split up. In some cases, the therapist is confronted with a fait accompli and has no alternative except to help clients cope with the aftermath of a breakup. However, if family members come to the therapist before committing any irrevocable acts, it is usually because at least one of them wants to maintain the family. In such cases, the therapist generally attempts to delay family breakup while initiating therapy, if only to test the goal of maintaining the family and its possible achievement.

Family Troubles as a Process

When we group together these types of situations encountered by the marriage and family therapist, we see that family troubles represent a process of escalation set into motion by a failure to achieve or to maintain constructed reciprocity. Personal limitations, interpersonal predicaments, and crises each represent a stage in that escalation. The major source of variation in each stage is the presence or degree of conflict.

First Stage: Limitations

Generally, the troubles brought to family therapy begin with personal limitations of one or more family members. These limitations become a problem when something occurs that family members cannot satisfactorily cope with or explain. The personal limitations may have been accepted previously by family members, they may have been longstanding sources of strain and disagreement, or they may be newly acquired (perhaps as a result of disturbed reciprocity).

Second Stage: Predicaments

When individual limitations become chronic sources of binds and problems to the family as a group, they grow into interpersonal predicaments. Inherently, predicaments inhibit family members' ability to engage in the joint problem-solving necessary to resolve their bind.

Third Stage: Conflict and/or Crisis

Interpersonal predicaments may or may not be associated with conflict. Even without actual conflict they may escalate into a crisis, although conflict exacerbates escalation by adding to the factors disrupting reciprocity. For example, conflict can make it virtually impossible for family members to interact as significant others. Thus, with or without conflict, interpersonal predicaments may escalate into crises. Also, family members' personal limitations infrequently precipitate a crisis without causing an interpersonal predicament or engendering conflict.

Initiation of Therapy

The therapist's first encounter with the couple or family occurs when problems, conflicts, or crises prompt them to reach out for help. The therapeutic process actually begins when the request for help is made. This step indicates that family members realize their need of professional assistance and their potential ability to benefit by it. The sociocognitive therapist schedules an initial visit with all the family members directly involved in the problem situation.

This may be a married or unmarried couple or a couple with their children. It may be an extended family grouping including siblings, parents, and close relatives in addition to any others who live with or are a functional part of the family group. If it is not feasible to set up an appointment with everyone who should participate, the therapist meets with as many as possible.

A CLINICAL TAXONOMY
OF FAMILY TROUBLES

To guide that initial encounter, the sociocognitive therapist makes an initial assessment or presumptive diagnosis in terms of the stages and major variations of the escalation process presented in Table One.

We will now consider the types of family troubles brought to the first therapeutic meeting as identified in Table One. These are based on actual cases treated by Hurvitz and we will follow some of them throughout the therapy process. Names of family members in these case examples have been changed to maintain confidentiality.

Personal Limitations That Do Not Cause Interpersonal Predicaments, without Conflict or Crisis

Sometimes family members enter therapy because disturbed reciprocity is attributed to one or more family members who have personal limitations. These limitations do not prevent generally satisfying and effective family interaction but are nevertheless perceived as an acute problem. Help is sought because family members recognize that unless the personal limitation is overcome, it may become the basis for an interpersonal predicament, conflict, or crisis.

70

TABLE ONE: CLINICAL TAXONOMY OF FAMILY PROBLEMS

| | CONFLICT | | CRISIS | |
	YES	NO	YES	NO
PERSONAL LIMITATION* — YES				
INTERPERSONAL PREDICAMENT — YES				
— NO				

*Assumed in all cases

Mrs. Wilson and her grandson, Michael: Enuresis

Mrs. Wilson was referred to Hurvitz by her grandson's pediatrician because of Michael's enuresis (lack of bladder control).

* * *

The grandmother explained over the telephone that Michael is the six-year-old son of Henry, Mrs. Wilson's son, and his former wife, Gloria. They were divorced shortly before the birth of their daughter, now two, who lives with Gloria's parents. Gloria has been in a state hospital since the birth of her daughter—Mrs. Wilson said she didn't know exactly why. Michael's father agreed to have his son live with him rather than be placed in a foster home, but quickly regretted his decision and asked his mother to care for Michael. That was two years ago. Henry promised to pay for Michael's keep, but he seldom visits and often neglects to give them the promised money.

Mrs. Wilson further reported that Michael is afraid of everything, does not want to be left alone, has to be taken to and from school each day, and cries when he is left there. He has various other limitations that make life very difficult for his elderly grandmother, but the one that most disturbs her is his daily soiling and nightly bedwetting. Despite the burden Michael places on her, Mrs. Wilson accepts the child as someone who needs help, which she wants to secure for him. Hurvitz advised her to make an appointment with the pediatrician for a complete checkup, with particular attention to Michael's genitourinary system, and then to call back for an appointment. About three weeks later she did so and an appointment was set.

* * *

Lilly and Arthur Hampton: Agoraphobia

Lilly Hampton called Hurvitz for an appointment.

* * *

She explained that she fears leaving her home unless another family member or someone else she knows very well is with her. Otherwise she feels that she may panic. She reports that she has had this problem for about eight months. For most of this time she believed she was the only one who had it. She is married and has four children, so that being unable to leave the house causes many problems. It places a burden on her husband and children who are very concerned about her.

She further explained that she is afraid to go out of her house alone because she is worried about being mugged or raped. She recognizes that she is more fearful than necessary, especially during the day, but she becomes so upset when she tries to leave the house that she usually gives up. She does force herself to walk to the corner of her street to watch for her youngest child when he comes home from school. She is also able to force herself to go to the market on the same corner if none of the children is available to go shopping for her.

About three weeks ago, she heard a psychologist on a radio talk show say that her problem is quite common and that psychologists can help people overcome it. Within the last week, she called a friend who once told her she had seen a therapist, who gave her Hurvitz's telephone number. She was given a late evening appointment so that her husband, Arthur, could bring her after work.

* * *

Personal Limitations That Cause a Crisis without Interpersonal Predicaments or Conflict

When one family member's personal limitations become a problem for others, despite attempts to accept and not complain, maintaining constructed reciprocity subjects the family to considerable strain. Commonly, the person does not recognize the limitation or acknowledge it as a problem for which help is required. After some time, the other family members feel unable to continue normally and demand that the individual "change her act."

The crisis frequently results in family members agreeing to a deadline for change and, when it is not met, requesting an emergency appointment from an agency, clinic, or therapist. They seek crisis intervention only and do not consider longer term therapy to effect the fundamental changes needed to restore family reciprocity.

Once the acute problem is resolved, spouses and family members relax back into their old patterns of thinking, feeling, and behaving. That is, until the strain builds up once again and there is another crisis. . . .

Ms. Hilliard and her son, Leroy: A delinquent

Ms. Hilliard, a single parent, called the therapist and reported that she has been having many problems with her 16-year-old son, Leroy Hawkins.

* * *

She said that he has already been in a lot of trouble, particularly at school. She had received complaints from the vice principal that he had hit one woman teacher, made sexual remarks to another, thrown a book out of a classroom window, and extorted money from elementary school children. Although she felt she could no longer keep trying to straighten him out, she wanted to give him another chance.

Ms. Hilliard said she tried to work, but her efforts to supervise Leroy cost her her jobs. Leroy had become such a burden to her that she could not give her other children the attention they needed. And she felt in danger of driving them away from her. They had given up on Leroy and did not consider him a member of the family.

She said yesterday Leroy was caught shoplifting in a neighborhood department store. When he acted smart-alecky toward the store security guard and refused to answer questions, the police were called. Leroy was taken to the neighborhood station, where the police learned his identity and called Ms. Hilliard. They told her that Leroy would be released to her custody but she would have to have him appear for a hearing. He would then probably be sent to a California Youth Authority Honor Camp.

Ms. Hilliard said that she had heard from women friends (who had similar experiences with their sons) that Leroy might be treated leniently if she could show the judge or hearing officer a letter stating that Leroy and his family were receiving therapy. She therefore wanted to make a therapy appointment as soon as possible, to which she would bring Leroy and the other children.

Hurvitz informed her that before he could prepare a letter, it would be necessary to see them both individually and together over a period of time. He also informed her that what she told him about Leroy was not promising. He might have to write a letter stating that while Leroy is participating in a therapy program, he isn't getting much out of it. Ms. Hilliard said she understood but wanted to go ahead, and an appointment was set.

* * *

Interpersonal Predicaments without Conflict or Crisis

Personal limitations can escalate into an interpersonal predicament without causing conflicts or crises. Although one family member may charge that another's limitations cause her own limitations and their interpersonal predicaments, these charges are not intended or delivered in a hostile way. Rather, the intention is to bring about more effective and satisfying family interaction. All family members recognize this and, although they declare each other's culpability, they do so in a helpful, nondestructive way. The personal limitations underlying the interpersonal predicament may or may not be known and acknowledged.

The Knights: Problems of communication

Mrs. Knight called for information about marriage counseling after receiving a referral from the county psychological association.

* * *

When asked what their major problem is, she said she really doesn't know if they needed counseling because they are not having serious problems. She explained that they aren't getting along as well as they would like. She asked whether the therapist would see them even though they weren't thinking of breaking up.

Hurvitz assured her that he saw cases like theirs and that she was wise to consider counseling. A late afternoon appointment was set for the next week, when both spouses could attend together.

* * *

The Stanleys and their children: Miscellaneous personal limitations

Mrs. Stanley called Hurvitz, reporting that she was referred by her gynecologist because she was continuously depressed.

* * *

She asked whether the therapist accepts Medicaid and whether she could bring three of her four daughters to the appointment. She had nobody with whom to leave them. When the therapist inquired about her husband, Mrs. Stanley said that he is a drinker but not an alcoholic. He had been involved with other women to whom he gave his money. She said he doesn't do that any more, adding that he used to call her names and beat her but he doesn't do that any more, either. When the therapist asked if her husband's behavior might be a cause of her depression, she replied that it used to be but was no longer. She said that while they don't fight any more, they don't get along as well as she would like, so she doesn't know why she is depressed.

Mrs. Stanley explained that she has three children by men to whom she was not legally married and one child by her husband, who was upset by the other three. She repeated that she is always depressed and does not get her work done. She said she stays with him because he married her even though she already had three children and he knew all about her past. She said she felt indebted to him and that when he is sober and has money, they have a nice family together. She also said that she knows he would never molest her daughters and therefore prefers to stay with him rather than take a chance with another man.

The therapist asked whether her husband would come to the appointment with her. She replied that she had asked him, but as she had expected, he refused. In fact, he refused to stay with the children if he was home when she went for an appointment. This is why she asked if she could bring her children with her. She assured the therapist that the children were well behaved and would not touch anything they should not touch. The therapist assured her that it was okay to bring the kids and that he would have something for them to play with. An appointment was set at a mutually agreeable time.

*   *   *

Interpersonal Predicaments with Conflict but without Crisis

Perhaps the most common type of marital and family problem seen by therapists is the interpersonal predicament with conflict. Simultaneous accusations and denials or admissions of limitations escalate (or degenerate) from enlightening and helpful discussion to acrimonious and spiteful arguments. The relationship and interaction based on constructed reciprocity breaks down, resulting in the same conditions that develop when personal limitations lead to conflict.

Yolanda Robison and David Tucker: Mutual dependency

Ms. Robison called for an appointment saying that she had to talk to someone immediately.

*   *   *

Sobbing, she said that she was given the therapist's name by a girlfriend who was a former client, but she couldn't remember her name. She asked whether she could come immediately to see him. The therapist told her that he could not see her that day, and offered to refer her elsewhere. She began to moan and what sounded like children trying to be helpful could be heard over the telephone. At no time did she respond to the therapist's questions concerning why she was calling or what was wrong. The therapist assumed that she didn't want to say anything in the presence of the children. Because the situation seemed to be an emergency, the therapist accepted Ms. Robison's suggestion that she drive to his office later that evening. It was only later that he learned about her mutual dependency relationship with David Tucker.

*   *   *

Interpersonal Predicaments with Conflict and Crisis

As discussed earlier, the family crisis represents the penultimate stage in escalation of family troubles. One or more family members threaten to leave the group or expel a member against the wishes of that individual or some other family members. Whatever the specific type, the escalating intrapersonal crisis is manifested in anxiety, depression, incapacity to perform one's social roles, and even physical illness. Of course, this exacerbates any personal limitations, interpersonal predicaments, and conflicts associated with the crisis situation.

The sociological perspective makes it clear that a cycle of ever-greater emotional crisis may be primarily attributed to family members' frustrated problem solving and an actual or anticipated loss of one's significant others. These cut deeply to the social-psychological core of feelings and the self.

Ms. Gloria Mackey and her daughters: Parent-child conflict

In this case, we see how known and acknowledged personal limitations can lead to interpersonal predicaments with conflict that escalate into crisis.

* * *

Ms. Gloria Mackey and her daughters, Sandra Williams, 14, and Michelle Mackey, 12, were referred by a pediatric heart specialist with offices in the same building as Hurvitz. This doctor had performed open heart surgery on Michelle several years earlier. After a follow-up office visit, he sent them down the hall to wait in the therapist's office until they could be seen.

The three family members appeared to have waited quietly and without hassling. However, the moment they came into the consultation room, Gloria began to complain, "I can't stand it. I can't take it any more." Without being asked, she said (all in a rush) that both girls are failing in school and they do not do their homework or their chores. They are always fighting about who is supposed to do what, they play cruel tricks on her, they do not follow their medical regimen, they are always on the phone or fighting about who is to use it — and more.

Although she leveled her complaints against both daughters, it became clear through her references and eye contact that they really were directed at Michelle, the younger girl. Gloria said that she knew Michelle is taking advantage because the cardiologist told her that she could do the household chores, which Michelle complained tired her. He also instructed Gloria to send Michelle to school daily. Michelle would feign illness and Gloria would then excuse her from doing her chores or going to school. Sandra often had to do Michelle's chores—which she complained about to their mother. When Gloria spoke, the girls constantly interrupted her, shouted at each other, and refused to answer any questions put to them.

When the therapist asked Gloria what the therapist could do to help, she replied that she wanted to place the girls in a foster home or other facility while she got a chance to rest. She began to recapitulate her reasons for this plan, precipitating another three-way shouting match. The therapist said that placing the girls is a serious undertaking that should be examined carefully before proceeding. Since the therapist had a scheduled appointment waiting, Gloria and her daughters were instructed to write down the pros and cons of the suggested course of action in a notebook. They were to bring the notebook to the next appointment, which was set for after school the next week.

* * *

Ross and Brenda Turner: Marital conflict

This case shows that personal limitations can be unknown and unacknowledged yet lead to conflict and crisis.

* * *

Mrs. Brenda Turner called the therapist, referred by a general practitioner with an office in the same building as Hurvitz. She asked for an appointment at the earliest possible time, explaining that her marriage of 25 years was turning into a nightmare. She asked about the length of the counseling process, about fees, and whether it was necessary to bring money to the first appointment. These questions were answered.

The therapist suggested that Mrs. Turner come to the appointment with her husband. She readily accepted although she wondered out loud whether her husband would come and if he did, whether she could talk with the therapist alone. A tentative appointment was set for the coming Saturday morning, when Mr. and Mrs. Turner could both come for an appointment.

The next day, Mrs. Turner verified the appointment and reported that she was surprised her husband had agreed to come without any urging. She again asked whether she could talk to the therapist alone. The therapist assured her that she would have an opportunity to do so.

* * *

ADVANTAGES OF THE TAXONOMY

The terms "problems," "conflicts" and "crises" are often used interchangeably by family therapists. They also use a host of neologisms specific to the school of therapy with which the therapist or author identifies. This may cause conceptual and clinical confusion. The processual model and nomenclature suggested by the clinical taxonomy indicate both differences and relationships among problems, conflicts and crises. Furthermore, instead of merely naming the family member's troubles — enuresis, alcoholism, extra-marital relationships, delinquency, parent-child conflict and the like — it describes the situation of family members through marital and family interaction processes. As will be seen in subsequent chapters, in the clinical setting this approach offers the following benefits. It suggests:

1. the general type of change activities appropriate to achieving the desired goal.
2. that families come to therapy for a variety of reasons not just because they have conflicts or crises.
3. whether greater efforts should be directed at individual or group change activities.

4. whether to gather history, investigate the cause of disturbed reciprocity, use objective instruments, or immediately use the basic sociocognitive method of learning and testing each family member's meanings.

Chapter Four

The Opening Phase
and the Tripartite
First Appointment

Chapter Three identified types of family troubles and explained how personal limitations become sources of interpersonal predicaments. These then escalate into situations of conflict and crisis. Examples were given of family members' first contact with the therapist. We now turn to the process of family therapy.

THE OPENING PHASE

During the opening phase, the therapist gathers information, determines the appropriate course of intervention, and begins the sociocognitive therapy process. The opening phase may continue for more than one appointment and overlap the second phase of the therapy process. It concludes with contract preparation between family members and therapist and among family members.

Establishing the Family Therapy Group

Sociocognitive therapy invariably proceeds on a two-track basis. The therapist works simultaneously with family members as individual social actors and as a social group. In both instances, the therapist facilitates change by entering and modifying family members' interactions.

To accomplish this, the therapist creates a *family therapy group* — a transient primary group consisting of the family members together with the therapist. Unlike natural primary groups, it is strategic. Serving as a model for the family, it provides an example of social relations that allow family members to achieve individual and joint objectives. This group provides a context for negotiating new meanings, joint reconstructing definitions, and changing collective reality.

Therapist's role. Within the family therapy group, the sociocognitive therapist operates as a participant observer in a much more active sense than social science researchers (Lofland, 1984). The therapist both participates in and manages the group process to facilitate emergence of new statuses, roles, and role relationships. These allow family members: (a) to experience more satisfying and effective significant other relationships and (b) to take increasing responsibility for maintaining their own constructed reciprocity.

Triadic structure. The family therapy group is also characterized by the deliberate formation of triadic relationships in which the therapist enters each family dyad as a significant other. As Hall describes it:

> In clinical work with dyads in crisis the practitioner functions as a third party in what might be called a "consultation triad" . . . [in which] the two-person relationship will be opened up and constructively modified. By sustaining an autonomous functioning position, while at the same time interacting meaningfully with each member of the dyad, the clinical sociologist may catalytically bring about change within the troubled dyad. (1989, p. 101)

The Therapist as a Significant Other

For the therapy group to acquire the form and life-changing impact of a primary group, the therapist cannot and must not remain external to the family members' interactions and manipulate them. Nor does the therapist act the role of all-knowing expert or father figure. Rather, the sociocognitive therapist interacts with family members individually and as a group in such a way as to provide a model for being a significant other.

In many ways, the sociocognitive therapist's interactions with clients are more like social conversation than what we generally think of as therapeutic communication. When family members talk, the therapist listens, supplies words they are groping for, and helps them express themselves more clearly so their meanings and feelings are understood.

When the therapist develops hypotheses about family members' behavior, he discusses his perceptions with them to secure feedback. He might tell them, "I'm not saying that's the way it is. I'm saying that if you look at it this way, you can do something about it." He not only recognizes but acknowledges that spouses and family members know more about their family than he does. He does not impose his perceptions and interpretations upon them. The family members are not presumed to be passive recipients of the therapist's profound insights or wisdom. They are partners in the therapy experience.

Becoming a significant other. Becoming a significant other means that the sociocognitive therapist puts himself on the line in a way that is essentially alien to many schools of therapy. He allows family members to see him as a fellow human being with his own limitations. He interacts with them on the basis of constructed reciprocity and engages in transformation by offering a surplus of some aspect of the significant other. This compensates for any real or perceived deficits in his performance or personality.

Again unlike many therapists, he does not withhold information about himself from the therapy process. In addition to drawing illustrative cases, vignettes, and metaphors from clinical experience, literature, fiction, movies, television, and other popular culture, the therapist uses himself as an example. He draws upon his own experiences and those of his own friends and family members. However, these revelations contain no more intimate information than would be divulged to a new friend; too much intimacy may cause embarrassment, discomfort, and harm to the therapist's credibility.

Information Gathering Tasks
of the Opening Phase

While group formation is the overriding strategic objective during the opening phase, the more immediate task of the first appointment(s) is to determine which services are needed by the group and which by the individuals. In fact, most of the opening phase is devoted to analytic, reflective, and directed discussion. By talking with family members — not talking at them or merely listening to them — the therapist achieves a preliminary understanding of the family members and their troubles.

The Four Questions

In Chapter Two, we introduced the Four Questions technique with reference to social perceptions. This is the basic method of directed discussion employed in sociocognitive therapy. In some form, it is used to probe family members' meanings and definitions of the situation, explore issues, and evaluate exchanges or interactions (either those observed during therapy or described in family members' accounts).

In this discussion technique, the therapist probes for acts (or perceptions of acts) of both *commission* and *omission*. What a person does not say or does not do can be as meaningful and have as much impact as what they say or do. The therapist questions each member of a family dyad about the "what" and the "why" of self-perceptions, other-perceptions, and metaperceptions according to the following pattern:

1. What did you think, say/not say, do/not do, mean, or feel? Why did you think, say, do, mean, or feel as you did?
2. What did the other think, say/not say, do/not do, mean, or feel? Why did the other think, say, do, mean, or feel as he or she did?
3. What did the other think you thought, said/didn't say, did/didn't do, meant, or felt? Why do *you* think the other thinks you thought, said, did, meant, or felt as he or she thinks you did?
4. What did the other think he or she thought, said, did, meant, or felt? Why do *you* think the other thinks he or she thought, said, did, meant, or felt as he or she thinks you did?

After asking these questions of one dyad member, the therapist asks the same questions of the other. Of course, the therapist does not ask the entire question as given in the pattern. As in any other form of research, the therapist does not ask double-barrelled questions. Rather, he asks about one thing at a time: thoughts (or perceptions), feelings, behaviors (acts of omission as well as acts of commission), or meanings as appropriate. To avoid vague generalizations, the therapist also specifies time, place, form, and event.

While the Four Questions are unwieldy in their general form, they resemble an algebraic equation into which any substantive problem or issue can be plugged. Preferably the reader will memorize this pattern of four two-part questions to be asked of each dyad member about the other. If these are kept in mind, many of the apparent difficulties that might be encountered in our later discussion of therapeutic situations will disappear like a California fog on a summer morning.

Using the Four Questions. It is most practical to tape record (with their consent) family members' discussion and then transcribe the pertinent information before the next appointment. This allows the therapist to study the replies and their implications for discussion with the family members. When recording this information, it is particularly helpful to do so in a way that answers regard the same topic.

For example, when investigating family members' overall mutual perceptions, transcribe together the following six "data dyads":

1. Jack's perception of himself and Jill's perception of him;
2. Jill's perception of herself and Jack's perception of her;
3. Jack's perception of Jill's perception of him and Jill's perception of him;
4. Jill's perception of Jack's perception of her and Jack's perception of her;
5. Jack's perception of Jill's perception of herself and Jill's perception of herself;
6. Jill's perception of Jack's perception of himself and Jack's perception of himself.

This tells the therapist how well each spouse or family member understands the other's perceptions of themselves and one another. Regardless of the content, recording information this way identifies discrepancies in family members' definitions of the situation. These may then be discussed with family members to generate therapeutic hypotheses. The discussion sensitizes each to the other's definition of the situation to increase skill in taking the role of the other. In turn, that will help family members engage in more satisfying interactions as significant others—one of the primary goals of family therapy.

Naturalistic Assessment

During the opening phase, the Four Questions technique is used primarily to make a naturalistic assessment of family members and their situation. By naturalistic assessment, we mean a conceptual model of situations and relationships as dynamic social processes. This model is built up from observations and other sources of information about actual behaviors, thoughts, feelings, and interactions (Lofland, 1976, 1984). It is important to keep in mind that naturalistic assessment is always *grounded* (Glaser & Strauss, 1967): the therapist lets a conceptual model emerge from observations rather than forcing the analysis of family members' interaction to fit a pre-established theoretical scheme.

Hence, as he speaks and interacts with all the family members, the therapist organizes a working model of family members' situation. He seeks evidence regarding personal limitations, interpersonal predicaments and conflicts, meanings and definitions of the situation, family members' stated and unstated values, goals and preferences, attempts and failures to re-establish constructed reciprocity, and tactics for coping and decision making. As a humanist, the therapist is not entirely "value free," rather he describes what occurs within the family in terms of reciprocity, justice, equity, and fairness.

Example of naturalistic assessment. The case of Yolanda Robison and David Tucker, introduced at the end of the previous chapter, illustrates a naturalistic assessment derived from use of the Four Questions.

> Yolanda complained that David isn't romantic toward her, that he doesn't hug and kiss her. David responded that Yolanda doesn't get dressed but wears her robe over her nightgown and doesn't remove her makeup for days at a time. Yolanda explained that she is uncomfortable about being alone in the

house when David goes to work at night. She stays awake until late and can only sleep after she drinks nearly a bottle of wine. Then she has to get up early to get the children to school, catches a few more hours of sleep and then gets up again to make David breakfast when he comes home from work. David said that his night maintenance job was the best he could find and that he doesn't plan to give it up because he is not only supporting himself, Yolanda, and their children, but sends money home every month to his wife and children. Yolanda agreed that David has a good job and that they need the money to get by. However, she said that she lives on a funny schedule in which she sleeps whenever she can, so she always wears her nightgown and robe.

Agenda for the Initial Assessment

Uncovering the family members' story is only part of the naturalistic assessment process. In addition, the therapist must determine whether and how he can help those who have come for help. This information cannot be obtained by direct questions because it involves analysis of accounts and interactions, not compilation of responses. This analysis addresses whether sociocognitive therapy is appropriate and, if it is, what the spouses and family members want for themselves and for their life together.

Are They in the Right Place?

Answering this question requires the therapist to evaluate three critical issues:

1. Does the family need sociocognitive therapy or some other type of assistance?
2. What are the spouses' or family members' goals for their marriage or family and do they agree about a therapy goal?
3. Does the therapist have the desire and capability to help these particular individuals?

Therapy needs. Discussion may reveal that family members are asking for help about the wrong problems or aspect of their problems. When the help needed can better be provided by someone else, the family therapist refers family members to the proper professional or to an appropriate service or agency in the community. For instance, an expressed concern about a child's disturbing school behavior may prove to be a woman's cry for help because of difficulties with the man she lives with. A request for marital counseling may reflect concern about what to do with an aged parent in the home. And a complaint about conflict between children may translate into a need for securing placement for an exceptional child.

Alternatively, the family members may lack the physical, psychological, and interactional competency to participate effectively in sociocognitive therapy. Anxiety and depression are to be expected and are displayed by the overwhelming majority of those who come to the therapist. However, threats of suicide and violent behavior merit careful monitoring. Family members should be advised to call the therapist for crisis intervention referral if a family member becomes acutely despondent or talks about harming himself or others.

The therapist also considers the issue of whether the family can afford his services. He inquires about family financial resources, sources of private third party coverage, and eligibility for public assistance. If the therapist and family members cannot work out a reasonably affordable fee schedule, they should be referred to a therapist, clinic, or agency they can afford.

Therapy goals. Goals and expectations for marriage or family as well as for therapy are usually volunteered by the family members. If not, the therapist secures the information through reflective, analytic, or directed discussion (perhaps using the Four Questions technique.) If a family member is reticent about stating a goal in the presence of others, the therapist may delay pressing for a reply until meeting with the individual alone.

In some cases, family members may harbor covert goals or may deny goals they actually hold. Each spouse may perceive the other's goal to be different from what is asserted. For example, both may claim to want to maintain and improve their marriage but one may actually want to prove that their marriage is not salvageable. Alternatively, both may actually want to save their marriage but one may believe that the other is actually trying to find an excuse for abandoning the relationship.

Assuming that goals and expectations are commensurate with sociocognitive therapy, the therapist must determine each individual's goals and the extent to which family members agree about them. The therapist needs to know each family member's definition of goals, each one's perceptions of the other's goals, and each one's perceptions of the other's perception of his goals. Therefore, the therapist applies the Four Questions technique.

Client/therapist match. Each therapist decides whether he wants to work with the particular couple or family and whether he has the skills, knowledge, competence, and theoretical orientation to help them. Sometimes, the therapist will not feel comfortable working with a particular family or individual on the basis of incompatible personal "chemistry," religion, ethnicity, or lifestyle. In such cases, the therapist should refer the family members elsewhere.

Are the Family Members' Realities Compatible with a Successful Therapy Outcome?

The therapist also needs information about the family members' beliefs, goals, and values. Using the Four Questions and other discussion techniques, the therapist uncovers family members' individual and joint realities. Once again, the therapist is primarily interested in three questions:

1. Do the spouses or family members have the same values and life goals?
2. Do the spouses or family members agree about the realities of their situation?
3. What are they willing and able to change?

Values and goals. It is clear that family members act in a way that is congruent with their values and directed toward their goals. However, a person's values and goals are not always clear to themselves or to anyone else; they may be ambiguous, ill-defined or unacknowledged. Because values and goals are related to statuses and shared meanings (which differ with each relationship) integration and consistency cannot be assumed. Family members, like everyone else, may hold mutually contradictory or incompatible goals and values and be unaware of it.

For example, men and women often marry without really knowing each other's values and goals. They assume that identical goals are derived from shared values or that their love will automatically align their goals and values. When their individual values and goals prove to be difficult or impossible to reconcile, they experience an interpersonal predicament (perhaps leading to conflict and crisis). At other times, couples find that goals and values have shifted over time, disrupting constructed reciprocity and triggering marital and family problems. The case of Yolanda Robison and David Tucker offers a provoking example:

> Yolanda Robison married her husband and David Tucker married his wife when each was a teenager in a small Southern town and both were happy with that lifestyle. After three or four years of marriage, Yolanda and David had become disenchanted with small town life. They imagined that they could find a better life in a large city offering them opportunities to make "big money," which had become very important to them. Each left his or her spouse and separately migrated to Los Angeles where they met each other. Neither divorcing his or her former spouse, they moved in together to establish a better financial situation for themselves.

The therapist can rarely elicit useful information about values and goals by direct questions. Family members may not have adequately focussed on their values and goals to articulate a meaningful answer to such questions. Rather, the therapist employs indirect or metaphoric lines of inquiry. These prompt family members to project their desires, wishes, and aspirations onto their reply. Examples might be:

- What did you want to get out of marriage or your family?
- If you had a magic wand and could wave it to make things different how would you like your life to be five years from now?
- What do you think your wife (husband) wanted to get out of marriage or your family?

If discussion reveals continuation of similar values and goals, the therapist may assume that the problems and conflicts are caused by unrelated personal limitations. If the therapist discovers dissimilar values and goals, he would probe to determine whether this was always the case. If not, what caused their values and goals to change and diverge? Regardless of whether or not they ever shared values and goals, the therapist edges family members toward development of them as a basis for more effective and satisfying family interaction.

Definitions of the situation. Each family member has a unique definition of the situation as well as a unique perception and interpretation (or image) of their lives problems, or conflicts. As a result, each constructs a different account of their common situation. Generally it is one that excuses or mitigates responsibility for troubles and blames them on others. The therapist must take indexicality and reflexivity into account and employ the disciplined analytic approach of a qualitative sociological researcher (Lofland, 1976, 1984) when making a naturalistic assessment of problems and conflict. Yolanda Robison and David Tucker again illustrate our point:

> She complained that David Tucker, who lives with her and her children, beat her. David denied her complaint. He said that she had difficulty falling asleep and drank wine at dinner to relax and help fall asleep later in the evening. Sometimes when she had been drinking, she became belligerent. She blamed him for various misfortunes and tried to beat him. When she was drunk, she bumped into walls and stumbled over furniture which caused bruises. Sometimes she cut herself. He said he tried to control her by holding her wrists until she calmed down or became exhausted from unsuccessful attempts to hit him. She would eventually start to cry. Later on, she would feel embarrassed by her behavior and claim that he beat her.

The therapist listens to each family account and then uses the Four Questions to elicit self-perceptions, other-perceptions and meta-perceptions. This is done to obtain information and to encourage and assist family members in taking the role of the other—to get inside the other's head and learn how and why the other perceives his reality.

Willingness to change. It is axiomatic that the therapist cannot (and should not) force clients to change anything about themselves, their lifestyle, or their relationships, that they are not willing to change. Therefore, it is essential that family members identify personal limitations or interpersonal binds they *are* willing to change in order to improve their relationship. This can be done using the Four Questions technique (as illustrated by the discussion of David's and Yolanda's personal limitations we have just considered).

Another issue is the extent to which family members agree about their own and others' desire and capability to achieve their therapy goals. When they consider their therapy goals, they evaluate both their own and others' desire to achieve their goal ("Do I want to achieve it? Does he/she want to achieve it?"). Each also evaluates his or her own and the others' ability to achieve the goal ("Can I achieve it? Can he/she achieve it?"). The therapist must consider these same questions.

Customarily in an interpersonal predicament, one or both spouses assert the desire and capability to fulfill the other's expectations. However, one may question the other's desire or capability and point to past experiences to justify these suspicions. The attacked spouse may then assert that the present predicament is different from past situations, which are therefore irrelevant. When this occurs, the therapist uses the Four Questions technique in a format like:

— Jill, do you have the desire and ability to be the wife Jack wants you to be?
— Jill, does Jack have the desire and ability to be the husband you want him to be?
— Jill, does Jack believe you have the desire and ability to be the wife he wants you to be?
— Jill, does Jack believe he has the desire and ability to be the husband you want him to be?

If each spouse or family member perceives the other as having the desire and capability, the situation is encouraging for the successful achievement of their asserted therapy goals. However, a positive outcome is less likely if each perceives the other as having neither the desire nor the capability and the situation is highly discouraging. In such a case, the therapist should ask the spouses why they assert the goal of maintaining their marriage.

Another aspect of this issue is whether the family members are actually willing and able to make the changes required to restore constructed reciprocity. In some cases, it is a matter of overcoming deeply entrenched personal limitations which, may offer secondary gains to the individual displaying them. In other cases, it is an explicit matter of giving something up in order to get what they want out of the relationship. Thus, there may be problems of capability when the individuals are unable to change personal limitations despite the desire to do so.

More commonly, family members may be unwilling to make or accept the costs or trade-offs required to achieve the stated therapy goals and their own goals for their family. One example would be a husband who feels unable to break off an extramarital relationship that threatens to disrupt the family, despite a professed desire to maintain his family. Although other options may be acceptable, it is most common for the negotiated resolution to involve terminating the outside relationship and rebuilding the family one.

Family Members' Negative Other-Perceptions

According to family members, the most important feature of the situation is almost always the limitations of the other spouse or family members. Family members have stories to tell that they feel will show how the others cause their troubles. They present various types of evidence to support their assertions. Generally, they explain how changing the other will improve the situation and that they want the therapist to do so because they have been unable to.

Being an audience. When family members come to the therapist, they want to tell their stories and have their accounts validated. If they cannot relate their accounts in their initial appointment, they perceive a lack of closure and continue attempting to tell their reviewed and rehearsed stories until they believe they have been heard. Then, and often only then, can they permit the therapist to introduce and attempt change activities.

Therefore, the therapist allows family members to tell their stories from their own perspectives. However, as is customary in daily life, they generally equate telling their stories with making complaints about the other spouse or family members. The therapist listens to their stories, complaints and all. He uses the Four Questions technique to probe beneath these surface accounts for evidence of personal limitations and perceptions of others' personal limitations.

Redefining the Situation

The sociocognitive therapist introduces and uses the term "limitations" instead of "problems," "shortcomings," and other negative terms. Thus, the therapist asks Jack:

—What do you feel are your limitations?
—What do you feel are Jill's limitations?
—What do you think Jill believes are her limitations?
—What do you think Jill believes are your limitations?

The therapist then asks Jill the complementary questions. And so on for each family dyad.

This method secures vital information about perceived limitations and begins to redefine the objects of complaints in instrumental terms (i.e., as limitations). It also reveals family members' awareness of the limitations that trouble other family members. The therapist inquires further about gaps in self- , other- and metaperceptions regarding limitations and then presents and discusses the missing data with each family member.

Strategies for Dealing with Complaints

Because complaints about others' limitations create a mutually depressing definition of the situation, it is wise to impose structure on complaints in the opening phase. In addition to redefining perceived flaws in behavior, thinking, and feeling as personal limitations, the therapist states that he has heard and recorded their complaints. Therefore it is unnecessary to repeat them. He may then comment about the positive aspects and elements in the family's life together. Once again, we use the example of Yolanda Robison and David Tucker's first appointment.

* * *

During their first meeting with the therapist, Yolanda and David began to argue about what they do or do not do that they know the other complains about. David reported that Yolanda would like him to stop smoking and he agreed that he smokes too much. When David admitted that he smokes too much, Yolanda admitted that she drinks too much and said that David wants her to stop. Each then said that he or she wanted to stop smoking or drinking. When asked what else they do or do not do that the other would like them to change, neither reported additional limitations.

The therapist then asked David what he would like Yolanda to do that she is not doing and what she is doing that he would like her to stop doing. David said she cooks the same things all the time. Yolanda was surprised to hear this complaint. David then said that she doesn't clean the house properly and Yolanda responded that she knew he would complain about that, even though it isn't true.

She repeated this response when David went on to say that she doesn't take care of her appearance. He explained that she doesn't remove her makeup for several days and nights or get dressed but goes around the house in a robe over her nightgown. Yolanda was embarrassed but admitted that this was true. However, when David said she lies, she became very upset and demanded to know what he referred to.

He explained that she lies when she says he hit her. Also she lied when they met, when she told him she wasn't married. He said that there were other things she lied about but those two things were enough. Yolanda acknowledged that she had lied about not being married but only because she didn't want David to leave her. David said they almost got married then, so they would have been bigamists and might have gone to jail. However, he was flattered that she lied because she didn't want him to leave her. She insisted that she does not lie when she says that David beats her. She raised her voice and shouted him down when he tried to defend himself on this point.

When Yolanda began to describe David's limitations, she repeated that he beat her. David was quietly angry and shook his head from side to side. She also said that David does not have time for them to do things as a family, that he is not romantic because he does not kiss her, and that he does not give her moral support.

David wanted to know what she meant by "moral support," but Yolanda could not explain it.

The therapist said that maybe she meant that David did not compliment her when she did something good (like clean the house when she did so). Or maybe she wanted him to say something good about her as a mother. To which David interjected, "I wish I could." Yolanda replied, "I am so a good mother. My children go to school every day, they are in the right grades and they do their homework." The therapist then pointed out that "I wish I could," was not moral support and that maybe she needed him to not chop her down. David asked, "Then how could she learn what she was supposed to do?" The therapist agreed that he had a point and suggested that David help Yolanda do her housework so she would be rested and better able to handle the children.

At this point, the therapist halted the discussion and outlined the limitations of each on paper as reported by the other:

Things David does or does not do that Yolanda wants him to change	*Things Yolanda does or does not do that David wants her to change*
1. He smokes too much	1. She drinks too much
2. He never has time to do things as a family	2. She doesn't care for herself; doesn't remove her make up, doesn't get dressed some days
3. He isn't romantic enough; he doesn't kiss Yolanda	3. She doesn't clean the house
4. He doesn't give Yolanda moral support	4. She cooks the same thing all the time
5. He hits Yolanda	5. She tells lies

After the therapist wrote this down and showed it to Yolanda and David, discussion about their limitations ceased. The therapist then spoke:

First, I want to comment that you have few serious complaints about each other and except for the lying and hitting — I mean the accusations of lying and hitting — the complaints are not critical. I also want to point out that neither of you complained about your sexual relationship, you didn't complain about his working and earnings, and you didn't really complain about how she handles the kids. If you don't have serious complaints about these roles, then you really don't have any problems in some very important areas of your relationship. So you're pretty lucky.

Yolanda, you seemed surprised when David said that you don't keep yourself as neat and attractive as you could. Didn't you know he feels that way about you?

Discussion followed about Yolanda's personal care and the difficulties she experienced with that because of her responsibilities for the children and the problems caused by David's night work schedule.

Then the therapist commented again.

You, David, seemed surprised when you said that you aren't as romantic to her as she would like. She said you don't kiss her and hug her the way she'd like you to. Didn't you know about that? I wonder whether there are other things like that that each of you doesn't like about the other that the other one doesn't know and therefore doesn't do something about.

Discussion followed about David's night work schedule, his sleeping during the day, and being up in the afternoon when the kids came home from school. David said it was wiser not to hug and kiss in front of the children because it would lead to sex. Yolanda said that it didn't have to lead to sex. David replied that, although it didn't have to, it usually did. Their interaction revealed that Yolanda and David have a basically friendly, even loving, relationship.

* * *

THE TRIPARTITE FIRST APPOINTMENT

The first appointment is typically two hours in length. It is normally recorded on either audio or videotape. In most instances, it is divided into three parts:

1. *The opening joint meeting* with both spouses or all the family members together.
2. *Individual meetings* with each spouse or family member alone.
3. *The closing joint meeting* with both spouses or all family members again seen conjointly.

The Opening Joint Meeting of the First Appointment

One-half to three-quarters of an hour is allotted for the opening joint meeting. When the spouses or family members are seated in the consultation room, the therapist requests permission to record the session. He defines the therapy situation and helps the family members discuss their reasons for seeking help. For example, the therapist might begin by telling them:

> I want you to notice the microphone. I'd like your permission to record our session this afternoon. I want to record it for the following reasons: First, paying attention to what happens during the session makes it too difficult to take notes. However, I'd like to have a record of our meeting so I can listen to the tape later sometime during the week and make some notes from it. Second, we may say some things that we'll want to play back and listen to. For example, sometimes there are misunderstandings or arguments and each of us has a different idea about how they started. If we have a recording we can play it back and listen to what happened. I think I can be of better help to you if I have such a record. Also you can take it home and play it if you'd wish and discuss it between yourselves. How do you feel about it?

The therapist then waits for a response and answers questions about the request. It is rare for family members to refuse to have the session recorded. The therapist proceeds to define the situation by describing the procedures to be followed in this first meeting and repeating information given to the family member who called to make the appointment:

> Before we get started, I want to tell you what will happen here during the next two hours. We'll all talk together for a while to try to get a general picture of the situation at home to find out what the problems are. I'll also try to learn what happens between you. Then I'll talk with each of you individually for a while. Sometimes family members want to tell me things about their problems that they are uncomfortable talking about in front of the others. Also, in this way I can get to know each of you better. Then all of us will get together to review your situation, to decide whether we can do anything about it, discuss what we can do about it, and determine whether we want to do it. You'll also have a chance to decide whether or not you feel you can work with me in the kind of personal relationship we'll have together. Any questions?

During this introductory portion of the session, the therapist requests permission to address the spouses or family members by their first names. Because the therapist's objective is to establish a significant other relationship, he also offers them the right to address him by *his* first name. Not all family members are comfortable with this. They may prefer to address the therapist as Mr., Ms., Mrs., or Doctor although they may be willing to have the therapist call them by their first name.

The therapist proceeds to assess the family members' situation. Generally he begins with the Four Questions and probes further through reflective, analytical, and directed discussion. As he questions and talks with the family members, the therapist observes their interactions. He evaluates their accounts to obtain information about their family culture, social structure, and interpersonal dynamics.

Handling Reluctance to Participate

Family members may differ greatly in their level of motivation to participate in family therapy. Some may have come only because others demand it or because of a court order. They may profess to want the therapist's services or believe they do but their behavior may contradict what they say, even to themselves. The therapist explains to such family members that he cannot help them unless they want to be helped and that they are only wasting everyone's time and money. They may even make matters worse if they agree to therapy but do not come to sessions or participate.

The therapist prefers that all the family members attend sessions even if they do not participate. When they attend there is always a possibility that they may be drawn into the family interaction by another family member's challenge or cajoling. Sometimes, the family member does not participate in the therapist's office but then discusses what was said and done with other family members back home. Virtually all family members who continue to attend sessions are eventually drawn into the therapy group interaction. This situation was illustrated by Leroy Hawkins:

> Leroy came to several appointments, sullen and uncooperative. He apparently came because he was told that participating in therapy would help him in court. He listened to the therapist without comment. But his mother reported that he told her, "That white doctor knows about black people." He was thereby encouraged to tell the therapist about the bind his mother put him in when she required him to see that the younger children did their chores but did not give him the authority to get them to perform their chores.

The Individual Meetings of the First Appointment

Following the opening conjoint session, the therapist informs them that he wants to talk with each of them individually. During the opening joint meeting, the therapist develops an overview of the jigsaw puzzle that is the family members' situation. He determines which additional pieces of information are necessary to complete the puzzle. He then secures this additional information during the individual meetings with the spouses and family members.

The Rationale for Individual Meetings

The method of holding individual meetings with family members has been the subject of considerable controversy (Fullmer, 1975; Gaines & Stedman, 1979; Nadelson, 1978). In support of this practice, Hurvitz states that:

> I hold individual conferences with spouses and family members because the family members I have counseled over the past 25 years have given me feedback to the effect that they want to talk with me, alone. Many times during the telephone intake call (which I take myself) when I inform the caller that I want to see both spouses or the entire family together, the caller asks whether he or she will have an opportunity to speak with me alone, implying that he or she wishes to do so. I assure him that I will. Also, early in my practice, when I saw spouses together for marital counseling, it was not unusual for one spouse to call me following an appointment to tell me something the spouse thought was significant but did not want to reveal in the presence of the other spouse.
>
> I continue to see family members alone because I believe that they are entitled to their secrets. I believe that the pressure therapists sometimes exert on family members to reveal information, thoughts, and feelings may harm them more than help them. Family members often have secrets which they have not revealed to the others. The information from individual sessions that is not disclosed to the others but which need not be concealed, will be revealed through continuing interactions in the group session.

Tactics for the Individual Meetings

The therapist uses the individual meetings to probe for information not revealed in the joint meeting, clarify discrepancies, and explore more deeply each family member's motivations for therapy and situational definition. The meeting gives the therapist an opportunity to learn, in confidence, each family member's perceptions and metaperceptions of the others and their concerns. Here again the therapist relies on some variation of the Four Questions technique. For example:

> When the individual meeting with Jack draws to a close, the therapist asks Jack, "What do you think Jill believes we've been talking about?" and "What do you think Jill will want to talk about when she comes in here in just a few minutes?"
>
> When Jack leaves and is replaced in the consultation room by Jill, the therapist asks her, "What do you think Jack believes we're talking about now?" "What do you think Jack and I talked about while you were in the waiting room?"

The replies reveal whether the family members are concerned with the same problem or conflict and define it in the same way. The replies also reveal whether family members perceive family interaction in the same way. If their concerns and perceptions of those concerns differ, these differences must be examined and resolved in the continuing therapy.

Seeing parents and children. At the first appointment parents and children are first seen together, the parents are seen alone, and then the children are seen alone. Lastly, the parents and children are again seen together. In this way, the children know that their information was not disclosed to the parents because the parents were not seen alone again. Information given by the parents can be used to direct discussion with the children.

The Concluding Joint Meeting of the First Appointment

After individual meetings with family members, the therapist again meets with the entire group. Throughout the first appointment, the therapist has been assessing the family members and their relationships. By the concluding joint meeting, the therapist has a pretty good idea of the spouses' and family members' interactions and relationships. He knows their personal limitations, interpersonal predicaments and conflicts, goals for therapy, and how each perceives their situation and one another.

Although the process may continue into subsequent meetings, the therapist now offers the family members a therapeutic hypothesis concerning their situation. He presents this hypothesis in the form of a summary assessment. By focusing reflective, analytic, and directed discussion on this assessment, the therapist helps family members to agree on a joint definition of their situation and to establish common therapy goals. If the agreement is to continue with therapy, the therapist then proceeds with the business of formalizing the therapy relationship.

The Summary Assessment

In the concluding joint meeting, the therapist presents the therapeutic hypotheses he has developed through talking with family members individually and together. This summary statement is neither intended nor presented as a definitive diagnosis of the family. Rather, it is set forth as a hypothesis and a basis for discussing whether and how to proceed with therapy.

After presenting the summary assessment to the family members, the therapist invites them to respond. If the family members have questions about the therapist's interpretation and evaluation of their situation, the therapist answers them. If they offer additions and corrections, these are incorporated into a revised summary. In the course of these exchanges, the therapist assists family members to negotiate a mutually acceptable account of their situation.

For example, in addition to assessing their overall situation, the therapist summarized an aspect of Yolanda and David's situation as follows:

> When Yolanda doesn't remove her makeup and wears her robe all day, David doesn't think she is kissable. He feels that she is being unfair when she complains about his expectations that a woman who wants to be kissed keep herself as clean as she can, whatever her circumstances. At the same time, it is his job that creates at least part of the circumstances that prompt her to wear her robe all day. She feels that it is unfair of David

to expect her to clean up and dress before she greets him in the morning. You are experiencing an interpersonal predicament in which each of you is attempting to do the right thing and make the best of your situation but your attempts to do so seem unfair and uncaring to the other person because they interfere with his or her own efforts.

Therapy Goals

Because the summary assessment is an instrumental hypothesis, it implies therapy goals to work toward in order to resolve crises and conflicts and restore constructed reciprocity. In presenting the summary statement and facilitating its discussion, the therapist simultaneously assists clarification of individual goals and definition of preferred therapy outcomes. The therapist then uses the Four Questions and other discussion techniques to help the family members identify and agree upon what they want out of their therapy. This becomes the overall therapy goal.

Identifying the Initial Problem

As discussed in Chapter Three, the overall assessment of the family members includes identification of an *initial problem* to work on. This is normally a relatively minor aspect of the overall troubles which family members can easily agree upon and which they can change without extraordinary efforts. He then nominates this problem for discussion and agreement by family members during the concluding joint meeting. For instance:

> While Yolanda's appearance and behavior was only one aspect of their difficulties, the therapist determined that it would be a good initial problem to work on. In subsequent sessions, he went on to mitigate this interpersonal predicament by training Yolanda to fall asleep by cognitive behavioral methods and without drinking (e.g., using self-hypnosis). His underlying strategy was to eliminate her need for drinking at night and enable her to obtain a full night's sleep before she awakened to get the children to school. She wouldn't have a hangover and

would have enough time and energy to clean up before David returned home from work.

Alternative Therapy Relationships

By this point, the therapist will have determined if family members require and can benefit from his services as well as if they want to continue therapy. If appropriate, he would conclude the joint session by proposing that family members seek services from another resource that the therapist recommends. Of course, they may decide to continue without professional assistance.

Separation counseling. Alternatively, if the spouses or family members came to a decision to part or discussion led to such a decision, the therapist may suggest separation counseling. A separation based on mediation and consideration of feelings and interests may result in a much less traumatic experience than the customary legal approach which fosters an adversarial relationship and may leave each member feeling manipulated or cheated.

Preparing for continuing therapy. Assuming that there is reason to negotiate continuing therapy, the therapist now obtains additional identifying information about the family members (including information necessary for third party payment). He negotiates fees and discusses any ground rules he wants to establish, such as policies regarding keeping appointments.

The Trial Period

One question asked by prospective clients when calling an agency, clinic, or therapist for information is "How long does it take?" Although the therapist cannot offer a specific reply, he informs the caller that it is his practice to set a trial period. During this time, the therapist intervenes to help the family members determine and achieve a therapy goal. Although family members may not reach this goal during so short a period, they can determine if they can work comfortably with the therapist. They can also determine if the principles and methods he uses are compatible with their desires and expectations and are likely to be effective for them.

As part of his closing summary, the therapist proposes that the initial contract be for a trial period of therapy (customarily of four to six weeks duration). The therapist offers information about the trial period, explaining the concepts and practices that guide his understanding of the family members' interaction and relationships and the change methods he employs. He explains how the continuing sessions differ from their first session together. They may consist solely of joint meetings or of joint meetings and concurrent individual meetings with one or more family members.

The therapist informs the family members that the trial period will be concluded with a summary and evaluation of their progress. This summary will be prepared jointly by the family members and the therapist. On the basis of this summary and evaluation, they will decide whether the asserted goals have been reached or show promise of being reached. They also decide if therapy can be concluded, should continue as it has been conducted, should be changed in some way, or has not been working and should be terminated (preferably by a referral to another therapist).

Homework

Homework is an integral part of sociocognitive therapy and the spouses and family members are introduced to it during the first appointment. Homework is one of the elements that changes therapy from a process in which the professional therapist is always in charge to a process in which the family members assume ever greater direction. It is a strategy that maintains and reinforces change efforts initiated during therapy as well as transfers symbolic control back to the family members and their autonomous efforts. In the authors' experience, homework creates as much or greater improvement in family members' interaction and relationships as the appointment with the therapist does.

Examples of homework. While homework may consist of structured assignments (such as the listing task given to Yolanda Robison and David Tucker during their session), some of the most productive assignments are interactive and open-ended. Examples of such homework assigned by Hurvitz have included:

1. Having family members share their feelings about important people and events and about each other. They are asked to then discuss what it was like for each of them as they communicated these things.

2. The therapist instructs the spouses, "Tell each other about the kind of couple you would like to socialize with; the kind of boy (girl) you would like your daughter (son) to meet, date, and marry."

3. The therapist advises the family members to discuss their appointments with him and to tape record their discussion (to be brought to the next therapy session).

4. The therapist encourages the family members to tell each other what they want from their marriage, family, work, school, or other major activity.

5. The therapist advises the family members to anticipate decisions they must make. Each member reports to the others why he or she favors a particular decision and defends it against the others. Following the event or situation which required the situation, the family members review and evaluate the decision and the process by which it was made.

6. The therapist advises parents to discuss their growing up experiences, thoughts, and feelings; difficulties with their parents and how they were handled; and problems which are comparable to those their children now face.

7. The therapist teaches the concept and practice of sentence completion. The family members are then encouraged to devise such tests themselves and to tape record and discuss their responses (which are reported during the therapy session).

8. The therapist invites each spouse or family member to report one incident that occurred at work, home, school, et cetera during the week. Every other family member is encouraged to ask three questions of the family member who is reporting an incident.

9. The therapist encourages the family members to discuss their fantasies, dreams, daydreams, and other ephemeral experiences (perhaps restricting them to those that can be discussed without any negative effects).

Chapter Five

The Change-Inducing Phase: I. Crisis Management

The opening phase of therapy gives way to the change-inducing phase. In this phase, the sociocognitive therapist takes the spouses and family members back along the path which led them from personal limitations to interpersonal predicament to conflict to crisis. He engages in activities which reduce the crisis to a conflict, the conflict to an interpersonal predicament, and the interpersonal predicament to personal limitations. In addition to applying the appropriate change concepts and methods, the therapist teaches them to the family members. Then they can help themselves and their significant others to overcome their limitations.

OVERLAP OF PHASES

The opening and change-inducing phases of therapy always blend and overlap to some extent, beginning with the first appointment. Because it is sometimes the only appointment family members attend, the therapist attempts to facilitate positive change in the course of information-gathering activities. For instance, we have already suggested that directed discussion using the Four Questions can improve family members' effectiveness in taking the role of the other.

A full-blown or impending crisis requires a somewhat different tack in the first appointment than was discussed in the previous chapter. Because family members often do not seek help until faced with a crisis, the therapist anticipates that each new pair of spouses or each new family may be experiencing a crisis. If there is evidence suggesting this, the therapist switches tracks and abandons general information-gathering activities such as filling out forms or investigating social perceptions. Instead, the therapist assesses the crisis and acts to bring the family members back from the brink.

SOCIOCOGNITIVE STRATEGY FOR CHANGE

The general strategy underlying sociocognitive therapy is to change unsatisfying and ineffective family relationships by changing how family members define their joint situation not merely "in their heads" but in action (Straus, 1989b). The key is getting them to stop doing whatever they have been doing and to interact in new ways. The therapist takes the initiative by providing a therapeutic hypothesis that redefines their situation. He also encourages them to act as if that instrumental hypothesis were true. As the family members do so, they reconstruct their joint reality at both the individual/subjective and group/intersubjective levels. Sociocognitive crisis intervention exemplifies this method of reality reconstruction, only on a more focussed and directive basis than is the case in the overall therapy process.

Sociocognitive Crisis Management

Because it is often associated with a precipitating event, the crisis is particularly amenable to reconstruction. In practice, crisis management through reality reconstruction involves a three-stage process: (a) retrospective reconstruction, (b) situational reconstruction, and (c) prospective reconstruction.

Retrospective Reconstruction

This process is based on an analysis of the exchanges which led to the crisis in order to determine what happened. During the initial joint meeting, the therapist informs the spouses or family members that he would like to know precisely what precipitated the crisis. He requests each to describe what happened and to permit the others to give their own accounts without interruption. The behavior, meanings, and feelings that led to the crisis will thus be revealed, better understood and simultaneously cooled.

The family members usually volunteer accounts of the escalation process that caused the crisis but their accounts always differ. Each starts his or her story at a different point and attributes what happened to different aspects of the situation. Each tends to justify his or her position and explain how he or she attempted to arrest the process that led to the crisis.

A variation of the Four Questions technique is used to move the story-telling process beyond self-serving accounts that blame others. The therapist:

1. Asks about what family members said or did and what each perceives the others as having said or done that may have caused the crisis.
2. Asks what each believes he or she may have done to prompt others to act in a way that caused the crisis. Or what others might have done that prompted each to act in a way that caused the crisis.
3. As patterns are detected, the therapist tracks them backward in time. He probes for the actions or events that may have prompted each set of responses until an obvious "ultimate" precipitant emerges or a tender issue is uncovered that has great emotional significance.

Situational Reconstruction

Once critical events or issues are detected, the therapist proceeds to help redefine the situation. He:

1. Engages in directive negotiating activities such as proposing face-saving concessions and compromises, breaking binds, and proposing and evaluating alternatives.
2. Offers information and advice, coaches and advocates, justifies and explains, and does real things to help them understand their situation and believe they can change it as they desire.
3. Takes a proactive role in engaging the family members, analyzing exchanges, and challenging or supporting interpretations.

These activities have two purposes. One is overcoming the family members' feelings of anxiety, demoralization, despondency, and despair stemming from the crisis. The second is bringing the family members to a joint definition so that they can do something to change their situation.

Prospective Reconstruction

Based on the two preceding phases, the therapist may propose a contract to maintain the marriage or family while trying to overcome the personal limitations or interpersonal predicaments that eventually led to the crisis. Once the crisis process has been clarified, family members have been led to accept responsibility for escalation, and a goal of maintaining and improving their relationship has been set, the therapist proposes an ongoing treatment plan.

Avoiding Premature Termination

The activities of retrospective and situational reconstruction are often adequate to cool out the family members and defuse the crisis. The family members may consequently believe that they have no further need for therapy. To avoid this impression, the therapist must make it clear that although the immediate crisis may have been resolved, the problems that caused their conflict remain. These problems may be attributable to family members' limitations or interactional process problems such as ineffective communication. The crisis is over but the malady may linger on. In such cases, the therapist uses the concluding joint meeting to offer a summary assessment, appropriate change activities, and a contract for continuing therapy.

In other cases, the therapist or the family members may see little or no hope for restoration of the marriage or family group. For example, it may become obvious that one or more members will not participate in a joint therapy program. In such cases, efforts are directed at assisting separation with as little trauma as possible — perhaps through separation counseling. However, if the crisis is acknowledged and there is even a slight chance that family members want to step back from the edge, the therapist involves them in continuing therapy.

CASE ILLUSTRATIONS OF CRISIS MANAGEMENT

Rather than proceed at a theoretical level, we will consider four actual cases in which the method of redefinition was applied in the first meeting. These illustrate both full-blown and impending crises. They show how crisis management focuses on redefining the situation as a workable problem and proceeds to develop a therapy plan agreeable to all family members.

Crisis Caused by an Interpersonal Predicament with Conflict: The Mackey Family

Ms. Gloria Mackey and her two daughters were referred by Michelle's open-heart surgeon when Ms. Mackey wanted to place her daughters in a foster home because she had great difficulty supervising and disciplining them. Reading at times like a popular novel, the following is an actual excerpt from the transcript of a troubled family's first therapy session. It begins a few minutes into the initial joint meeting.

As discussion unfolds, you will see Hurvitz using the Four Questions technique to probe family members' accounts of their situation and to offer and test an instrumental hypothesis about Michelle's behavior. Reflective, analytic, and directed discussion concerning that hypothesis has the secondary effect of behaviorally redefining the situation. This cools them out, breaking the cycle of escalating conflict and defusing the desperation which prompted the immediate crisis. Therapeutic hypotheses are proposed that both give hope for changing the situation and define it as in the family's mutual interest to remain together (at least for a trial period).

Therapist: As I understand it from what you've been telling me, you and Michelle got into a typical argument, the kind that are pretty common in your house, and you got fed up or you lost control and

Gloria: I didn't lose control. I knew what I was doing. I had enough from that child. I told her that. I told her, "I've had enough out of you. I can't take it any more. Your father doesn't want you and I can't handle you. I'm going to ask Dr. Hicks to send you to a foster home.

Then you'll see how good you've got it here. You'll
want to come back home and do things right, like I tell
you.''

Therapist: Michelle, what's your picture of what happened?
Michelle: Huh?
Therapist: What's your picture of what happened?
Michelle: What's the use? Everybody is gonna believe what she
tells them.
Therapist: Try me.
Michelle: (Shakes her head, ''No.'')
Therapist: What was that part about ''your father doesn't want
you''?
Gloria: Go on, tell him.
Michelle: (Shakes her head, ''No.'')
Therapist: Michelle, have you had fights like that before and your
mom said she'd send you to a foster home?
Michelle: (Looks to mother.)
Gloria: Go ahead. You can tell him everything. I won't be
mad.
Michelle: She says that all the time.
Therapist: So you just don't pay attention to her, is that it?
Michelle: I guess so.
Gloria: But this time you went too far. I made an appointment
with Dr. Hicks and we came to see him today like I
told you. And he sent us up here to you. Because that
child can't live with me anymore.
Therapist: This all happened when?
Gloria: It was last Friday.
Therapist: Well, let's find out what happened. What did Sandra or
Michelle say or do to cause what happened?
Gloria: Sandra didn't say anything, but Michelle told me to
shut up.
Therapist: Why did she tell you to shut up? What did you say?
Gloria: I said that if she don't act like a member of this family
she can find herself another family she wants to join.
Therapist: What did she say that caused you to say that to her?
Gloria: She stuck her tongue out at me. I saw her when I turned
around. I was standing by the sink and I had my back

	to her. She even gave me that finger thing. That's an ugly thing for a girl like her to do to her mother.
Therapist:	Ms. Mackey, how do you think Michelle would describe what happened?
Gloria:	What do you mean?
Therapist:	I mean I would like you to try to tell me what happened from Michelle's point of view? Pretend you're Michelle and tell me what happened.
Gloria:	You'll have to ask her. I don't know how that child thinks.
Therapist:	Can you try? Please.
Gloria:	If she thought about it at all, she thought, "My crazy mother is saying the same thing again. I don't have to listen to her. She'll never do what she says."
Therapist:	Michelle, is that what you thought? That your mother made other threats like that in the past and nothing ever happened?
Michelle:	Huh?
Therapist:	Did your mother ever threaten you before and nothing ever happened?
Michelle:	Maybe, I don't know.
Therapist:	But you've had scenes like that in the past?
Michelle:	Huh?
Therapist:	Michelle, why do you do that?
Michelle:	Do what?
Therapist:	Make me repeat what I said when you heard me?
Michelle:	I didn't hear you.
Therapist:	Now listen: have you had scenes like that before?
Michelle:	Lots of times.
Therapist:	Are you tired?
Gloria:	She does that. When she's blocked she makes like she's tired. But you can't tell when she is and when she isn't, so you have to be careful—even when you know she's putting it on.
Therapist:	OK. Now, Sandra, what do you think happened? What I mean is what happened from your point of view?
Sandra:	I don't know. I wasn't there when it all took place.
Michelle:	Yes you were. You were there from the beginning.

	You always make it seem like you don't know what's going on.
Therapist:	You don't sound so tired, Michelle. (To Sandra) Were you there?
Sandra:	I came in the kitchen to sharpen my pencil three or four times. You're mixed up about that.
Therapist:	Let's let that ride for the moment. Michelle, can you tell me what happened from your point of view?
Michelle:	I stuck out my tongue at her when she said she wasn't going to take us to the show. She promised us and now she was backing out — like she always does. When I did that I was real angry and I didn't know she was going to turn around.
Therapist:	OK. Ms. Mackey, what happened that you said you wouldn't take them to the show?
Gloria:	I gave those kids instructions about doing the dishes, cleaning the table, putting the stuff away, and so on because I was going to go out for a while. And I expected them to get that done. But when I came back, I saw they didn't do anything. That made me angry.
Therapist:	How do you think Michelle saw what was going on?
Gloria:	She thought it was a joke. She always thinks everything I tell her is a joke. I have always done everything that has to be done for that child and she doesn't appreciate it.
Therapist:	Michelle, did you know your mother believed you treated that situation like a joke? That you didn't clean up the way she asked you to, and then you made fun of her?
Michelle:	I didn't make fun of her. I didn't do the dishes because I was waiting for Sandra to do her share. She always lets me get started first and she says she's doing her homework so my Mom says not to bother her. But just as soon as I'm finished, then she comes out and says she finished her homework and is ready to help.
Sandra:	That's a lie and you know it. Any time I don't do anything to help her it's because we made a pact and I did

	the whole job myself yesterday so she would do the whole job today.
Michelle:	Only sometimes. Sometimes you hide in your room 'til I'm finished. You know it.
Sandra:	Stuff it. You think you're smart. You're a liar and you know it.
Therapist:	Let's get back to what happened, OK? You say you didn't do the dishes because Sandra didn't do her share. How did you think your mother felt when she came home and saw the dishes weren't done?
Michelle:	She began to holler at me.
Gloria:	That's not right, Michelle. First I asked you whether you felt okay, right? Remember? Then you began to hem and haw, and finally you said that you did your homework first. So I asked if I could see your homework. You told me to get it out of your bedroom. I said, "No, you go get it," and then you said something like, "Like Hell I will." You remember that, don't you?
Michelle:	I said I was too tired.
Gloria:	You didn't say anything like that. You began to whimper and cry. You do that when you're in a corner. I know that I didn't take care of all my business, but you just can't learn. I tell you, what goes around comes around. You'll get yours some day.
Therapist:	What happened before you went out?
Gloria:	We ate. First Sandra and me talked. She was frying some chicken and I was cooking some greens. She was telling me about something that happened in school. It was about a fire drill, wasn't it?
Sandra:	Yeah. It wasn't nothing important. Just talk.
Therapist:	Where was Michelle?
Gloria:	She was in her room listening to records or watching TV. She don't have nothing to do with us when we got work to do. But she'll come when it's time to eat.
Therapist:	What happened then that might have caused some of the trouble that came later?
Gloria:	Nothing. Nothing that I can think of.

Michelle:	Yes there was. You got that phone call. She got that phone call from Mr. Mullins.
Gloria:	That's right, I did. But that didn't—it wasn't important.
Michelle:	A call from Mr. Mullins ain't important? Wow! When she gets a phone call from Mr. Mullins she gets all unstrung.
Therapist:	(To Ms. Mackey) Who's Mr. Mullins?
Michelle:	Mr. Mullins is her lover boy. When he calls her she gets all excited and she don't care about nothing.
Therapist:	You seem to be pretty upset about her friendship with Mr. Mullins. What's the matter?
Michelle:	Upset? Me? I don't know. She acts like a little girl. Like we don't know what she's doing with him.
Gloria:	I don't hide that from you. Mr. Mullins is my friend. We go places together. He helps us out. If it weren't for Mr. Mullins we wouldn't have half the things we got.
Michelle:	Yeah, but you know what I mean. He's her lover and she would rather do for him than for us.
Gloria:	That's right. I said that Mr. Mullins is my friend. The doctor knows what that means. But you're starting the same story if you say that I don't take care of you because of him. It's just the opposite. Because of him I can take care of you better. Isn't that right?
Sandra:	I guess so. Yes.
Gloria:	You know what her problem is? She's mad because Mr. Mullins does more for her than her own daddy. Mr. Mackey, he's in town. He don't live far from us. But he don't do nothing for his child. She wanted a radio that you wear on your head and the earphones fit over your ears. Well, she asked her daddy—she calls him on the phone and sometimes he'll talk to her—for that radio. But Mr. Mullins is the one who got one for her. So why should she be so mad if he is my friend?
Therapist:	Do you think this is what caused everything that happened?
Gloria:	I never thought of it that way. But now that you say

that, it sounds right. You know, like an answer that brings everything together. Yes, I guess I do. Her daddy is just no good. But if anyone dares to do or say something against him, she gets all knocked out of shape. I used to be sorry for her. You know, she's just a child, I thought. But he never — and I mean never — visited her in the hospital when she had her operation. He don't regard her like she is his child. There's something about that and it bothers her. Okay, I can understand that. But why does she take it out on me?

Therapist: Michelle, how do you feel now?

Michelle: (Shakes her head as if to say, "Don't bother me.")

Therapist: Ms. Mackey, how do you think Michelle feels now?

Gloria: I think she's mad at me for telling you about her daddy. She'll take it out on me. She'll find a way. When she gets mad her mind works to get even. I know, she's done it before, lots of times.

Therapist: Sandra, how do you think Michelle feels now?

Sandra: Like my mother said, she's mad at her. She gets like that.

Gloria: When she gets like that you better watch out because she's going to do something to cause you trouble to get even.

Sandra: That's right. She gets mad and she wants to get even.

Therapist: Do you want to tell us how you feel, Michelle?

Michelle: (Shakes her head, No.)

Therapist: Can I tell you how I think you feel?

Michelle: (Shrugs her shoulders.)

Therapist: I think you feel rejected, for one. Do you know what that means? It means that you feel left out or pushed away by your mom and Sandra. You feel like an outsider in your own family so you feel unimportant, maybe even worthless. Maybe you feel this way because of the operations — like you are imperfect and no one can love you if you aren't perfect. So if you aren't perfect, why should you try to do your best in school or do your chores at home? I also believe that you must ask yourself, "Why did this have to happen to me?"

You might also think, "I didn't do anything to deserve such a problem. Somebody else in my life, maybe in my family, did something bad and I'm the one suffering. That's not fair." Then maybe you think your mother or your sister are the ones who did something bad and you're angry at them. It's true that your mother does things for you, but when she complains you may believe that she isn't doing them because she loves you but because she has to. But I don't think that's true. Maybe you also feel, "How can anybody love me if my own father doesn't care for me?" That's an understandable feeling, even if it isn't true. And maybe you think your mom and Sandra don't care about you because your father has caused them a lot of trouble and in some way they blame you. This also makes you feel hurt and sad. I think your most important feeling is being depressed and feeling rejected and unappreciated. When your mom and Sandra don't understand your feelings, then you get angry and do things to try to get attention or provoke them. But that's not a smart thing to do. You just upset them more. I want you to know that I'm not saying what I'm saying is true. I think that's one way to look at what your feelings are. If we look at your feelings in this way, then maybe we can change the way you and your mom and Sandra get along together. Do you know what I mean? How do you feel now?

Michelle: (Shrugs her shoulders. Her eyes become wet.)

Therapist: Ms. Mackey, how do you feel about what I've just said?

Gloria: I don't know. I never thought of it that way. I only know that child makes me miserable.

Therapist: Sandra, how do you feel about what I've just said?

Sandra: I don't know.

Therapist: I'm not saying the way I explained Michelle's problem is true. What I am saying is that the way we have been explaining her problems before have caused us to behave in a certain way to her. And that way hasn't helped her to change in a way that we would like to see her change. So the question is: If we want Michelle to behave in a different way because of the new way that we're trying to explain why she behaves like she does, then what would we do that we aren't doing now and what are we doing that we should stop? I think, but I don't know, that the expression on Michelle's face shows that some part of what I said is important to her, and maybe true, too. We won't answer my questions now; it's something we'll all have to think about. But we also have to question our explanations about everyone else in the family. To reconsider them and to think of different explanations that will lead to new ways to behave to them and with them. And maybe by behaving differently to them, each of them will become able to behave differently to us. Do you understand what I mean? (All remain silent.)

Therapist: This is the first time since we've met that no one has anything to say. It seems as though it's too important to say anything.

Gloria: Well, I know what to say. She can't make life miserable for us just because he don't act like her daddy.

Therapist: Is there anything we can do to bring him back into the picture?

Gloria: Why would you want to do that?

Therapist: I don't know. I just wondered whether doing something like that would give her a better feeling about things. I was just thinking out loud.

Gloria: I don't want him around me. He's just trouble for me — and for her too. He's full of promises but no action. But you can see that it bothers her.

Therapist: From what just happened here it seems as though we learned something that is important to her. We sort of went backwards from what happened on Friday night that upset you so bad and we ended up with Michelle's feelings about her daddy and you and Mr. Mullins. Was that something you expected?

Gloria: No. I didn't see that connection.

Therapist:	Now that we made that connection, as you call it, do you think other times when she does things that bother you that the same reason is the cause of it? Do you think it's this feeling about her father and the way he acts to her, and about Mr. Mullins being your friend and that he does things for her that her father doesn't do for her?
Gloria:	I don't know. Like I said, I never thought of it that way. But you know, whatever the reason is, it's got to stop.
Therapist:	You're right about that. But maybe we have a new way to understand Michelle's feelings and why she feels that way. That should help us understand what's going on in her head. Maybe that will help us work out something to change things.
Gloria:	I'm willing to try anything. But I want you to know that everything I've tried up to now hasn't worked. So I don't know.
Therapist:	You know, of course, that it means everybody has to be together. It means that for now everybody in the family has to be in your house with everybody else.

Hurvitz's Assessment of the Mackey Case

The joint meeting described in this transcript was then followed by individual meetings with each family member alone. Based on the information generated in these discussions, Hurvitz's assessment of the family's basic situation was that:

> While each family member contributes to their collective troubles, Michelle is the central person in the family conflict. All of the family members saw through the threat to place the girls in a foster home or Juvenile Hall. Ms. Mackey was really only angry about Michelle, but she threatens both girls because she doesn't want it to appear that she favors Sandra. Ms. Mackey knew that the girls no longer believed her threats and therefore she felt that she had to do something to make it appear that this time the threat was one she would carry out. The dramatic visit

to Dr. Hicks and the therapist was supposed to serve this purpose.

Hurvitz analyzes the transcript as showing that the encounter started off lamely, when he said that Ms. Mackey "lost control" of the situation at home and she challenged his assertion. This concerned Hurvitz whose anxiety increased when he could not get Michelle to speak to him. She made him repeat his questions until he expressed his irritation at her.

Michelle's behavior, doubtlessly determined by her definition of the situation, is used to deflect attention from what needs to be done by the individuals involved rather than by the therapist. This ploy would allow her to continue to manipulate because of her heart condition and thereby win the encounter. Michelle may have felt that her behavior gained her a little victory over a new enemy. The therapist cannot resist telling Michelle, "You don't sound so tired." He does so to express his irritation at her manipulative behavior and let her know that he recognizes it as such. But, to an extent, he falls into the trap from which he wants to save Ms. Mackey.

When Michelle uncharacteristically gives a sharp and quick response to Sandra, the therapist remarks on it. This lets her know that he is observing her and that, although he wants to be on her side, he will not justify everything she does at home or in the office. He notes that Ms. Mackey and Michelle scapegoat each other while Sandra makes tentative coalitions with each of them.

The therapist's attempts to have Ms. Mackey take the role of the other revealed her perception that Michelle regards her as crazy, someone that Michelle does not have to mind. This contrasts strongly with Ms. Mackey's belief that Michelle *ought* to perceive her as being the helpful mother. The one who provides for Michelle and cares for her in all necessary ways despite her meager income and lack of opportunity. Therefore, her metaperception is very disturbing to Ms. Mackey. It is the basis upon which she interacts with Michelle.

She does not recognize that Michelle is trying to get even with her for revealing that Michelle's father rejects her. The therapist suggests this instrumental hypothesis which, whether or not it is correct, it may be wise to accept provisionally in order to prompt a better relationship between Ms. Mackey and Michelle. After the possibility of bringing Mr. Mackey back into the family was shot down by Ms. Mackey, the therapist brought attention back to this therapeutic hypothesis. Having discovered a new way of interpreting Michelle's behavior, Ms. Mackey was willing to step back from the brink and try something new. As the therapist defines it, this means that everyone in the family had to remain together. The crisis was, at least temporarily, resolved.

The same result (a cooling out of the crisis situation) and the same information could have been achieved by some other approach. However, the value of reality reconstruction is that it simultaneously focuses on the presenting problem, introduces exchange analysis, involves the family in a discussion, and maintains the family unit while offering a breathing space for positive actions.

Assessment of Individual Family Members

Hurvitz also arrived at a preliminary assessment of the family members as individuals and their parts in the conflict situation.

Michelle. Michelle devalues herself because of her bad heart, surgery and the resulting scar, and continuing sickness that keep her out of school (among other things). She feels further devalued because her own father denies her. And if her own father rejects her, how can anyone accept her? However, she cannot account for her feelings of being rejected based on reasons that others cannot see (e.g., her illness and her father's rejection). Given her common sense problem solving perspective, Michelle knows there has to be a tangible reason for her rejection, something that others can notice. She creates a self-fulfilling prophecy by fooling around and being truant at school and by overacting her invalid role and goofing up at home. The school authorities and her mother then complain about her behavior and reject her. This places the blame for her negative self-feelings on other people who treat her badly. At the same time, her interaction with other people has become a kind of game she wins when they allow her to have her way because of her heart condition.

Ms. Mackey. Gloria opened the appointment at a high pitch of anger which she maintained throughout the interview. Her feelings are compatible with her expressed desire to place her children in a foster home or Juvenile Hall. Her anger, initially focussed on her daughters, spills over against the therapist because he did not immediately accede to her request. However, it began to appear that she expressed that anger to support a spoken desire that she did not really want. She may have been covertly pleased with the therapist's refusal to agree that her daughters should be sent away and his face-saving way to withdraw from the brink. This contradiction between her overt behavior and her covert thoughts was later confirmed during the individual meeting. At that time, by taking the role of Devil's Advocate, the therapist prompted her to lay out the pros and cons of placing the children versus keeping them, and Mrs. Mackey chose to keep them.

Gloria presented herself as an unhappy person. This was revealed even more clearly during her individual meeting than during the initial joint meeting. She complained about everything she discussed with the therapist. She was large, awkward, and slow-thinking in contrast to her daughters who are average height, graceful, and quick-witted. In her ethnic and socioeconomic group, having daughters age 13 and 11 at age 43 put her out of phase with her women friends. Most of them are not much older but are grandmothers. She seems to hold these things against her daughters.

In her individual sessions she also reported several experiences in which she was victimized by men, including the fathers of both daughters (who were only half-sisters). She complained that even Mr. Mullins had other women friends and seemed to be nicer to the girls than their mother. She sometimes felt she had to compete with her daughters for Mr. Mullins' attention and she was upset with them about that, as well. She also continued to look for a man with whom she could feel secure. For this reason, she belonged to an informal club of women who arranged house parties to which they invited eligible men. As these parties took up a great deal of her time, she often left the housework for her daughters to do. She would then complain that it wasn't done promptly or properly.

In a vague way, Ms. Mackey believes she has been saddled with an imperfect child as punishment for her liaison with Michelle's father. She is angry at herself for resenting Michelle and angry with herself for the affair that produced the child. She is also angry with Michelle whose behavior and claims of being tired or ill she perceives as being manipulative and provocative. Nevertheless, she is afraid to express her anger against the child out of fear of causing something bad to happen. When she does express hostile feelings about the child, she tries to make up for them by rewarding both girls in some way.

The girls, knowing this pattern, tease their mother into angry outbursts predictably followed by simple punishments because they know that these will be followed by disproportionate rewards. Thus, although Michelle complains that her mother did not take them to the movies as promised, it was far more common that Ms. Mackey would take them after she said she would *not* do so. For instance, during a later session a chart was prepared which listed the girls' school and home chores. It was agreed that if the girls did their outlined chores, they would be taken to Disneyland. The girls did not fulfill their responsibilities but Gloria took them to Disneyland anyway. She explained, "They get so few pleasures."

Sandra. Sandra has learned to keep out of the quarrels between her mother and sister. In fact, she tries to ignore them in order to avoid becoming upset. Although she says "I didn't see nothing," it was clear that she had observed what occurred. She feels ambivalent about Michelle. She resents her sister for making her life more difficult, being manipulative, and squirming out of her chores. At the same time she feels sorry for her little sister who has had open heart surgery. Sandra therefore feels guilty for resenting Michelle but is not above adding to her difficulties if she can do so without being exposed.

While at times she has gained from Michelle's attempts to manipulate their mother and make her look like a fool, Sandra does not want Michelle to do this in front of a stranger. This accounts for the protective aspect of Sandra's verbalizations and silences during the initial joint meeting. Sandra is also aware that Michelle tries to blame her for some of her own limitations during their discussion with the therapist. Although Michelle apparently succeeds when Ms. Mackey scolds Sandra when Michelle is in fact responsible, this type of interaction is a game of sorts. Gloria scolds Sandra because she wants to be easy on Michelle due to her illness, but

Gloria then makes it up to Sandra by some special attention. Since that special attention is more valuable to Sandra than the scolding, she is willing to accept the blame and the special attention or reward that follows. In this way, the characteristic interaction of all three family members is continually reinforced.

Unanswered Questions

The therapist wondered if Ms. Mackey realized she needled Michelle as sharply as she did. If so, was this a way to get even with Michelle? Or was Gloria unaware of the effect of her remarks about Michelle's father on Michelle? Further interaction during the Opening Phase was planned to clarify this issue. Another crucial question was whether Michelle could define what she is freely given as of equal value to what she now gets by manipulation. In this way she would not feel that she had to continue this behavior that sets up continuing conflict. Also in question was whether she could relax her demands by enhancing her understanding and tolerance of her mother's and sister's needs.

Therapy Plan

A therapy program for the Mackey family was outlined as follows and then (in sanitized form) written into a therapy contract to which all parties agreed:

1. Review the family's activities between appointments to examine exchanges, interaction, problems, and conflicts and determine changes required to resolve problems and conflicts.
2. Explain to Ms. Mackey that placement in a foster home for one or both daughters would likely cause greater problems for her than trying to change things at home.
3. Explain to the girls that their mother's decision to place them in a home was a desperate message about how difficult they were making life for her.
4. Prepare a contract that outlines the girls' chores with an appropriate award for performing them (a trip to Disneyland).

5. Explain to the girls the consequences for their mother when they do not do their chores.
6. Explain to the girls that their mother may have an adult relationship with a man without taking something away from them.
7. Offer Michelle an opportunity to ventilate her feelings about her father.
8. Help Michelle increase her self-esteem, learn to make life choices, and develop a more responsible attitude toward her life.
9. Help Sandra increase her self-esteem and overcome depressive feelings about herself and her situation.
10. Secure a tutor for Michelle to help her catch up with her school work.
11. Engage or enroll both Ms. Mackey and Michelle in a program of assertion training.
12. Ms. Mackey to join Weight Watchers or participate in another weight reduction program.
13. Ms. Mackey was urged to discuss with Michelle's physician whether her activities should be restricted in any way.

Crisis Caused by a Personal Limitation with Conflict: Leroy Hawkins and His Mother, Mary Hilliard

Ms. Hilliard brought her son Leroy Hawkins to the appointment. Friends told her that he might fare better in court on charges of shoplifting and extorting money if she could tell the hearing officer that the family was in therapy. The crisis was that Leroy might be removed from the family by the authorities, thrown out by his mother, or run away on his own.

The therapist discovered that there was a serious problem with the family role structure. For instance, Ms. Hilliard complained that when she put Leroy in charge of her other children, he would push them around or hit them when they did not do their chores. They would complain to their mother who then scolded Leroy. He was in a position of having the responsibility but not the authority to see that jobs were done. This is an example of an interpersonal predicament based on an ambiguous and inherently contradictory role definition (sometimes termed role conflict). The family's role structure was selected as the initial problem to work on. At the same time, activities would be initiated to ameliorate Leroy's negative interactions with non-family members.

The therapist was pessimistic about the chances for a successful outcome based on his assessment that Leroy was not committed to change. However, he agreed to provide services because he could at least help the family members improve their relationship. A tentative therapy program was outlined as follows:

1. Review Ms. Hilliard's and Leroy's activities between appointments to examine their interaction and institute changes required to resolve problems and conflicts.
2. Prepare a contract specifying acceptable mutual behaviors for the therapist, Leroy, and Ms. Hilliard after a basic understanding has been established with Leroy.
3. Devise a chart for all the children's assignments so that they can each know and perform their chores.
4. Relieve Leroy of his responsibilities for supervising the younger children at home.
5. Inform Leroy about shootings of teenagers in the black community that were being reported in the newspaper and his mother's concern that his activities might make him a target.
6. Inform Leroy about the need for leaders in the black community and that he is messing up when he should be preparing for a leadership role.
7. Assign Leroy the task of bringing in clippings from newspapers about activities in his neighborhood, especially those that indicate problems. This would be structured as a game by rewarding him for every relevant clipping he brings that the therapist does not.
8. Investigate the possibility of transferring Leroy to another school as he requested because of his negative reputation in his present school.
9. Initiate a tutoring program for Leroy.
10. Write to the court and school authorities indicating Leroy's participation in family therapy and request feedback about his behavior and any changes that might occur.

11. Plan for the other children to participate in family therapy sessions with Ms. Hilliard and Leroy.

Crisis Caused by Conflict over Unacknowledged Personal Limitations: Ross and Brenda Turner

Sometimes spouses or family members have conflicts whose causes they claim to not know. In such instances, they customarily state that their difficulties are due to problems of communication. The therapist works with this definition of the situation but does not accept it as being more than a common sense account. In fact, the therapist anticipates that uncovering what is actually going on may trigger a crisis that the family members' communication problem had been suppressing.

Secrets

As the therapist explains, the cause of poor communication is often the unwillingness to talk because of anxiety that secrets may be revealed. Family members may charge another with a limitation or doing or not doing something that causes their difficulties. Family members may deny the accusation or acknowledge their alleged limitations but claim the cause is something the accusers are doing or not doing. Alternatively, the accused may claim that the limitations or problem behaviors have existed but have not been overcome or improved. The accusing family members may persist in the same allegations or may find new limitations to complain about.

Sometimes the therapist discovers that the accuser is actually hiding a secret and following the strategy of "the best defense is a good offense." In marital situations, this is often an extramarital relationship. Between parents and young adult or teenaged children, the secret is generally a relationship or activity that is contrary to the parents' values and goals for the child.

Because one or more spouses or family members may harbor secrets, the individual appointment takes on great significance and must be skillfully managed to uncover the facts. Once secrets are revealed, the pros and cons of disclosing them to others are discussed. The therapist points out the effects of the family member's behavior or limitation on the other family members. He also shows how it causes them to experience limitations and leads to interpersonal predicaments between all family members.

The therapist suggests several outcomes that are possible. The family member may decide that he can no longer prevaricate about his behavior. He may therefore choose to leave the family or be forced to leave by other family members. Alternatively, the crisis may be overcome and the conflict resolved when the family member decides to re-establish effective and satisfying interaction with significant others and do whatever has to be done to accomplish this objective.

Example: The Turners

Brenda Turner informed the therapist over the phone that her marriage was turning into a nightmare. She also felt she and her husband, Ross, had a communication problem.

* * *

In the opening joint meeting of their first appointment, she said that he complained about her constantly. When she corrected the behaviors that he complained about or denied that the complaints were valid, he conjured up new limitations to complain about. Although their conflict was not expressed physically, Ross disparaged her at home, to their friends and relatives, and avoided her sexually. He assaulted her self-concept and made her feel so worthless that she began to fear that she was going crazy. Ross Turner accused Brenda of being unable to handle her household responsibilities and the children effectively. Mrs. Turner denied this. Brenda said she wanted to maintain their marriage and became very disturbed by Ross's accusations against her.

In their individual meeting, the therapist informed Mr. Turner that his behavior could only be interpreted as due to being involved with another woman. He denied this. Mrs. Turner made the same accusation which he denied again during the concluding joint meeting. However, it was decided to continue with a few more sessions to explore how to help the Turners with their relationship. Thus, the opening phase continued simultaneously with the initiation of change-promoting activities.

In the course of the following counseling sessions, Ross admitted that he had been having an affair. He stated that he had decided to end the extra marital relationship and try to repair his family and home life. Shortly after he made this decision, Brenda was informed by an anonymous phone call about Ross's affair. She was very disturbed by her realization that she had been suffering from accusations about non-existent inadequacies made to excuse her husband's involvement with another woman. She decided that she wanted a divorce.

* * *

Thus, the severe conflict initially brought into therapy escalated into a full-blown crisis situation as a result of change-producing activities. At this point, the therapist shifted gears and focussed on crisis management. A tentative therapy program was outlined as follows:

1. Explore with Ross how the inability to communicate was connected to his fear that he might reveal his affair if he communicated freely with his spouse.
2. Offer both spouses training in effective communication, bargaining, decision making, and problem solving.
3. Review their continuing interaction to examine their exchanges.
4. Help the Turners prepare a contract stating their desire to maintain and improve their relationship and indicating what each has to do to achieve this goal.
5. Ross to end the extramarital relationship.
6. Train Ross in thought stopping regarding his former friend (see Chapter Seven).
7. Help Ross and Brenda develop freer sexual behaviors.
8. Brenda to forgive her husband and try to make their marriage work.
9. Turners to participate in social activities together and develop new mutual friends.

Therapeutic Contracts

Assuming that the consensus is to proceed with therapy, the therapist begins overcoming the family members' interpersonal predicament through joint efforts toward maintaining the family. The necessary change activities are typically defined in three contracts proposed during the concluding phase of the first meeting: (a) between therapist and family members, (b) among the family members themselves, and (c) by each family member with himself or herself.

These contracts spell out the therapy goals and provide an objective standard against which progress can be measured. They remind each party of agreed-upon responsibilities. Although contracts can take the form of a verbal understanding, they are best formalized in writing.

The written contract. The written contract between therapist and family group, for example, outlines the therapy goals in terms of behaviors, thoughts, and feelings that are to be changed. The terms of the other contracts are negotiated with the therapist's assistance so that they are explicitly agreed upon by all family members.

It is helpful to use an attractive format for the contract (perhaps using printed forms with multicolored artwork or doing it with a computer and good quality printer). It can then be framed and placed in a prominent place in the home. Family members can remind themselves of their own and others' expectations and use the contract as a motivating device. Additionally, the displayed contract prompts them to talk at home and remind each other of their agreements and common goals.

Contingency and good faith contracts. The contracts used in sociocognitive therapy are of one of two types. *Contingency contracts* identify a quid pro quo such as what therapist and family members agree to do or what one family member agrees to do contingent on another's actions (Azrin, Naster & Jones, 1973; Hickok & Komecheck, 1974; Knox, 1971). The therapist agrees to provide sessions and exert himself on behalf of the family members. They, in turn, agree to attend and participate in the meetings, pay the fee, do homework, and do what is necessary to achieve their agreed upon goals. Such contracts mean that each agrees to fulfill their part contingent upon the others fulfilling theirs. This situation can lead to stalemate if either party defines the conditions of agreement as not being met.

However, the contracts among and between family members should preferably be of a second type—the *good faith contract* (Weiss, Hope & Patterson, 1973). In this form, each party agrees to act voluntarily toward the agreed-upon goals and then to reinforce themselves for doing so. In this way, each is responsible for fulfilling his part of the contract. Each receives a reward for doing what the other wants but does not wait for the other to do anything first. In effect, this eliminates the difference between the contracts made among family members and those they make with themselves. Deftly handled by the therapist, this can become a type of game or contest in which each tries to outdo the other to become a supportive significant other.

Example of a Good Faith Contract: Ross and Brenda Turner. It was difficult to work out a contract with the Turners. In part this was because Brenda took to heart the therapist's statement that what they said they wanted was like getting remarried. Carrying this symbolism to an extreme, Brenda suggested that Ross promise to "love, honor and cherish" her, while she would promise to "love, honor and something else, but I don't know what—certainly not 'obey.'" The therapist explained that the contract he was referring to was much more specific and related to their particular situation. After considerable hemming and hawing and awkward joking, the following contract was devised:

> I, Ross Turner, desiring to re-establish a loving and faithful relationship with my wife, Brenda, herewith promise to do the following:
>
> 1. I will compliment her about all the things I have neglected to compliment her for in the past.
> 2. I will demonstrate my affection for her by kissing her when I come home from work and by snuggling with her when we go to bed.
> 3. I will propose two or three different things to do together or with the children for a Saturday evening or on Sunday.

4. I will call home at least once during every working day (unless it is impossible to do so — and then I will explain the reason when I get home).
5. I will answer all my wife's questions about my activities during my day at work (because I understand that she has reasons to be concerned about my behavior).

I will do all the things I have named above without any expectation of any consideration or favors from my wife, but simply because I want to demonstrate my love for her and desire to re-establish the kind of feelings we had together for nearly 25 years.

Signed, Ross Turner   Witness

I, Brenda Bryant Turner, desiring to re-establish a loving and faithful relationship with my husband, Ross, herewith promise to do the following:

1. I will accept my husband's compliments with grace and will not look for any special meaning in them.
2. I will accept his demonstrations of affection and I will respond to them like I did when we first got married.
3. I will refuse to talk with others about our family crisis and I will not bring it up at home.
4. I will participate in all the activities we plan to do together or with the children.
5. I will look forward to the future and not back to the past.

I will do all the things I have named above without any expectation of any consideration or favors from my husband, but simply because I want to demonstrate my love for him and desire to re-establish the kind of feelings we had together for nearly 25 years.

Signed,   Witness
Brenda Bryant Turner

As the contract was being signed, the therapist explained that they were establishing a good faith contract. He told them that such a contract included provisions for demonstrating one's pleasure and gratification when the other fulfilled their conditions. That is, if Ross fulfilled his part, Brenda could reward him in some way, he could reward himself, or the therapist could reward him in some way. The same held for Brenda. Both Mr. and Mrs. Turner said they were sure the opportunity would arise to reward each other. They were amused as they said they would find ways to do so.

CODA

When the spouses or family members resolve their crisis by deciding to remain together there may be a simultaneous resolution of their conflict, interpersonal predicaments, and underlying personal limitations. This result may be due to re-evaluation and redefinition of the situation and consequent changes in family members' interaction and self-interaction. Alternatively, it may be due simply to the decision to remain together. This decision may have fostered a renewed commitment to the affirmative elements of the family. As is more often the case, the procedure of deciding to remain together does not catalyze a sufficient reconstruction to permit the effective and satisfying interaction and relationships. The therapist then continues with the reduction process.

Chapter Six

The Change-Inducing Phase: II. Resolving Conflicts and Interpersonal Predicaments

Crisis management enables spouses or family members, on their own or with the therapist's assistance, to apply the coping processes of joint decision making, bargaining, and problem solving. This does not mean that everything is now sweetness and light between the family members. It does mean they no longer believe that their inevitable next step is over the brink. The movement to crisis has been halted. In this chapter, the sociocognitive therapist continues the reduction process to resolve conflicts and interpersonal predicaments that escalate into a crisis situation.

WORKING WITH THE COPING PROCESSES

There are three major processes by which spouses or family members determine, establish, and maintain common meanings:

1. *Decision making* is the process of choosing between two or more alternatives without necessarily implying a compromise.
2. *Bargaining* is the process of coming to an agreement through compromise.
3. *Problem solving* is the process of resolving a perplexing situation or condition.

All three interactional processes require the participation, meanings, and feelings of two or more family members. Each enables the family members to cope with various conflicts and problems, adjust to others' meanings, and thereby maintain constructed reciprocity. Obviously, these processes shade into one another. Decision making may require bargaining; decision making and bargaining may be required for problem solving; bargaining and problem solving may be required in decision making.

Viewed from the family group's perspective, these function as *coping processes*. Successful decision making, bargaining, and problem solving are given little attention in the course of everyday interaction. They are the means by which the family members resolve interpersonal strains and deal with environmental challenges. However, when unsuccessful, they have serious consequences for the family members. Their failure triggers or exacerbates the escalation of limitations into predicaments, conflicts, and crises.

From a therapeutic perspective, these serve as the basic *reduction processes*. The therapist helps family members engage in effective decision making, bargaining, and problem solving. These, in turn, transform, convert or reduce the crisis to an interpersonal predicament (with or without conflict). Next they reduce the interpersonal predicament to family members' personal limitations. The personal limitations are then overcome by appropriate change methods or activities.

Decision Making

Typically, the first reduction process used with the spouses or family members is decision making. Once a crisis has been reduced through reconstruction, the family members must decide whether the escalation process shall be consummated by the separation of the spouses or breakup of the family. In situations of severe conflict, they must decide whether they want to restore satisfying and effective interaction before change-producing activities are initiated. In other cases, the first decision to be made is what they want as their therapy goal.

Decision Making Applied to an Interpersonal Predicament with Conflict: Yolanda Robison and David Tucker

The process by which the sociocognitive therapist helps with decision making is best explained by example. We turn again to the interpersonal predicament with conflict experienced by Yolanda Robison and David Tucker.

1. *First appointment*. Yolanda called to make an emergency appointment. She only said that she had a problem and did not mention David. She came to that appointment with her seven-year-old daughter. In her discussion with the therapist, she complained that the man she lived with, David, beat her and that these beatings had recently become more severe. She said she had been unable to get him to stop and came to the therapist to get him to stop beating her. She had not told the therapist about this over the phone because David said he would not participate in any kind of therapy.

Hurvitz notes that when Yolanda reported that David beat her, it was not because she wanted to leave him. Therefore a crisis did not exist. Yolanda said that basically David is real nice — that is, the "real David." Other times "he is not himself" and that is when he beats her. She said she wanted the therapist to help David be nice all the time.

2. *Assessment meeting with adult family members alone*. Despite Yolanda's assertions that David refused to participate, the therapist telephoned him and he agreed to come to an appointment. When he came with Yolanda and all three of her daughters, the therapist continued the opening phase with a modified tripartite appointment. Initially, the therapist spoke with David and Yolanda together:

Yolanda repeated her complaints about David and refused to acknowledge her heavy drinking. David denied beating her. He stated that when Yolanda became drunk, she would attempt to fight him and he would simply try to hold her wrists so she could not hit him. Her bruises were caused by falling and bumping into walls and furniture. One time David took her to a hospital as she demanded and Yolanda made such a commotion that he could not tell his side of the story. He also learned that it was better not to contradict her because she only elaborated her accounts when he did.

3. *Assessment meeting with the children alone*. Next, the therapist met with Yolanda's three children for a joint session. The children knew about the conflict between Yolanda and David. When

they were asked what they wanted for themselves, all three children said they wanted their mother to stay with David.

> The children were given an opportunity to play with dolls. At that time they were asked to make a family and tell the therapist a story about that family. When they did so, the therapist asked whether the father ever hit the mother. The children said he did not and that they know why the therapist asked them that question about the dolls. As they did again later during individual meetings, the girls told the therapist, "Don't believe my mother. David doesn't hit her. Jimmy hit her. David helps her. She drinks a lot."

4. *Evaluating alternatives: least desired choices technique.* Now, in an individual meeting with Yolanda, the therapist asked her to list on paper all the choices she could make about her relationship with David. That is, all the possible alternatives available to her. Together with the therapist, Yolanda listed:

— Stay with David and hope he changes.
— Leave David and go back with Jimmy.
— Go back to Alabama.
— Leave David and live alone with my children.
— Keep company with David when I'm on my own while he changes.
— Stop drinking so David won't fight me.

After Yolanda made this list, the therapist typed them on a sheet of paper. He then sliced them apart. He discussed each alternative with her and asked her to rank them from the *least undesired choice* (the one she disliked the least or liked the most) to the *most disliked choice* (Bell, 1977). Her ranking was:

— Keep company with David when I'm on my own while he changes.
— Stay with David and hope he changes.
— Stop drinking so David won't fight me.
— Leave David and go back with Jimmy.

— Leave David and live alone with my children.
— Go back to Alabama.

The therapist next held an individual meeting with David and followed the same procedure. David came up with the following ranking of alternatives:

— Stay with Yolanda and her children and let her drink.
— Keep company with Yolanda while separated from her.
— Try to help Yolanda change.
— Live alone and forget Yolanda.
— Find another woman to live with.
— Go back to my wife in Mississippi.

5. *Stress testing meanings and definitions.* The therapist then held a joint meeting with Yolanda and David. The purpose was ostensibly to compare their least undesired choices and discuss their implications. The real agenda for this portion of the session was to stress test their individual and joint definitions of the situation:

> Yolanda said that, although she preferred to go out with David while she was on her own, she didn't really know if that was what she wanted. She knew she didn't want to break up with David and didn't want to have to try to find another man. She said David is the nicest man she knew and maybe it was best to hold on to what she had. She kept saying she hoped David would change and began to admit that maybe she wasn't being fair to him. David said that he preferred to stay with Yolanda, but she would have to stop the drinking. His next choice was to go out with Yolanda while they were separated.

During this joint session, the therapist confronted Yolanda and David about the scene of drinking and fighting they displayed at home. Clearly, because of David's schedule they lived in a kind of topsy-turvy world. It was also true that they had greater financial resources together than each would have alone. But they needed to examine whether the greater material benefits were worth the grief they caused each other. He told them they had to consider some serious questions. For example:

The therapist asked Yolanda to explain why she had stayed so long with David if he treats her so badly. Is David a cause of her drinking? If so, how does he cause her to drink more if he says he is trying to help her? If she continues to stay with him under these conditions, wouldn't she eventually lose her self-respect and her children's respect? And then wouldn't she no longer be a fit mother for her children? If he did not beat her as she claimed, why does she say that he does?

The therapist asked similar questions of David:

Why does he stay with someone who calls him a liar and who causes so much trouble? Why does he keep trying to stop her from drinking when doing so puts him in danger of being accused of wife-beating? If she lies about him the way he says she does, how can he respect himself and continue to live with her? If she continues to lie about him, wouldn't it be better for him to ask her to move out?

The therapist offered a therapeutic hypothesis that was deliberately paradoxical in order to help them test their meanings and feelings (Seltzer, 1986). Recall that he had already come to accept the provisional hypothesis that neither Yolanda nor David really wanted to break up. Instead, they were mired in a very serious interpersonal predicament with conflict that threatened to force them over the brink.

The therapist said that the conflict in their home might have such damaging consequences that perhaps it would be better for them to consider some type of separation. Staying together and fighting might cause Yolanda to be severely hurt and unable to care for her children. David could be arrested for wife-beating and sent to jail. The children would grow up in a home in which the parents were having bad fights. And they might also be hurt. Clearly, they were learning that such fighting is the way people live in families. This could have a bad effect on them. Perhaps it would be better for them to separate before the situation worsened.

This was a very unexpected turn for Yolanda and David. It immediately sobered them.

> Yolanda backtracked and said maybe she had exaggerated her beatings. David added that perhaps he was too rough with her when he tried to stop her from fighting him. The therapist told them that it would be a good idea to consider the various alternatives they had and decide which one would be best.

6. *Ballot technique for forging a joint definition.* The therapist then turned back to their lists of alternatives. As their least liked options, both listed leaving the other and finding another person to live with, living alone, or returning to the South and their original spouses. As their least disliked alternatives, both listed staying with the other and hoping for the promised changes or separating but remaining friends. The therapist prepared a ballot consisting of the two least disliked options. He typed out the following on a sheet of paper:

> To stay together and hope for/promise to change   Yes   No
> To keep company while we don't live together   Yes   No

> Each was then asked to circle "Yes" for one statement and "No" for the other, depending on which choice they preferred. This was conducted as a secret ballot. Each folded their paper and handed it back to the therapist who then read and announced their choices.

> On the first ballot, Yolanda circled "No" for "Stay together" and "Yes" for "Keep company . . ." while David circled the first "Yes" and the second "No."

Because each chose a different option, a second identical ballot was prepared (today this exercise could more easily be done using a computer and printer). Yolanda and David were told that they could vote the way they did the first time or they could change their vote. This time Yolanda and David both circled "Yes" for "Stay together . . ." When the therapist announced the result, Yolanda began to cry. David put his arm about her and comforted her.

7. *Outlining a therapy program*. At this point, the therapist outlined a tentative therapy program:

1. Work out a contract between David and Yolanda based on the information secured from them (Yolanda's early morning appearance and behavior was selected as their initial problem).
2. Review interaction between meetings to examine exchanges.
3. Instruct David and Yolanda in behavior modification (reinforcement of desired behaviors, thoughts, and feelings in the other).
4. Yolanda and David to discuss divorcing their spouses (so that each would regard it as a sign that they were not thinking of leaving the other).
5. Yolanda and David to prepare a budget to use their joint income more wisely.
6. Yolanda and David to prepare a chart outlining the children's chores to help them be aware of and perform their assignments.
7. Yolanda to see her physician to determine whether there are any physical problems that contribute to her limitations (e.g., chronic tiredness).
8. Therapist to teach Yolanda relaxation exercises to help her fall asleep.
9. Yolanda to investigate Alcoholics Anonymous to help control her drinking before it becomes more serious.

In helping with decision making, the therapist may help them overcome irrational or ineffective assumptions or algorithms. This may involve training in rational choice (Dawes, 1988). The therapist may also wish to employ a more structured decision-making approach, such as the Robinette model for conflict resolution (Robinette & Harris, 1989).

Bargaining

Bargaining becomes the central reduction process when the spouses or family members hold divergent positions which create conflict or interpersonal predicament but offer potential for reconciliation. In such a situation, the family members usually make negative attributions about one another's overt or covert motives, intentions, and purposes. They tend to engage in deception. Each tries to figure out the other's intention in order to act preemptively while concealing his own. Bargaining offers a way out of this situation through compromise.

The Bargaining Structure

Various factors influence bargaining processes within the family or in the therapy setting. These include the social, physical, and issue components of the bargaining structure.

1. *Social components* include: (a) the audience and its composition (family members or non-members, adults or children); (b) family members or others attempting to serve as intermediaries; (c) the number of participants, their relationships, and division into coalitions (adults against children, all against a scapegoat, or one parent and set of children against another); and (d) participants' social characteristics (age, health, economic security).
2. *Physical components* constrain the process and symbolize aspects of the conflict. These include: (a) the context of the bargaining (e.g., family's home or therapist's office); (b) specific location (living room, kitchen, or bedroom); and (c) other aspects of the setting (arrangement of the room, presence or absence of time limits).
3. *Issue components* include: (a) the number and type of issues involved, (b) the way they are presented, and (c) the extent to which they have similar salience or importance for participants in the bargaining situation.

The Bargaining Process

Before bargaining, the spouses or family members recognize (or are helped to recognize) that an impasse has been reached and action cannot be taken until it is resolved. At the same time, each implicitly or explicitly determines a bottom line condition or need which is not subject to compromise. The bargaining sequence proceeds as follows, assuming that the participants cooperate and the situation is free of intransigence:

1. Jack makes a proposal to Jill (after identifying a fall-back position were it rejected). In doing this, he may bluff in the sense of asking for more than he expects.
2. Jill responds to Jack's proposal as a demand with a counter-proposal. She also identifies a fall-back position and she, too, may bluff.
3. Jack re-evaluates his position and, expecting Jill to re-evaluate hers, makes a proposal Jill is more likely to accept, but which is still better than his fall-back position.
4. Jill reconsiders her position, evaluates the new proposal, and either accepts or makes a new counter-proposal.

Each continues making new proposals with greater concessions until one or both reaches a compromise position. Or until they come to their own bottom line positions beyond which they are unwilling to compromise. Sometimes, dyads can live with unresolved differences depending on the centrality, salience, and meaning of the issues. Each also has to consider whether the proposed compromise or failure to meet their bottom-line position leaves no alternative but to end the relationship.

Initial Tactics. Early tactical moves are critical because initial proposals and counter-offers set a basis or context for subsequent proposals. That is, they establish the joint definition of the bargaining situation. Therefore, the therapist (as intermediary) attempts to facilitate the best possible initiation of bargaining.

Assessment. As the bargainers pursue a mutually acceptable agreement, their proposals and counter-offers reveal the individual's cooperativeness and openness to redefinition of the situation. The therapist observes which family members are cooperative, competitive, individualistic, willing to settle for a small gain, or demanding a big gain. Using the Four Questions technique, he evaluates the family members' perceptions of each other, their intentions, and the intentions they attribute to others.

Similarly, he questions perception of the other's purposes and goals, the other's strategy and tactics, and how they plan to respond. The therapist also discovers the ways family members influence each other, such as threats, promises, capitulation, or "guilt tripping." He evaluates the effects of the social, physical, and issue components of the bargaining situation. He seeks to modify them, if possible, to facilitate compromise and reduce the number of issues requiring bargaining.

The Therapist's Negotiating Activities

The family members whom therapists counsel have been unable to solve their problems or resolve their conflicts on their own. The therapist uses various negotiation activities when the family members are unable to bargain effectively on their own. These activities include overcoming obstacles to concessions and originating face-saving concessions and compromises.

Overcoming obstacles to making concessions. One of the principal routes is by working out a compromise in which they achieve reciprocity, justice, equity, or fairness by mutual concessions or adjustments. This requires that family members agree to change their behavior in some way. However, they will not agree if they believe they are being imposed upon or taken advantage of. Or if they are not really committed to maintaining and enhancing their marriage and family. Such a situation causes a stalemate in therapy.

The therapist uses resources and techniques to overcome such stalemates and enable bargaining. Family members begin with generalized or global perceptions and complaints. The therapist helps them to focus on specifics and identify one action to take by way of a concession. Five ways in which the sociocognitive therapist accomplishes this are:

1. *Carrying proposals*. The therapist carries proposals from one family member to another that enable them to develop rapprochement:

    [The therapist tells the husband] She said she'd withdraw the divorce action if you would move out of the house and agree not to see her for six months.

    [The therapist tells the wife] He said he's willing to accept your proposal but he'd like to work it out so that the six months would end a couple of weeks before Christmas. He said that would be a good time for a family reunion after such a long separation. Is that OK with you?

2. *Suggesting accommodations*. The therapist suggests accommodations that enable the family members to have an effective and satisfying family life:

[The therapist tells the husband] You say you want to maintain the marriage. Okay. So instead of coming here and complaining about her, can you suggest one change you can make to help both of you get along better? For instance, you're always griping about the way she keeps the house clean. But if she tries to clean the house the way you want, she'll be too tired to stay awake with you in the evening and she'll want to go to bed early. So then you'll complain that she's avoiding you sexually. Ease up on your demand for her to be the perfect housekeeper. If she keeps house the way she takes care of herself—it seems to me that she's pretty careful about her appearance—I would guess the house is in good shape, too. I think that if she felt you eased up about the housecleaning she'd feel better about you, and your sex life would improve.

[The therapist tells the wife] You say that you want to stay married. Okay. So instead of coming in here and complaining about him, can you suggest one change you can make to help both of you get along better? For instance, you've complained that he always wants sex when you're tired. But if you don't get together on the weekend when you're not tired, he's going to want sex during the week. And when he isn't satisfied sexually, he finds something unrelated to complain about—usually the way you keep the house clean. So if you would be more responsive sexually, I think he'd feel better about you and quit griping about the housecleaning.

3. *Bargaining out agreement*. The therapist bargains out an agreement between family members in accord with their therapeutic goal:

[The therapist tells the mother] What do you want him to do before you'll agree to let him have the car? What do you think he'll accept and what do you think he'll reject?

[The therapist tells the son] What do you think your mom wants you to do before she'll agree to let you have the car? What are you willing to accept and what aren't you willing to accept?

4. *Stating the need for concessions.* The therapist informs the family members that each must offer some concession in order to achieve the kind of family interaction they assert as their joint goal:

[The therapist tells the wife] You've complained about him and told me all the bad things he does and why he's so difficult to live with, and he's done the same. Now, please tell me one thing that he's complained about that is justified — even if only a little — that you are willing to change to achieve the kind of marriage you want. Keeping the house cleaner, seeing that the kids go to school every day, getting them to school on time, preparing dinners instead of sending out for hamburgers or fried chicken and that sort of stuff — which do you think is the easiest for you? Let's start with that.

[The therapist tells the husband] I'm sure that not all the complaints she made about you are true — any more than all you made about her are. When people come here, they justify their position by telling me as much that is bad about their partner as they possibly can. Sometimes I wonder why they want to stay with someone who has all the shortcomings they say their husband or wife has. You know the complaints she has about you. You say you want this marriage to work out. So tell me which of her complaints you think are justified and which ones you are willing and able to do something about. You must know you have to give something to stay together. What's it going to be?

Originating Face-Saving Concessions and Compromises

The therapist also helps the spouses and family members to resolve their differences by proposing and eliciting concessions and adjustments. This is one of the therapist's most difficult and important tasks. The therapist must convince family members that they are not being asked to give up so much that they become unwilling to give up anything at all. To accomplish this, the therapist must present them with face-saving compromises that modify their position to enable change to begin.

Face. Each human being attempts to appear wise or at least intelligent, competent, and effective in his own eyes and in those of significant others. Therefore, each tries to avoid people or situations which cause him to lose face. *Loss of face* means acting or being acted toward in such a way that the individual appears foolish, incompetent, or inadequate. It is relative to, and associated with, a person's status (in both the family group and larger world) and subsequent role performances and expectations.

When an individual is threatened with a loss of face, he attempts to find a means to *save face*. That is, he wishes to avoid the loss of esteem or dignity. A person who perceives a loss of face may retaliate against those who caused or witnessed it. He may withdraw from the situation in which he lost face, respond with an alibi, redefine the situation with a joke, or use other defensive mechanisms available to cover and/or compensate (see Goffman, 1967).

When significant others cause each other to lose face, their relationship deteriorates to retaliation and recrimination. The therapist therefore cautions clients against making statements that cause the loss of face. He also proposes face-saving compromises and solutions to their differences.

Tactics. One approach to helping save face is enabling them to back out of an untenable situation. This is illustrated by the case of Ross and Brenda Turner. In this case, a crisis was resolved once Mr. Turner's affair was brought to light and he agreed to terminate it in order to renew his marriage. Then, the key to resolving their remaining conflict proved to be helping Mrs. Turner withdraw her demand for a divorce after she had told her family and friends she was going to leave her husband.

In many cases, the therapist discovers a contradiction between family members' underlying feelings and assertions made about each other. Or a contradiction between their desired outcomes and goals. In such cases, the sociocognitive therapist assists conflict resolution on the basis of the definition *exhibited* in their behaviors,

thoughts, and feelings. He uses these rather than the surface definitions *expressed* in their statements, complaints, and recriminations
made to each other and the therapist as a manifestation of their
conflict. This is seen in the case of Ms. Osea Jefferson and her
daughter.

*   *   *

Ms. Jefferson came to the therapist because she was having difficulties with her man friend. They had been intimate friends for many
years. Now that Ms. Jefferson's only child, Sharon, was graduating
from high school, they were discussing marriage. In the course of
her sessions, Ms. Jefferson often mentioned Sharon, a bright and
attractive young woman who is "college material."

One day, about six weeks before graduation, Ms. Jefferson
brought her daughter to the appointment because Sharon told her
she is pregnant. Ms. Jefferson was very disturbed about the pregnancy because Sharon is the child of her own premarital pregnancy.
She had learned how hard it is for an unmarried woman raising a
child alone to work and get an education. Ms. Jefferson had to quit
high school and work in laundries to support herself and her child.

Sharon told her mother that she planned to have the baby and live
with the father, an unemployed teenager who quit school in the 10th
grade. Ms. Jefferson tried to explain the foolishness and danger of
such a plan. She pleaded with and finally threatened her daughter.
Ms. Jefferson told Sharon that if she went through with her plan,
she would cut Sharon off. Sharon said she didn't care. She said she
loved the child's father and was going to live with him. Following
another argument about her plan, Sharon moved out of her mother's
house into the home of the boy's family. The conflict thereby
turned into a crisis.

Once Sharon was gone, Ms. Jefferson returned to the therapist
disturbed and confused about the situation. She asserted that, since
Sharon decided to have the baby, she didn't care that Sharon had
moved away. However, while she was hurt and angry, it was obvious that she wanted to maintain a friendly relationship with her only
child. The therapist responded to Ms. Jefferson's sense of loss and
her fear that it might be permanent. She was cautioned against mak-

ing any statements that assumed the permanence of her break with Sharon.

The relationship between Ms. Jefferson and Sharon became so strained that it prevented them from coming to joint appointments. The therapist wrote to Sharon at her boyfriend's address (given to him by Ms. Jefferson). He asked Sharon to call him, which she did. The situation was reviewed with Sharon and an appointment was set for her. Additional appointments were then made.

During her meetings, Sharon acknowledged that she needed more than love to establish a family. She was dependent on her mother in many ways. Ms. Jefferson had been so eager for Sharon to finish high school that she had made few household demands on her and Sharon wanted to learn from her mother. She was also anxious and frightened about having her child without anyone in her family to help. Therefore, she was willing to accept some of the proposals her mother made for continuing association.

Sharon agreed to delay her marriage until after the child was born. At that time, a decision would be made about the best arrangement for her, the child, and the child's father. In turn, Ms. Jefferson accepted that Sharon would have the child and that Sharon and the child's father would move into their own place as soon as she became eligible for welfare assistance.

After several individual meetings, both women came separately to a joint meeting. Amid tears, they professed their desire to maintain their mother-daughter relationship albeit with necessary modifications.

* * *

The therapist's shuttle diplomacy overcame the crisis and permitted everyone involved to maintain a friendly relationship without losing face.

Problem Solving

The third basic reduction process is problem solving, in which group members work out joint lines of action to overcome negative or unwanted conditions. An interpersonal predicament (with or without conflict) makes it difficult or impossible for the family members to cooperate in this fashion. Additionally, the predicament itself may be the result of the family members' lack of adequate problem-solving skills. In the present context, we refer to the methods by which a therapist helps family members to overcome such barriers and engage in satisfying and effective problem solving.

Interactional Problem Solving

Problem solving involves casting about for alternatives, following one line of action until it becomes blocked, casting about again and then trying another line. Which line is taken and how it is pursued is largely dependent on the sequence of individual events and choices. Often the goal is redefined or other problems identified in the course of problem-solving action. In this case, the entire process may change direction, branch unpredictably, and acquire an open-ended character.

Problem solving is not, as is often presented, a straight-line process in which one step follows another in a formal sequence leading to a preconceived goal. It is therefore impossible to prescribe a correct and systematic approach to problem solving. To a great extent, success is dependent upon the creativity and commitment of the therapist and family members. However, problem solving in interpersonal interaction tends to progress through a general sequence of stages (see also Reid, 1985):

1. Recognizing that a problem exists
2. Defining the problem
3. Researching the situation
4. Identifying and evaluating alternatives
5. Implementing an agreed-upon solution
6. Monitoring and reviewing progress
7. Maintaining changes achieved

While we present these in linear sequence, problem solving is actually an iterative process. One may cycle through any or all parts of the process several times. Each time one uses what has been learned in attempting one line of solution to modify, refine, or redirect the next attempt. Furthermore, stages overlap and interact, so that the skills, information, or decisions central to one phase may be required in a slightly different form at another stage. The therapist needs to be aware of these stages to identify gaps or discontinuities in the family members' problem-solving approach and to help them work through the process. We will briefly consider each of these seven basic stages.

Recognizing that a problem exists. Obviously, unless one is aware that a problem exists, nothing will be done to solve it. However, in many situations only some of the interactants perceive a problem. Those who do not recognize the problem (or experience it sufficiently) may not cooperate in solving it. They may have a vested interest in denying or not perceiving a problem. This may be because they obtain gratification from the present situation or simply because the existing reality is the basis for their status, identity, and conduct. Thus, one spouse may not accept the existence of a problem because he or she is unwilling to consider the possibility that they do not have a stable and happy marriage.

The therapist may need to help one or more family members recognize the problem that has brought other family members to therapy. Family members commonly require training in problem-detecting skills. This may require learning how to challenge assumptions and be more sensitive to discrepancies between what is expected and what actually occurs.

Defining the problem. An individual may be aware of a problem but may be unable to identify what it is. He may be unable to express it in words or only be able to label it with generalities, common-sense categories, or other categories drawn from a problem-solving perspective. This may take the form of "I feel something is wrong but I don't know what" or complaints by one dyad member about the other's attitude.

The first step in defining a problem is identifying the features that create a problem for one or more interactants. In other words, one constructs an interaction hypothesis to account for the problematic features of the interpersonal situation. As we have discussed, interaction hypotheses may be either terminal or instrumental. Terminal hypotheses tend to reify and perpetuate any problems or become sources of problems themselves.

Therefore, the therapist helps family members develop the skill of generating instrumental hypotheses about perceived problems. In the therapy situation, he works to develop specifically therapeutic hypotheses. In both instances, *a problem in interpersonal interaction should be defined in relation to the specific behavior of the individuals involved.* This not only shifts focus away from generalities ("He's like that.") to the concrete and observable situation but also enables therapist and family members to agree upon, modify, and monitor progress in changing specific aspects of their interaction and relationship.

Researching the situation. The sociocognitive therapist employs the tools of the symbolic interactionist social researcher in assessing and understanding behaviors, thoughts, feelings, interactions, and relationships. Furthermore, he trains family members to apply basic forms of these skills on their own. This research extends beyond obtaining information about family members' situation and conduct to organizing that information at a conceptual level.

Therapist and family members alike generate interaction hypotheses based on actual instances of conduct. They test and continually refine those hypotheses by reference to further instances of observed behaviors, thoughts, and feelings. When the hypothesis accounts for (or takes into account) new observations without further modification and all the family members agree it satisfactorily models their interactional realities, a point of closure has been reached (Glaser & Strauss, 1967).

This does not mean the hypothesis is right or is the only way to model the situation. It may even require further refinement (or even abandonment) at a later time. Rather, it means that the problem-solving process can proceed to the next step using the organized information as a working hypothesis.

Identifying and evaluating alternatives. Once a therapeutic hypothesis has been defined and agreed upon, problem solving moves on to identification of possible solutions. As we have discussed, each interaction hypothesis implies a set of solutions. Alternatively, possible solutions can be generated through brainstorming or similar exercises.

In any case, solutions initially advanced by family members tend to be self-serving or at least framed from the individual's limited, personal viewpoint. It is therefore necessary to help family members to examine each other's proposed solutions. The therapist can help by pointing out individual family member's blind spots. He encourages each to take the role of the other and perceive the problem and the proposed solutions as the others perceive them. The Four Questions technique may be helpful in this regard.

The proposed solutions must also be considered in relation to the family members' individual and joint values and goals. They will each offer solutions that are compatible with their own values and goals but which may conflict with those of other family members. The therapist helps the family members consider each solution's advantages and disadvantages. This should be done from the perspective of each family member and in relation to its effect on the family members' continuing interaction.

Finally, alternative solutions must be tested — both to ensure that they are workable and to evaluate their possible short- and long-term benefits and costs for each member and for the group. One method is reflective, analytical, and directed discussion with family members and interested, informed others of proposed solutions' implications and possible consequences. Other methods suited primarily to use in the therapist's office may also be adapted for the back home situation. These include role-playing, imaginative rehearsal of applying solutions (see Chapter Seven), and practice in the real-life situation for a designated period of time.

Implementing an agreed-upon solution. Once possible solutions have been evaluated and tested, a choice must be made. It is wise to define that choice as *provisional* (for a designated period of time) in order to learn if it has the potential for achieving the desired purpose. Agreement and commitment by all concerned may be recorded in a contract. As discussed earlier, doing so facilitates monitoring progress and holds family members accountable to enact their agreements.

Once a choice is made, the solution must be implemented. A basic principle of sociocognitive therapy (and, all clinical sociology) is: *the way to be changed is to act changed* (Straus, 1982, 1989). At the same time, symbolic interactionist social psychology recognizes that one acts in accordance with one's meanings. Therefore, implementation of change should involve activities of cognitive change or re-definition of the situation by the individual family members.

The therapist encourages testing the agreed-upon solution for a predetermined period of time as suggested above. It is essential that all the family members understand what is expected of them. They must also recognize their responsibility for fulfilling their part of the agreement in order for others to fulfill theirs. Family members should prepare for the possibility that the solution's introduction may send unexpected shock waves through the family. This may require redefinition of constructed reciprocity and development of new expectations for reciprocity, justice, equity, and fairness.

Monitoring and reviewing progress. The family members and therapist then monitor the effectiveness of the chosen solution. For the therapist, this process depends upon feedback from the family members. The therapist is particularly interested in whether problems arise during implementation and how those problems are solved, whether family members are fulfilling their responsibilities, and whether it is more difficult for some than others.

After a period of time, family members are invited to review and determine if agreements and commitments are being observed and if they are achieving their asserted values and goals. They are also trained to do this when solving problems on their own. If the solution being implemented does not appear to be leading to the desired objective or if the solution is not working in some other way, then the problem-solving process is repeated.

Maintaining changes achieved. As a humanist, the sociocognitive therapist is committed to the empowerment of clients. This means that he transfers control of ongoing interaction to the family members. It also means that the therapist cannot cut family members off without some support in their natural environment. The external influences that helped cause their personal limitations and interpersonal predicaments will still be there. The people with whom they interact will constrain them to be "themselves" as these others have defined them. Thus, there is great pressure to return to old behaviors, thoughts, and feelings and transfer these back to family interactions (Hurvitz, 1967; Straus, 1977).

The therapist must therefore make provisions to help maintain and further gains in the back home situation. These include checkup appointments at designated intervals or follow-up calls by the therapist on a regular basis for a period of months. In addition, the therapist refers family members to community groups and activities which will serve as a natural support system or help develop alternative formal or informal social support systems to stabilize gains.

Redefinition: Interaction Hypotheses and Problem Solving

The therapist helps the family members to recognize the same problem and define it ever more specifically in behavioral terms. Such a process requires the spouses or family members to:

1. Work out a definition of the situation that family members can agree upon;
2. Formulate interaction hypotheses to explain their behavior, thoughts, and feelings in such a way that something can be done to change them;
3. Determine what each can do to prompt and reinforce the behavior, thoughts, and feelings desired in the other to enable all of them to change in accord with their asserted goal.

Example: Charles and Linda Knight. When Mrs. Knight called for an appointment, she said she did not really know if she and her husband needed counseling. She said they were not having serious problems and were not thinking of breaking up. Hence there was no conflict. However, they were not getting along as well as they wanted to and they did not know why. Thus, there was an interpersonal predicament perceived in terms of having a problem. The Knights were unable to pinpoint the cause of their unease or otherwise define their problem on their own. This appeared to call principally for a problem-solving approach, as was confirmed during the course of naturalistic assessment.

The redefinition process is illustrated in the following excerpt from a joint meeting with the Knights during their second therapy appointment. It is annotated to point out stages of the problem-solving process and other relevant features:

Therapist: Linda, why do you think he's so upset when you call your mother? (*Recognition of the problem*)

Mrs. K: He thinks it takes me away from my housework and taking care of the kids. Besides, he thinks it's in the nature of women to gossip and that it's a low kind of thing to do. Maybe he thinks we're plotting against him. I don't know. (*Offering explanations of one's own and the other's behavior, thoughts, and feelings*)

Therapist: Why might he think that?

Mr. K: That's ridiculous.

Mrs. K: I know it's ridiculous, but you just might think that.

Mr. K: Of course it's ridiculous — and I don't think that.

Therapist: Well, what you said may or may not be true. If he thinks that it's in the nature of women to gossip and he really believes that and he behaves toward you as though that's true, then there isn't very much we can do about the situation.

Mrs. K: Was he angry because I call my mother when he — ? I don't know. I know he's asked me lots of times not to call her. Is he angry about that?

Therapist: Well, there's another way to look at it. Maybe he became angry not because you call your mother despite his repeated requests to you not to do so, but because not acting according to the way he wants is a sign to him that he isn't as important to you as he wants to be — as he's tried to become. So he wonders, "Why doesn't she do what I would like her to do?" and then he's disappointed in himself and angry at you for making him feel disappointed with himself. (*Defining the problem*) I'm not saying that's the way it is. I'm saying that's another way to look at it. Charles, does that express how you look at it?

Mr. K: Yes. I guess so.

Therapist: How do you feel now?

Mr. K: How do I feel? I feel kind of good that this came out, that it has been put in words. Maybe if you said it she'll understand it because I don't think she'll understand it if I told her what you said.

Therapist: Oh? Linda, how do you feel about that comment?

Mrs. K: I think that's ridiculous.

Therapist: But how do you feel?

Mrs. K: I feel put down. Like he thinks I'm not smart enough to understand such ideas. Maybe that's why he doesn't talk to me the way I want him to. Maybe he just thinks I wouldn't understand his feelings so there is no use in discussing them with me. I just hope that's not so.

Mr. K: I feel put down too. You put me down when you do the kind of things I ask you not to do.

Therapist: So we've got a situation in which each of you puts down the other one or rather each one feels that the other puts him down. If this happens when you try to communicate, no wonder you each have the feeling that you have problems communicating — especially when you won't tell each other what the other one is doing that makes you want to quit talking with him. Well. Let's think about that for a while. That was an interesting thing that came out and it shows us something we have to work on. But what other reasons can you think of that would explain why he's so angry when you talk to your mother?

Mrs. K: Sometimes I think he's unhappy because his mother doesn't call me and I don't call her.

Therapist: Well, that's possible. Perhaps he is unhappy because you don't talk to his mother because she doesn't call you. But you can't control what his mother does. You still haven't shown how things can be changed.

Mrs. K: Sometimes I have the feeling that he's upset when I talk to my mother because he thinks I regard my mother as more important to me than he is. (*Offering explanations for one's own and the other's behavior*)

Therapist: Well, we don't know whether that's true or not, but it sounds reasonable. And it also ties in with what we just talked about — he must feel put down — and you know what that feels like.

Mrs. K: Do you feel that way too?

Mr. K: (Nods his head Yes)

Mrs. K: I'm sorry, dear . . .

Therapist: Let's say that's true. What can you do about it?

Mrs. K: One thing I can do is to call him [at work]. I guess I
               stopped doing that because I was busy with the kids
               and then I didn't know when is a good time to call him
               and he complained that I was taking up his time.

Therapist: Oh? Well, why do you think he felt that way about it?

Mrs. K: I think that he was unhappy that I used to call him and
               repeat the gossip that my mother had just told me. And
               frankly this was about members of my family that he
               doesn't care much about. Actually I don't mean that. I
               mean that he's not interested in that kind of informa-
               tion about them. (*Securing and organizing informa-
               tion*)

Therapist: You heard him say he'll send you a signal to call him
               [discussed in an early part of the session]. What do you
               think about that?

Mrs. K: I think that's wonderful. I'm looking forward to it.
               (*Identifying possible solutions*)

Therapist: Do you think it will solve your problems?

Mrs. K: It sounds like the best idea we discussed so far. (*Evalu-
               ating possible solutions*)

Therapist: Are you ready to call him or respond to his calls in such
               a way that he will want to talk to you during the day?

Mrs. K: I know I am. Yes.

Therapist: Well, what can you do that will make it easy and pleas-
               ant for him to call and will give him the feeling that he
               did a good thing?

Mrs. K: I guess what I can do is tell him I appreciate his calls.
               Not repeat the gossip like I used to. Tell him I miss
               him. And refer back to the good time we had the night
               before, perhaps.

Therapist: That sounds like an excellent idea. Well, why don't
               you try that and see what happens. (*Testing possible
               solutions*) How does that sound to you?

Mr. K: Okay. Why?

Therapist: How do you feel?

Mrs. K: Kind of excited.

Therapist: That's why . . . You seem to have worked things out.
               That's great. Now. You understand this isn't going to
               solve all your problems but it will remove at least one

irritant. If there continue to be problems between you, we'll have to examine other aspects of your relationship. Okay? All right, when do you want to start this new system?

Mr. K: Let's start on Monday, okay?

Mrs. K: Okay. (*Implementing the solution*)

Therapist: There are still a couple of things we have to work out. First, if the problem about the phone calls wasn't the real problem but was the surface expression of it — you know, if something else that you didn't bring up is what's really bothering one or both of you — then we'll expect to see some new irritant develop. That is, you'll discover something else that's bothering you. If you notice some new irritants, question each other about them and pay attention to your feelings when you discuss these things — and remember to bring them up when you come back here. (*Monitoring the solution via homework*) Do you understand what I'm talking about?

Mr. K: You mean maybe there's some underlying reason for our problems.

Therapist: No, I don't mean "underlying." I mean another reason or reasons which are expressed in this way. "Underlying" in our setting is taken to mean reasons that have their source or cause in an individual's unconscious and which are unknown to him or her. These reasons tend to be destructive or shameful, and they are demonstrated in irrational or anti-social behavior or they are denied and expressed as defense mechanisms. These include denial or repression, itself, and also rationalizations, projection, overcompensation, and others. What I mean by "another reason" is a reason that the individual knows but which he doesn't reveal because it would expose him as having a hidden agenda. That is, he doesn't really want what he says he wants and therefore didn't intend to work things out the way he said he did. Okay? Now there's another piece of business we have to consider. That's whether or not we want to write down your agreement about Charles sending Linda a signal so she will know that it's okay to call him. Maybe we would include the fact that she won't tell you the kinds of things you don't like to hear, gossip things that aggravate you. But she would tell you that she appreciates your call.

Mr. K: What do you mean, "write down"?

Therapist: Well, it's not unusual for people to make an agreement that helps them change to write it down — like a contract — and it serves as a guide and as a reminder for them.

Mr. K: What do you think?

Mrs. K: I think it's cute, but I don't think that's necessary.

Therapist: Okay, I agree. So let's make this arrangement: If you guys come back and tell me you weren't able to keep your informal agreement, then we'll consider the idea of a written contract more seriously. Okay?

Mr. & Mrs.
K: Okay.

Therapist: How will the fact that you're working out your difficulties affect other people you have something to do with? How will it affect your children? They're pretty young and I suppose the effect can only be good, but we ought to consider that. And how will it affect your parents — especially your mothers who are pretty involved with you? And what about your brothers and any sisters-in-law you might have? (*Exploring impacts for/of social support system*)

Mrs. K: I suppose that my mother will be disappointed if she calls me and finds out I'm on the phone. She'll want to know who called me. The rest of the family aren't that involved with me. There's no reason I shouldn't tell her, is there?

Mr. K: Look, she's not trying to break us up. I guess she's kind of lonely; that's mostly what it is. She's lonely and she wants to have someone to talk to. I think it would be better to tell her at the start that we're going to try to talk together about noon. Then if she calls about that time you won't have to cut her off. She'll know not to call then. And you can call her at a different time. I don't want her to think we're neglecting her.

Mrs. K: Isn't he a nice guy?

Therapist: You are a very nice couple. Do you think she'll be as cooperative as he says?

Mrs. K: I think so. She misses me but she won't do anything to make things more difficult for us.

Therapist: But we understand that you'll say something to her so she won't have any reason to feel cut off, and so she won't try to make you feel guilty.

Mr. K: I think Linda will handle it okay. (*Implementing the solution*)

Therapist: I'm pretty sure she will, but I'll check with you each time you come for your appointment. If things are going the way we would like them to, that's all the checking I'll do. If there seems to be some kind of problem, I'll call to remind you during the week. (*Monitoring the solution*) Is that okay?

Mr. K: That's okay, but I'm pretty sure it won't be necessary.

Therapist: And now there's one more thing about this plan: Check it out together—decide whether it's giving you what you wanted it to give you without causing any other problems with any family members—or causing you problems on your jobs—because it might do that if somebody thinks you're making all those calls out or if you're tying up the line. And when you come in, we'll examine all the aspects, okay? (*Evaluation*)

Discussion of Case Example. The foregoing exchanges occurred during Hurvitz's second appointment with the Knights. Both Linda and Charles are bright young adults and were cooperative clients (as revealed in the record). They were quite ready to end therapy after the second appointment, but wanted to attend all four sessions of the trial period. After the second session, they asked some questions about sexual behavior—perhaps to show off their comfortable and mutually-exciting sexual relationship. They could not understand how they could have such a satisfying sexual relationship while their communication problem brought them to therapy. Their sessions became a social event. They asked many questions such as people do if they meet a psychotherapist at a social gathering. These included questions about psychologists on the radio, psychological therapies advertised in the community, self-help books, about disciplining children, group therapy, therapist training, and why the therapist's office was in an increasingly poor section of Los Angeles. The Knights sent Hurvitz a thank you card several weeks after their last appointment.

Chapter Seven

The Change-Inducing Phase:
III. Overcoming Personal Limitations

Sociocognitive therapy always proceeds along the dual tracks of helping the family members as a group reduce interpersonal difficulties and overcoming individual personal limitations. Sometimes helping the family members to overcome personal limitations unravels their interpersonal problems. At other times, when crises, conflicts and interpersonal predicaments are reduced, personal limitations resolve on their own. More often, however, there is a synergistic relationship between progress at these two levels.

OVERCOMING PERSONAL LIMITATIONS

The therapist works with family members to overcome personal limitations as part of the overall therapy plan. Family members may agree about who has a limitation and that family member may acknowledge it. However, personal limitations may also be unknown and unacknowledged, or a family member may be accused of having a limitation by those whose limitations are actually causing disturbed equilibrium.

The therapist must therefore help family members to identify personal limitations that cause or exacerbate the family's troubles. The therapist then organizes a therapy program to overcome these limitations. Behavior limitations are approached through interventions that are primarily behavioral. Limitations involving thoughts and feelings (including fear that failure will bring with it a loss of love) are typically handled by cognitively oriented interventions.

Sociocognitive Intervention Theory

Symbolic interactionism recognizes a complex, recursive relationship between the triad of cognition, behavior, and social context. Humans act in accordance with their cognitions and associated feelings. These are largely prompted or evoked by taken-for-granted definitions of the situation (realities or schemata [Neisser, 1976]). However, behavior and its results feed back upon and prompt, reinforce, or modify cognitions, feeling, rules, meanings, and beliefs. Virtually all the patterns and contents of cognition (including rules for behavior) are learned in social interaction. Hence they reflect the social context comprising the individual's real world.

Based on these insights, the sociocognitive approach guides the family members to think, feel, and act in ways that will establish new meanings supporting their individual and joint values and goals. That is, the family members are helped to establish new definitions of the situation through which it becomes "only natural" to act in accordance with their values and goals.

Three aphorisms capture the essence of sociocognitive interventions to achieve these objectives:

1. The way to be changed is to act changed.
2. To make it natural to act changed, change the subjective reality.
3. Enlist significant others to facilitate rather than sabotage your change efforts.

Involving Significant Others

The sociocognitive therapist involves other family members in discussion and other activities to change their meanings and definitions regarding the family member with known and acknowledged personal limitations. As part of this, the therapist acts to restore or upgrade the other family members' motivation and ability to act as significant others.

The other family members constitute a primary group for the troubled individual. Hence they serve as that individual's most intimate social context. The therapist works with them to:

1. Determine whether the family member's limitations serve the others (i.e., if they gain from it in some way) who may attempt to maintain those limitations and sabotage efforts to overcome them.
2. Teach family members how to help the individual to overcome the limitation and prevent its recurrence after conclusion of therapy.
3. Help the other family members make necessary adjustments in order to live with the changes made by the family member with the limitation. This includes changes in the family group brought about by elimination of that limitation.
4. Help family members understand and empathize with the one trying to overcome his or her personal limitation in such a way as to bring about positive redefinition of that individual's status, role, identity, or character (promoting more supportive interactions in their roles as significant others).
5. Find substitute gratifications for those family members who gained from the personal limitation, thus eliminating any opposition or resistance to attempts to overcome the limitation.
6. Assist the other family members to make reciprocal changes in their own behavior, thoughts, or feelings to facilitate both success in overcoming the personal limitation by the family member who "has" it and restoration of constructed reciprocity during the process of change and afterwards.
7. Restore, catalyze, or strengthen activities and relationships by which family members serve as a support network for each other, thus obtaining the invaluable stress-buffering, mental, and physical health-promoting benefits of social support (House, Landis & Umberson, 1988; Pilusuk & Parks, 1986).

BEHAVIORAL AND COGNITIVE-BEHAVIORAL INTERVENTIONS

We will now consider some of the behavioral and cognitive-behavioral interventions that may be employed to help family members overcome their personal limitations. This discussion provides a sampling of relevant approaches and techniques while showing how cognitive-behavioral interventions can be adapted to sociocognitive practice.

Behavior Therapy

Behavior therapy radically breaks from earlier methods that depended on insight into unconscious causes of undesired thoughts, feelings, and behaviors. Instead, conditioning techniques modify observable behavior through positive or negative reinforcement based on the principles of learning theory. Originally, behavior therapy was deliberately mechanistic. It paid no attention to, even denying the reality of, unobservable phenomena such as thoughts or feelings (Carpenter, 1984; Skinner, 1965).

By the early 1970s, it had become commonplace to bring the mental dimension back into behavioral interventions, resulting in a cognitive-behavioral approach. Thoughts, mental images, and feelings are identified as covert behavior which can be modified used to bring about covert conditioning. Cognitive-behavioral interventions represent variations on earlier, purely behavioral methods. They follow the same principles (e.g., operant conditioning). They are also often called by the same names with the addition of the qualifier "covert" to signify that they are at least partially performed in the head. The sociocognitive therapist draws on virtually the entire armamentarium of behavioral and cognitive-behavioral therapy (Bandura, 1969; Eppstein et al. 1988; Falloon, 1988; Gambrill, 1977; Graziano, 1971; Kromboltz, J.D. & Krumboltz, H.B., 1972; Meichenbaum, 1978; Patterson, 1975; Stuart, 1980; Williams, 1984).

Adapting Behavior Modification

While behavioral and cognitive-behavioral techniques often work, the sociocognitive therapist defines the situation very differently: *humans respond to stimuli according to the meaning those stimuli hold for them.* Conditioning works only to the extent that we define the situation as dictating that we have to behave in a certain way. That is, human behavior is controlled by imagination of its consequences. Imagination is something the person does, not an event or a mechanical response. However, it can be shaped, manipulated, or blocked (Blumer, 1969; Wirth, 1931).

The sociocognitive therapist goes beyond conventional operant conditioning to define therapy for its participants and ensure that the intended meaning of reinforcers is clear to and accepted by the subject. The potency of methods by which behavior is modified depends less on what the reinforcers are or how often they are applied than what they mean to the subject.

Sociocognitive interventions treat the individual as a group member. They recognize that human beings carry their reference group of significant others in their imagination. Thus, whenever possible, the therapist defines the therapeutic situation in a way that deliberately mobilizes the self-judgement process inherent in the "looking glass self":

> A self-idea of this sort seems to have three principal elements: the imagination of our appearance to the other person; the imagination of his judgment of that appearance; and some sort of self-feeling, such as pride or mortification. The comparison with a looking-glass hardly suggests the second element, the imagined judgment, which is quite essential. The thing that moves us to pride or shame is not the mere mechanical reflection of ourselves, but an imputed sentiment, the imagined effect of this reflection upon another's mind . . . (Cooley, 1902, p. 8)

Operant Conditioning

Perhaps the most widely employed behavior modification technique is operant conditioning. It is based on the premise that the frequency of a desired behavior can be increased by providing a positive reinforcer (reward) or decreased by providing a negative reinforcer (punishment). Normally the therapist relies on positive reinforcement to increase the frequency of desired behaviors.

The therapist typically seeks to establish a complex behavior. To accomplish this, simple behaviors are elicited through operant conditioning and then chained. This is known as *shaping:*

> Shaping involves Skinner's method of *successive approxima-*
> *tions* whereby the subject is reinforced for pieces of behavior
> in increasing degrees of similarity to the final, desired re-
> sponse. For example, if we want to increase the behavior of
> walking on the hind legs in the rat, the rat would first be rein-
> forced for lifting one leg one inch, then one leg two inches,
> two legs one inch, and so forth, until the response of walking
> on the hind legs had been properly shaped. The method of
> successive approximations is used very effectively in psycho-
> therapy. (Kroger & Fezler, 1976, p. 64)

It is advisable to start with and increase the most complex behaviors that approximate the desired conduct and are already in a family's repertoire. It may not be easy to obtain information about an
individual's desirable behaviors from the others. This is because
family members tend to emphasize the others' limitations to explain
problems and conflicts. If affirmative statements from others are
not forthcoming, the therapist can ask the family member with limitations about himself or herself and then check with the others.
Alternatively, family members can be asked to keep a log of desirable and undesirable behaviors.

When the family members describe their desirable and undesirable behaviors, the therapist asks how to change the situation to
reduce the undesirable and increase the desirable behaviors. This
prepares the family members for the methods and techniques that
will be used to help them increase certain behaviors and decrease
others. In effect, this trains them in their new role as co-facilitators
of change. This simultaneously initiates a process of cognitive redefinition prompting formulation of instrumental hypotheses, and
encourages the family members to perceive their interaction in a
different way—one which may never have occurred to them.

The sociocognitive therapist prefers to work with the family
members to devise behavioral interventions that they can adminis-
ter. This places the family members in the role of co-therapists,
defining a joint reality in which they change and control their own
lives. It trains them for long-term autonomy at the same time that it
facilitates generalization by moving therapy out of the office and
into the "back home" situation.

Example of shaping desired behavior: Ms. Wilson and her grandson Michael Wheeler. As introduced in Chapter Three, Michael Wheeler was the fearful and enuretic grandson of Ms. Robertina Wilson:

*   *   *

Michael had developed a habit of hiding in his room after school. He would remain there for a long period and then come out running, saying things about a monster that scared him. It was thought that removing the TV from his room would encourage him to come out and watch television in the living room, with the other family members, but that did not work. One day he calmly came out of his room to show his grandmother a picture he had colored in the therapist's office. When Ms. Wilson reported this to the therapist, he informed her that this situation offered a way to modify Michael's behavior, to get him to spend more time outside of his room.

Ms. Wilson was advised to prepare a score card on which to note the length of time Michael stayed outside his room with the family over the period of one week. She was then to compute the average number of minutes per day and record this information as a baseline.

Meanwhile, the therapist mailed her similar pictures for Michael to color, which the therapist told him over the phone to show to his grandmother when completed. Ms. Wilson was encouraged to devise ways to keep Michael interacting with her and other family members. When he stayed outside his room longer than he had stayed the day before, he was to be rewarded with something concrete that was gratifying to him. Assisted by the therapist, Ms. Wilson decided that a set of motorcycle decals in which Michael had expressed interest would be an appropriate reward.

Since the decals were too expensive for continuing gifts, a token economy was devised: Ms. Wilson prepared colored slips of paper on which she printed, "GOOD FOR ONE TWENTY-FIFTH OF A VALUABLE SURPRISE." One was to be given to him each time he spent more time out of his bedroom with his family than the day before. By the time Michael had earned all 25 vouchers, he appeared to be coming out of his bedroom comfortably and interacting with the other family members in every room in the house.

* * *

Cognitive Interventions

Cognitive-behaviorists sometimes focus on mental acts to the virtual exclusion of the traditional application of overt stimuli: "The astonishing discovery is that shaping behaviors is possible as a psychic experience solely" (Tugender & Ferinden, 1975). Under the rubric of cognitive therapy, others have developed therapeutic approaches working from the other end, so to speak. These focus on changing what one thinks or says to oneself in order to change behavior (Beck, 1976; Burns; 1980, Ellis, 1974). Cognitive interventions are well suited to sociocognitive family therapy, although they may need adaptation to more directly encompass the sociological imagination, meanings, and situational definitions.

Discussion Tactics

Analytic, reflective, and directed discussion offer the most basic framework for cognitive redefinition of meanings and situations. Typically, this involves use of the Four Questions technique. Some specific discussion techniques employed by Hurvitz merit our consideration here.

Challenging negative definitions: Leroy Hawkins. The therapist may confront family members who belittle and disparage themselves or other family members. He informs them that he has had experience with many more people than the family members have. The therapist explains that he is therefore a more reliable and impartial judge of the family members' qualities or abilities. When confronting and challenging family members, the therapist does not demean or invalidate but takes advantage of his status and authority to suggest an alternative to the family member's definition of the situation.

If it is a case of self-deprecation, the therapist may say that he knows that the individual has the potential to be a more effective person than he regards himself to be. Such support may help change self-concepts and facilitate efforts to attempt new behaviors. It also helps family members attribute new meanings to situations or objects which then enables them to respond differently. If it is a case of a family member continually disparaging others, the therapist takes the same approach with the person's evaluation of other family members:

> Actually, Leroy, I'm in a better position than you are to judge whether or not your mother is being fair to you. You very likely don't have any other experiences in the position of mother to you, whereas I know a lot of mothers pretty well. I'm sure you're aware that I see a lot of mothers and their teenage sons — many who have pretty much the same kind of problems you and your mother have. So let me assure you, on the basis of my much greater experience with mothers than you have, that your mother is a pretty capable woman, one who really cares about you and wants the best for you. And if you were to listen to what she is saying instead of turning her off the moment she tries to get through to you, I'm pretty sure that you would recognize that it's true.

Fostering cognitive dissonance: Ross Turner. Another approach to using discussion involves creating or exacerbating conflict within the family member's definition of the situation. Hurvitz based his approach on the concept of *cognitive dissonance* (Festinger, 1957, 1964). When a person's actions, cognitions, feelings, or perceptions are inconsistent with his established or desired beliefs, understandings, meanings, or feelings, the resulting "cognitive dissonance" causes discomfort. He tries to reduce this by acting to establish consistency among his cognitions and actions.

The therapist accentuates or catalyzes this process by pointing out and emphasizing the dissonance between thoughts, feelings, or overt behavior and asserted meanings, goals, and preferences. The therapist also encourages the family member to consider changing those behaviors and cognitions as a way to relieve the stress and discomfort they provoke. This is accomplished by reviewing the information he or his significant others present in the course of discussion. Again, the sociocognitive therapist emphasizes the aspect of implied judgment inherent in the concept of the looking glass self:

You say you don't approve of philanderers and don't want to be thought of as a philanderer. You say you think of yourself as a good family man and want others to think of you that way, too. But the fact is that your relationship with Angela can only be called philandering and if you want to regard yourself as a good family man, you'll quit seeing her. Or, if you don't want to quit seeing her, you've got to recognize that you aren't the good family man you'd like to think you are. You've got to make the decision, Ross.

Lecturing the family members: Leroy Hawkins. The sociocognitive therapist uses his or her status and authority to lecture, scold, or sermonize the family members to encourage them to overcome personal limitations. A key tactic in this regard is to learn the culture and life situation of clients and to use and invoke that knowledge, particularly language, symbols, and metaphors. For example, the therapist tells teenagers and children who do not understand their mother's difficulty budgeting welfare allotments that their demands upon her are uninformed. He scolds them for being selfish and unreasonable and sermonizes until they acknowledge their unenlightened approach and promise to be more understanding of her efforts to provide for her family with the meager resources she receives from "the man."

A similar type of lecture is given to youths and young adults who are self-destructive (e.g., messing up in school, fighting to show off, drinking and using or selling drugs) and community destructive (e.g., vandalizing schools and public buildings):

The therapist scolded Leroy Hawkins by telling him that he should take advantage of whatever education and learning "the man" offers, to use it against those who oppress and exploit him. The man who oppresses him and his family, his brothers, and their families is pleased when they quit school, when they shoot other young men like themselves or get themselves shot, or when they get drunk or high. Then they are not dangerous to "the man." But someone like Leroy, who knows what is going on in his community, who wants to see things change, who has leadership potential, and who can become a leader of his people like King, and others who have been leaders of his people through the ages, people he never heard of yet, must take his place alongside these leaders. His people need leaders while he is wasting himself instead of preparing to serve them. He must learn to read now, before he is given time to learn in jail; he must read and study now, before he is given time to read and study in jail; he must get a library card and use his neighborhood library before he is given time to read and study in a prison library. He must learn and stay out of jail.

The therapist's status, the knowledge revealed by the lecture and the intensity with which it is given, all make an impression on some young people. This may turn them around as was the case with Leroy Hawkins.

Playing Devil's Advocate: Doris Mackey. The therapist may find it helpful to play "Devil's Advocate" when encouraging family members to choose between alternatives. The therapist attractively presents the opposite position from that taken by the family member about an issue. This requires the individual to examine her position more carefully and understand its implications better. During his individual session with Doris Mackey (who wanted to place her daughters in a foster home) the therapist tried to point out the pros and cons of her decisions. The pros were outlined as follows:

1. She won't have to spend the time she now does caring for her daughters. She will gain freedom to do things for herself that she has been unable to do until now.
2. She will have the time to rest that she needs to care for her own health.
3. She will have the opportunity and time to socialize as she desires and to meet and cultivate new men friends.
4. She will have the time to go to school to get a General Education Diploma (the equivalent of a high school diploma) which she has always wanted.
5. She will find it easier to diet because she will have to prepare food only for herself.

6. She will convince her daughters that she is serious about the problems they cause her.

After the therapist presented these points, Ms. Mackey became uncomfortable. She said, "Those are good reasons. I never really thought of them, except maybe that I could take better care of myself." She became thoughtful and then asked, "Does this mean you think that would be the best thing for me?" The therapist quickly responded, "Oh, no. I wanted to give you a picture of the things that could help you decide. Those were the points on one side. Now I'll give you the points on the other side." The therapist then enumerated the cons:

1. Her daughters may regard her act as giving them away, as deserting them, and they may resent her from that time on.
2. Her daughters will not regard her act as a desperate effort to survive but as punishment, which they will hold against her from that time on.
3. Her family may regard her as a bad mother, one who regards her social activities to be more important than the welfare of her children.
4. Her friends may also regard her as a bad mother, especially if she is able to compete better.
5. Her friends may accuse her of giving up her children because she is "man crazy" and getting a man is more important than raising her children.
6. She may develop guilt because of her own feelings about placing the children and because of criticism from her family and friends. Then she will take the children back and they will learn that she can't live comfortably if she places them. Therefore, she won't be able to threaten them with placing them in the future. It is likely that they may become even more difficult to handle after such experiences because they may also want to get even with her or punish her for what she did.

The therapist explained to Ms. Mackey that he was not urging her to make a particular choice, although he could state a preference. He was helping her to make a decision on the basis of his awareness of the pros and cons of the available alternatives.

Rational-Emotive Therapy

Hurvitz frequently employed rational-emotive therapy or RET (Ellis, 1974, 1984; Ellis & Grieger, 1977) to facilitate cognitive restructuring. More recent forms of cognitive therapy (Beck, 1976, 1988) and cognitive-behavioral intervention (Williams, 1984) would be similarly appropriate.

Principles of rational-emotive therapy. RET focuses on irrational learned beliefs that are responsible for disturbed and distressing behavior, thoughts, and feelings. When self-defeating and negative emotions arise from beliefs, people behave in such a way as to reinforce them. It is therefore necessary to change these beliefs. In RET, this is done through reflective, analytical, and directed discussion that examines the family member's personal realities and identifies the central irrational philosophies of life (i.e., problem-solving perspectives) by which the person lives and which she repeatedly tells herself. The therapist points out how certain beliefs lead to limitations and suggests how to challenge and overcome these beliefs, replacing them with meanings that do not lead to inappropriate behavior, thoughts, or feelings.

As the following example shows, Ellis's concepts and practices are applied by helping family members to recognize that they are often disturbed because another does not behave, think, or feel the way they believe the other should. Some of these expectations are brought into a marriage and may be based on the individual's values. Others may be based on information dispensed by the communication media, friends, or relatives. The expectations spouses have of each other, parents have of their children, and children have of their parents and each other may not be realistic. Or they may be realistic but the others may be unable to meet them.

The family member who fails to meet another's expectations may be complained about and identified as having a personal limitation. In fact, their responses to failing to live up to others' role expectations may become problems in their own right. However, the basic limitation is the behavior, thinking, or feeling associated with the unrealistic definition of the situation held by the complainer. Such issues are discussed in family therapy group meetings that permit all family members to rethink and clarify their perceptions of each other.

When a particular individual's self-perceptions or other-perceptions are challenged, she must decide how to deal rationally with the situation. The therapist participates by offering alternatives, urging experimentation, building self-esteem, and fostering similar participation by the other family members. By working in the joint session rather than individual meetings, the therapist accomplishes a secondary objective of modelling how the family members can work together to overcome perceived limitations. He also initiates them into this practice.

Case example: Sandra Williams. During an early joint family session in the change-inducing phase, Sandra Williams, the 15-year-old daughter of Doris Mackey, made a startling statement: "I wish I was real sick so you would let me do what I want to do all the time. I'm sorry I'm healthy." Then she began to cry. Sandra obviously was expressing her jealousy and resentment of the privileges permitted her 12-year-old younger sister, who had open heart surgery two years before and had learned to fake asthma symptoms to frighten her mother. Attention turned to her and she was encouraged to express additional thoughts and feelings about being ill:

* * *

Sandra reported that she regarded herself as the less favored child. She said she has to clean up after the others and is never appreciated or complimented for her achievements or efforts. She said she feels like an outsider in her own family.

Sandra was asked to recount specific incidents that illustrated and explained the cause of her feelings. However, instead of continuing to complain about favoritism at home, she reported an incident that had occurred at school during the past week. Some of the girls in the high school she attended were organizing an off-campus sorority. Other girls had received invitations to an organizing party, but she had not. Her failure to receive an invitation was very disappointing to her and she feels bad because "it means that people don't like me and don't want me to be their friend." She began to cry again. She said she is ashamed that she was not sent an invitation, that nobody likes her, that she feels worthless, and that the girls who she thought were her friends were only pretending to care about her.

Ms. Mackey and Michelle were surprised at Sandra's behavior and did not respond. The therapist expected her mother and sister to offer Sandra support, but they did not come through. This troubled the therapist more than Sandra's concern that she did not receive an invitation.

The therapist informed Sandra, her mother, and her sister that what Sandra told herself (that she feels ashamed and worthless and that nobody likes her) is based on self-defeating thinking. He pointed out that Sandra was making at least two mistakes in the way she responded to not getting an invitation. First, the information that she had not been sent an invitation could be wrong. Second, the conclusions based on the information, correct or not, were wrong.

The therapist suggested that there were other explanations to account for the lack of an invitation. Maybe no first semester ninth graders were invited, maybe an invitation was lost in the mail, maybe she will be invited to another party for girls who are school leaders. The therapist asked Ms. Mackey and Michelle whether they could offer other explanations. Ms. Mackey said maybe someone on the committee thought Sandra had other plans for the date of the party. Michelle proposed that Sandra was on the second half of a list because her name is Williams. She added that when Sandra learns which girls were invited to the first organizing party and which to the second one, she will be happy she was not invited to the first.

The therapist then said that regardless of whether these explanations were true or false, it is not true that she is a valuable person because she was invited or a worthless person if she was not. Sandra is and can be an important person because she is unique. The only thing that can make someone worthless is if she believes she is and acts as though she is.

Then the therapist recapitulated the whole experience with Sandra. He discussed her feelings about the experience with her. He proposed alternative explanations and examined Sandra's feelings about them. Then, on the basis of information she gave him, he suggested she call her girlfriends on the student council, girl's athletic league, and honor roll club, to learn if all of them had been invited.

The therapist also tried to help Sandra think of herself as a competent person in a pretty rough family situation—one in which her feelings are to be expected. There are many things she does well and she ought to tell herself this. She should think positively about herself because thinking negatively causes others to think negatively about her and will bring about results she does not want. If she thinks positively about herself she may cause other people to think positively about her. This may bring about results that she does want.

Ms. Mackey joined the discussion. She pointed out to Sandra that if she was partial to Michelle it was because she had been very seriously ill and much had to be done for her. Ms. Mackey said she appreciated all the extra work Sandra did and apologized for not having told her how much she appreciated it and how happy she was with Sandra. She said that her life would be much more difficult if not for Sandra.

Even Michelle participated in a serious way. She said that she did not know that she caused Sandra to be so unhappy. Michelle appeared to have a sincere understanding of Sandra's position. She said that any club that doesn't want Sandra for a member can't be much of a club. And if it is going to be a real good club, then Sandra will have to be invited. Mother and daughters kissed and promised to try harder to make life easier for each other.

*   *   *

Hypnosuggestive Procedures

The sociocognitive therapist may also employ allied techniques that fall outside the mainstream of both cognitive-behavioral and traditional psychological interventions. These involve having a subject think, feel, and imagine along with what Barber terms *hypnosuggestions*:

Hypnosuggestions are ideas or communications presented to others or to oneself in the same *goal-directed, serious, and expectant manner* as suggestions are presented in situations traditionally labelled as *hypnosis*. Hypnosuggestions have a unifying thread in the intentional way they are presented even though the way they are worded may differ vastly . . . It is important to note that some hypnosuggestive procedures do and others do *not* include suggestions of the type commonly included in hypnotic induction procedures, e.g., suggestions for deep relaxation, calmness, drowsiness, and "letting go" of extraneous concerns. (Barber, 1983)

To work effectively with hypnosuggestions, a subject must shift mental gears. That is, the person must actively be immersed in the alternative realities suggested to a point where the sense that "it's only make-believe" can be suspended and responses are allowed to happen and flow. While this is usually conceptualized as an altered state or trance (Weitzenhoffer, 1989), cognitive-behavioral and contextualist researchers think of it in terms of thinking, feeling, and imagining along with suggestions (Barber, Spanos & Chaves, 1974; Sarbin, 1984; Sarbin & Coe, 1972; Straus, 1977, 1978).

Those procedures that incorporate a formal induction procedure are typically referred to as hypnosis. Virtually identical techniques may be given other names (e.g., guided imagery, relaxation, autogenic training, affirmations, applied meditation, neurolinguistic programming, visualization, biofeedback) while procedures described or identified as hypnosis may involve no formal induction (e.g., Erickson, 1980; Erickson, Rossi & Rossi, 1976). For details about hypnosis and hypnosuggestive techniques, the reader should consult a variety of texts. Each tends to be written from a specific theoretical perspective and endorses or provides information on a specific set of techniques (e.g., Araoz, 1985; Araoz & Negley-Parker, 1988; Bowers, 1983; Edmonston, 1988; Gibbons, 1979; Kroger & Fezler, 1976; Kroger, 1977; Lankton & Lankton, 1986; Schorr, 1980; Weitzenhoffer, 1989).

Sociocognitive Application of Hypnosuggestion

Hypnosuggestive procedures are often combined or adapted for use with cognitive-behavioral tactics (Kroger & Fezler, 1976; Barber, 1983). For instance, covert reinforcement may be achieved by defining the situation such that the subject experiences an immediate, pleasurable reward each time that he thinks, feels, or behaves in the desired way (or even imagines doing so). The therapist coaches the subject to imagine herself in a real world situation behaving as she would prefer and then to imagine feeling the pay-off. This is defined as what the person will naturally and automatically do and feel in the back home situation. The family member is told to rehearse and practice this (perhaps in the context of self-hypnosis) until it becomes mental habit (Straus, 1984, 1988).

Many practitioners tape record at least the first hypnosuggestive session and have the subject play back and listen to the tape several times before the next appointment (Barber, 1983). This is intended as reinforcement and initiates a transfer of control back to the subject from the therapist (Straus, 1977). Barber (1979) suggests that the person imagine saying the words to herself while listening to the tape and then listen to the tape *entirely in her imagination* as a means of internalization and a bridge to less formal self-suggestion. In effect, these techniques insert the hypnosuggestions into the individual's self-interactions (background thinking).

Relaxation as Method and Strategy

Relaxation procedures and the moderate-to-profound psychophysiological relaxation they engender have an extremely important place in the therapist's armamentarium. They have come to be considered an indispensable part of many cognitive-behavioral procedures such as desensitization to overcome anxieties and phobias. Relaxation procedures are a direct means of stress reduction and management. In addition, relaxation provides access to many phenomena of psychophysiological self-control (Barber, Spanos & Chaves, 1974) and may serve to normalize physiological and psychological processes (Jacobsen, 1974).

Many individuals are chronically tense and anxious as a result of their socialization, the vast number of pressures and conflicting demands made on them by social groups and institutions, and frustrated attempts to achieve the contradictory values and goals of the American Dream. They commonly use prescription or non-prescription drugs and psychoactive substances to relieve these anxieties and reduce psychophysiological stress.

For such individuals — a majority of those seen by the sociocognitive therapist — relaxation training can serve as homework enabling family members to release everyday anxieties and tensions and restore equilibrium. Many are unaware of what it means to *not* feel tense, anxious, or stressed. Relaxation procedures provide a break between the goal-directed activities of school, work, and homemaking and social, recreational, and family-directed activities during the evening and weekend. In addition, training family members to produce and experience profound relaxation is a useful way to begin teaching them how to keep calm and relaxed in real-life performance situations.

Inducing relaxation. Relaxation is one of the simplest and most effective means of letting go of everyday realities and immersing oneself in thinking, feeling, and imagining along with hypnosuggestive procedures (Edmonston, 1981). At the same time, hypnosuggestions can be used to evoke deep relaxation, as in the classic type of hypnotic induction suggestions like, "Your feet are relaxing, your knees are relaxing, your entire body is relaxing, your eyes are closing and you are getting very, very sleepy . . ."

Relaxation can also be induced by overt methods such as Jacobsen's progressive relaxation (1974). In this method, the subject is guided to tense and then relax one muscle group after another. The result is both physical and subjective relaxation. There is evidence to suggest that covert methods are more effective in calming the mind and reducing cognitive stress while overt methods are more effective in reducing physiological stress and neuromuscular tension. Therefore, we follow Jacobsen and others in recommending that the practitioner combine both types of relaxation procedures.

Case example: Lilly and Arthur Hampton. Mr. and Mrs. Hampton came to her initial appointment together. They appeared to be an intelligent couple in their early 40s. Mr. Hampton said he is a house painter. However, he does not work regularly and therefore his wife and children receive Medi-Cal assistance. As will be seen, Hurvitz employed hypnosuggestion, defined as "relaxation," along with behavior modification techniques (desensitization and reciprocal inhibition). Hurvitz's description of the intervention also demonstrates the painstaking way he defined the situation for the family members:

*   *   *

In their joint meeting with the therapist, Lilly Hampton reported that about six months earlier, she and her husband had taken their children to a drive-in to see a Pink Panther film (a comedy). All of a sudden, for no explainable reason, she became frightened and wanted to go home. As she reported this incident, she began to hyperventilate and the therapist asked her to lie down on his couch.

Arthur Hampton took over telling the story. He said that his wife was not a fearful person. While some of the other members of her family were afraid or lightning or insects, she was not afraid of anything. She was not even afraid during the big Los Angeles earthquake of 1971, when many people became panic-stricken.

Arthur said that when the incident occurred, Mrs. Hampton could not offer an explanation for her sudden fear. He said that he and his wife tried to recall what in the movie might have upset her, but they couldn't think of anything. Neither could he think of anything that happened earlier that day or at the drive-in that might have disturbed her.

However, after this event she became fearful of leaving the house. Several days later, she began to explain her fear as being due to the rapes and muggings that occurred in their neighborhood. He said that he could not recall anything having to do with such things in the movie. No one in her family or any of her close friends had anything like that happen to them and, although there were such experiences in their neighborhood, none had occurred in the immediate vicinity of their home. He said that, as plausible as her explanation might be, it was something she thought of later to make it easier for her to tell people that she had this fear. They would not be as likely to think she was crazy as if she had a fear she could not explain at all.

With Lilly lying on the couch and Arthur sitting nearby, the therapist told the Hamptons that, whatever frightened Mrs. Hampton, it could not be understood from the information both of them gave him. However, that did not mean that she could not be helped.

The therapist explained that when Mrs. Hampton thought of leaving the house she began to get nervous and uptight. However, if she could be relaxed when she thought about leaving the house, the relaxation would overcome the feeling of being nervous or anxious. There is a way that this is done. It has two parts. The first part is to help her relax very deeply. The second part is to make a list — called a hierarchy — of steps that starts with something that hardly makes her nervous at all, goes on to steps that are more likely to make her nervous, and then to the step that makes her the most nervous.

He said that one of Mrs. Hampton's problems is that when she thinks of leaving the house, she doesn't think of the little steps along the way but of the final step, the one thing she can't do. And that is step out the door and walk to the sidewalk, the corner, and beyond. Because she thinks of the final step, the one she can't do, she can't start the process at all. However, if she were to think in terms of the very first step in the process, such as making a list of things to get at the market or putting on her coat, and then listed some of the other things that had to be done before she stepped out of the door, and was relaxed when she did the things, it was possible to help her.

The therapist informed Mr. Hampton that it was important for his wife to have a cassette tape recorder (which he then described in detail). The therapist explained that a recorder was important because he could give Mrs. Hampton only two appointments a month and it would be very difficult to use the method he had described on such a schedule. Mr. Hampton said he was concerned about his wife and would get a recorder.

The therapist informed the Hamptons that the recorder would provide a message to relax Mrs. Hampton, which is the first part of the method. Whereupon the therapist set up his own recorder, inserted a cassette and read a hypnotic induction procedure to Mrs. Hampton but omitted specific references to hypnosis (i.e., suggested relaxation only). The message relaxed Mrs. Hampton and the therapist told her that each time she listened to the session she would relax more than she had the time before. He also included remarks to the effect that her limitation was commonplace, that it in no way indicated that she had a weak mind, that listening to the cassette would achieve the same relaxation as listening to the therapist in his office, that she was a cooperative student, and that she was a person who could learn this technique to overcome the fears she reported to the therapist.

Mrs. Hampton was then "awakened." The cassette was rewound and given to her. Her husband was asked to secure a recorder so she could listen to the cassette several times before returning for her next appointment. He was reminded that the second part of the method required them to prepare a hierarchy that described getting ready and leaving the house to go to the market or the corner (where she waited for her child to come home from school), as had been explained earlier in the meeting.

The Hamptons returned for their next appointment with a small tape recorder and a very inadequate hierarchy consisting of only four steps. The therapist asked several general questions and then worked with them to develop a much fuller hierarchy.

*   *   *

Dramaturgical Interventions

Dramaturgical interventions are associated with or derived from psychodrama or sociodrama (Duhl, 1983; Glassner & Freedman, 1979; Howe, 1978; Moreno, J. 1972 & 1975; Moreno, Z., 1975; Satir, 1972, 1982; Star, 1977; Yablonsky, 1976). These methods integrate behavioral and cognitive aspects of situational definitions with a nonverbal and dynamic dimension. This is done within the framework of acting out and/or representing perceptions of relationships. Such methods have a powerful emotional and therapeutic impact (Glassner & Freedman, 1979). We will briefly discuss two of the dramaturgical interventions frequently employed by Hurvitz as an example of how this approach can be adapted by the sociocognitive therapist.

Sculpting

Sculpting has a distant relationship to the childhood game of "statues." It is a method of eliciting a nonverbal message from the family members about how they perceive their relationship and interaction. The method has three parts: (1) the therapist's introduction of the method and instructions about the process, (2) the family members' fulfillment of the instructions (their performance), and (3) the therapist's and family members' discussion of the results. An example cited by clinical sociologist Harry Cohen illustrates this process:

A young boy ran away from home several times. Yet it seemed as if his parents treated him well at home. It looked as if he was at fault for running away, not appreciating his good family life . . . The therapist decided to use a form of sociodrama to show visually how the act < — > react structure of the family was perceived by family members. The therapist asked the boy to play a game of "statue" with his parents. She asked him to move his parents around the room and mold their bodies as he wished. They were to remain "statues" just as he left them. Then he was asked to do the same for himself.

The results were striking. The boy positioned the parents on the far side of the room, arm in arm, free arms waving as if saying goodbye. He positioned himself, dejected, standing by the door, ready to leave. In the boy's perception he was not running away from home, but his parents were in an alliance with each other and were pushing him out. He perceived the family structure as mother and father . . . together with him as an outsider being told goodbye. And he was caught and blamed for leaving. So he felt more the outsider and left again. The parents were asked to "sculpt" their feelings toward their son. The therapist took this into account, too, in her clinical attempts to restructure the family in order to eliminate the running away. (1985, pp. 50-51)

Role playing

Role playing is a type of behavioral rehearsal based on the individual's ability to take the role of the other. It can be done jointly with all or several family members, by an individual family member with the therapist, or with the assistance of the therapist's staff in the situation being role played. This method, involves dramatization and verbalization of behavior, thoughts, and feelings. It can change each of these processes through the role playing itself and by subsequent review, evaluation, and discussion. Role playing is learning by doing. It is most effective when it uses real-life situations the family members experienced or will experience and engages them in such a way that they act spontaneously in the scene they create.

Role playing can be used as: (a) an assessment tool, (b) a therapeutic intervention, or (c) a means of training family members in a no-risk situation for effective performance in real-life situations. Subsequent evaluation, feedback, review, and reflective discussion are an integral element of the role-playing process. They are essential to achieving its full power as a means of sensitization, redefinition or preparation for coping. Whenever possible, group discussion should be encouraged. It provides a variety of viewpoints and sensitizes participants to the multiplicity of perspectives, perceptions, and meanings associated with any interaction or situation.

Self-Management Practices and Homework

An essential part of the sociocognitive intervention for overcoming personal limitations is teaching each family member to act as change agent. This involves training the person in self-management. We mean this literally. The family member learns to modify thoughts, feelings, and behaviors by strategically communicating with his or her self. Self-management techniques serve several invaluable functions throughout the course of sociocognitive family therapy:

1. As homework, reinforcing the change process between appointments, facilitating generalization (i.e., transfer to the back home situation), and internalization of new realities;
2. As a means of practicing and honing new skills taught during therapy sessions;
3. As a means of transferring control of the change process from the therapist to the family members (individually and as a group of significant others);
4. As a means of redefining the family members' joint reality by encouraging each to act in new, desired ways between therapy appointments;
5. As training and role induction for open-ended cooperation and joint coping among the family members to last beyond termination of therapy;
6. As self-management practices through which each family member can maintain results and open-endedly optimize performance, interactions, and relationships after termination of therapy.

These methods represent a translation of the methods used by the therapist or the family members to the individual using them on her own. Virtually all cognitive-behavioral techniques can be adapted for use as self-management practices. Some techniques may be performed together with a friend or another family member. Others are best performed privately. Many can be performed either overtly and behaviorally or covertly and symbolically. That is, the individual might overtly engage in some kind of activity or performs some kind of record keeping. Covertly, she might perform the same activities entirely in her imagination. Many of these techniques can be performed cooperatively by one or more family members, either to facilitate change by an individual with personal limitations or as homework by the group to reduce conflicts and interpersonal limitations.

Straus has published two manuals of sociocognitive techniques for assessment, evaluation, and resolution of personal limitations and improvement of relationships (1988, 1989). The more recent of these includes detailed instructions for use by dyads and larger groups. Fezler has also published a recent book describing ways individuals can use guided imagery on their own (1989).

Specific Self-Management Techniques

As we have suggested, virtually any of the cognitive, behavioral, and enactment techniques employed by the therapist can be adapted to homework and self-management practices. Conversely, the therapist can have family members engage in imaginative/hypnosuggestive activities to elicit thoughts, feelings, and information during the therapy session itself. Some of the methods employed by Hurvitz have included:

1. *Imaging* — fantasy or role playing in one's head; imagining the experience of actual or make-believe present, past, or future situations.

2. *Imaginative rehearsal* — actually rehearsing performance in various situations under various conditions or trying out alternative lines of action either to elicit associated thoughts and feelings or practice skills and behaviors prior to performing them in the real world.

3. *Goal focusing* — selecting a goal derived from values and, preferably, an image of that goal, then recalling that goal or image each time there is an opportunity to act in accordance with or contrary to it. In some forms of this technique, the person establishes a ritual of telling themselves that they choose to behave in accordance with that goal.

> Leroy Hawkins, who wants to become a professional football or basketball player, agrees that it is necessary for him to finish high school as well as to get an athletic scholarship to college. When friends suggest ditching school, he visualizes his goal and this helps him reject their suggestion.

4. *Self-monitoring* — observing and recording the incidence and/or situational contexts of one's thoughts, feelings, and behaviors; best performed overtly, providing feedback in some graphic form for behaviors or as an intensive journal for thoughts, feelings, and interactions (Straus and See, 1985).

5. *Thought stopping* — shouting "Stop" out loud (perhaps while visualizing a stop sign or other appropriate symbol) or in one's imagination in order to change or stop undesired thoughts or feelings; alternatively, one might snap a rubber band placed around the wrist.

6. *Thought substitution* — switching mental tracks and thinking different thoughts in place of undesired cognitions; overt methods include changing to a pleasure-bonded activity (such as a hobby, visiting people, or watching a television comedy show).

7. *Self-reinforcement* — rewarding oneself for performing desired behaviors, thinking or feeling or doing as desired, or administering a punishment for not doing so; reinforcers may be overt (e.g., treating oneself to a sweet or a pleasurable activity or denying the same) or covert (giving oneself mental strokes, telling oneself "You goofed," or using hypnosuggestive procedures to give oneself pleasurable or unpleasurable feelings or experiences).

CODA

Our purpose here has not been to present an introduction to the principles and practice of cognitive-behavioral, hypnosuggestive, or dramaturgical methods to overcome personal limitations. The novice is urged to study these methods at conferences, conventions, institutes, workshops, and similar programs, from textbooks, or apprenticeship with colleagues who have greater experience. However, it has been our intention to inspire exploration of the rich possibilities of sociocognitive interventions and use of creative imagination in developing, adapting, and applying such methods. In fact, we feel that the clinician can play a valuable role as a researcher who devises, evaluates and reports new methods and applications (e.g., Straus, 1977, 1981).

Chapter Eight

The Termination Phase and Beyond

Termination is really a misleading term for the final phase of therapy. Therapy is actually a transitional phase or punctuation between stages in the life of the family group. Termination marks the conclusion of one process of relationship and the beginning of another process and different kind of relationship. It is the therapist's responsibility to prepare the family members for life after termination.

THE TERMINATION PHASE

During the termination phase, therapist and family members review the progress and outcome of their relationship and consider what comes next. Family members are prepared for the phasing out of the therapy group and reliance on the therapist as a significant other. The final sessions complete the task of returning symbolic control to the spouses and family members. They also establish a framework for reinforcing and supporting the family members' gains from their therapy experience.

Deciding When to Terminate Therapy

Sociocognitive therapy is terminated when it appears highly likely that the family members will persevere to achieve their goal. The therapist observes the family members, watching for the signs that suggest mutual understanding and rapprochement. The primary criterion for evaluation of progress is fulfillment of recorded or cognitive contracts, demonstration of commitment, and progress toward asserted goals.

Readiness for termination is perhaps most easily determined in situations without conflict. If the family members came to therapy because of one family member's personal limitations and there is no conflict, the therapeutic task is completed when the limitation is overcome and the new behavior is incorporated into more effective and satisfying interaction. For instance, if the spouses (or a parent and child) are in an interpersonal predicament without conflict, the therapist evaluates the commitment to their contract and if they are working to fulfill it. If they demonstrate the skills necessary to overcome their limitations and resolve their problems, then the therapist informs them that therapy will conclude after the last appointment of the trial period.

Signs of Progress in Marital and Family Therapy

There are various indications that therapy is achieving the goal of overcoming personal limitations, interpersonal predicaments, problems, and conflicts and enjoying more effective and satisfying interaction. Indicators of progress may be displayed behaviorally before they are expressed verbally. The therapist looks for some or all of the following:

1. *Early signs*. One of the first signs of positive change is when one family member comments, "He's trying," and the other responds, "She's trying, too." Another early sign of positive change is when a family member states, "We're talking with each other more," or "We understand each other better," and the others agree. The family members also report that they "make allowances" and overlook little things that they may have complained about in the past. They explain that these things are not worth arguing about or they are not so important because there is evidence that the other is trying to overcome them.

2. *Transformation*. A crucial indicator of real progress is when family members report that their significant others practice transformation. Of course, they do not describe changes in those words. Instead, they report that a spouse, parent, or child who was unable to perform or demonstrate a particular behavior, meaning, or feeling "made up for it" by performing or demonstrating another ap-

propriate one. In this way, they re-establish and maintain constructed reciprocity.

3. *Joint action*. Initially, one spouse (the wife, for instance) may complain that her husband is doing something she desires not because he cares for her but because the therapist instructed him to do it. The husband may respond with a similar complaint. When they recognize that the other is doing something according to the therapist's instructions, they do not remark about it but participate in the undertaking. They report cooperative activities such as family observances of anniversaries, birthdays, and holidays. They volunteer information about the spontaneous use of short-term contingency contracts instead of attempting to force or constrain each other to do as they desire. They do not scapegoat each other, but resolve their predicaments and binds by problem-solving methods.

4. *Acknowledging positive changes*. The family members report their limitations in the past tense. For example, they comment about when they "used to fight" about something. They report that they resolved their differences by more effective communication and question whether these differences are important enough to bring to the therapist's attention. All the family members agree with one family member's comment that a particular difficulty was resolved to the satisfaction of the others.

Whereas family members were originally concerned about whether any desired changes would occur, they now report that changes have occurred and they expect further changes. They also inform the therapist that unreported limitations are also being overcome. For instance:

> A wife whose impulse buying was an acknowledged limitation which she wanted to overcome begins to wear her wedding band. The absence of the wedding band was not reported during the initial discussion of changes desired by the other. However, the absence of the wedding band was obviously something that irked the husband. He is pleased to see it now because of its symbolic meaning to him and the other family members.

5. *Improved sexual relationship*. During an early appointment, spouses may report that they do not have sexual intercourse as often

as other couples of the same age, health, and living circumstances. They are often embarrassed to acknowledge this. Subsequently, it may appear that they have sexual intercourse "for the benefit of the therapist." For example, they tend to have sexual intercourse the night before their therapy appointments. This was the last chance they could do so before coming to the office where they would have to report it to the therapist.

As therapy progresses, spouses report positive changes in their sex life. For example, the husband may report more spontaneous sexual intercourse and that his wife is more sexually accessible and responsive even though this was not a central complaint voiced in his discussion of therapy goals. The wife reports that her husband is more affectionate without demanding intercourse and that he is less likely to become disturbed if she says she does not want to have intercourse.

6. *Supportive interactions*. The family members may defer to one another, hand each other tissues, permit the other to choose the more desirable seat, touch each other, and display their affection for one another. In general, the family members become more aware of and polite to each other. There is a relaxation of tension among or between them. The family members may report that they are more relaxed or more content. They call each other pet names. They display friendly humor, laugh, and make light of their earlier differences and joke with each other in various ways. In response, the therapist notices himself relaxing when interacting with the family members.

7. *Treating the therapist as a friend*. The family members express an interest in the therapist's family and may call him by his first name as they were invited to do at the outset of therapy (or they ask about doing so). Reflective, analytical, and directed discussion become social conversations. The family members ask questions about the principles and methods which guide practice. They want to know if something that was done at a particular time was done purposefully to help them.

8. *Requesting fewer appointments*. The family members hint that they can get along without the therapist and suggest further appointments be held less frequently (e.g., every other week or on an as needed basis). They may also call to cancel a scheduled appointment stating that they can get by without it. When family members

communicate such requests, the therapist needs to be aware that they might be signs of premature termination rather than satisfactory progress.

The Decision to Terminate

If all has gone well, therapy can be terminated after the agreed-upon trial period, sometimes well before. If more time appears needed, the therapist considers suggesting an extension of their relationship or refers them to therapy elsewhere. Otherwise, the therapist prepares the family members for termination and for follow-up evaluation.

As previously discussed, the sociocognitive therapist does not start with the premise that family members should stay together. Nor does he judge the success of therapy on whether that is, in fact, what occurs. Rather, in the course of therapy family members may determine that their goals and values are incompatible or that their situation precludes effective and satisfying interaction and relationships. One or more family members may have been resigned to a breakup from the start and participated only to confirm or demonstrate that their differences were irreconcilable. In any case, as therapy proceeds, the family members themselves decide whether they want an end to their relationship or an improved relationship.

Family members' requests for termination. If they want to end the relationship, family members will announce this at the end of the designated trial period (if they remain in therapy that long). They say that they have tried, that further therapy will not change things, and that it is now time to separate. In such a case, the therapist has little alternative but to accept their decision to terminate therapy (although he may suggest separation counseling).

On the other hand, if they want an improved relationship and perceive that therapy is aiding them, the family members may decide to work on their own and use the therapist as a resource person or for feedback. The statement of such people that they are ready to discontinue therapy can usually be trusted.

Premature termination. However, the relationship between family members and therapist may be prematurely terminated by family members before they achieve their asserted goal. This is commonly a result of opposition or resistance from unstated preferences, covert goals, or unacknowledged values held by one or more family members but not shared by others. It may also stem from family members' belief that therapy cannot help them or that the particular therapist and his methods cannot help them. Or it may come from a lack of desire, interest, motivation, or willingness to change. It is also possible that there is a real mismatch between the therapist (and his approach) and the values, beliefs, style, needs, interests, problems, or background of the family members.

The overwhelming majority of clients who decide that therapy is not working or is not for them, terminate without discussing it with the therapist (Beck & Jones, 1973). Therefore, the therapist is always concerned about clients' premature termination.

The sociocognitive therapist's basic strategy for preventing this is to catalyze the formation of a primary group in which family members perceive and relate to the therapist as a significant other. The bonds formed are often enough to overcome the impulse to quit therapy when the going gets rough, results are not fast enough, or a hidden agenda becomes threatened.

The Final Appointments

As the end of the trial period approaches, the therapist plans for a concluding appointment. He assigns homework to maintain changes achieved during therapy and enable family members to act as their own change agents after therapy. The therapist considers his accountability and determines the effectiveness of his work.

During their final appointments, the therapist performs the following tasks:

1. Secures the family members' evaluation of their therapy experience.
2. Offers his review of the family members' therapy experience as a closing summary.
3. Obtains their agreement to attend a follow-up session one month to six weeks after termination to determine if therapeutic changes are being maintained.
4. Requests that family members participate in continuing follow-up evaluation activities.
5. Tells family members how to maintain the gains made in therapy.

6. Assigns homework both for family members' continued development and to enable the therapist to research therapy outcomes.
7. Informs the family members of useful community resources.
8. Encourages family members to investigate and participate in activities that strengthen family life for all members of the community.

Preparing for the concluding appointment. At the conclusion of the next-to-last appointment of the trial period, the therapist explains that the next appointment will conclude the agreed-upon trial period. He requests the family members to come prepared to discuss what they have accomplished, what they have yet to accomplish, and if they want to set a different goal. The therapist instructs them to prepare an evaluation of his activities including the ways he was and was not helpful. He informs them that he wants this feedback to modify and improve what he does to help people who come to him for therapy.

The Concluding Appointment

The concluding appointment may occur at the end of the trial period or at the conclusion of successful therapy. As outlined earlier in this chapter, during the concluding session, the therapist performs certain tasks on behalf of the family members. He attempts to get the family members to perform certain tasks. Some part of the concluding appointment is used to follow up and phase out ongoing assignments.

The family members' closing summaries. The therapist requests family members to present their reviews and evaluations of their therapy experience. This is done so that the therapist can incorporate elements of the family members' statements into his or her review and evaluation. Whatever the family members choose to talk about is something that is somehow important to them. The therapist can use any positive comments to reinforce the achievements and value of therapy for them. He can also use any negative comments to consider other ways to help them achieve their therapy goal.

In most instances, the family members consider evaluation to be a simple statement of thanks to the therapist for his services. If the husband or father participated in therapy, he is usually delegated to offer such a statement. A small number of husbands and fathers want to critique the therapist's efforts and engage in a discussion or debate about his theory and methods. The therapist should not become entangled in such a debate but should always reinforce and thank each family member for any contribution.

The therapist's closing summary. Following the family members' evaluation and review of the therapy experience, the therapist:

1. Discusses if and how well the contracts between all parties have been fulfilled.
2. Reviews the extent to which every family member has made the changes he wanted, changes others wanted him to make, and changes he wanted in others. The therapist also notes any positive changes that were not named as desired by family members at the outset of therapy.
3. Reviews the use of therapist's services as demonstrated by exchanges at home, following requested advice, asked questions, and similar ways.
4. Examines the meaning of the therapy experience to determine if it affected the family members' lives so that they feel differently about themselves and each other.
5. Presents the family members' characteristic interaction at the start of therapy: the binds they impose upon each other; their expectations; their individual limitations that became interpersonal predicaments, problems, and conflicts; their difficulties in bargaining and compromising, decision making, and problem solving.
6. Reviews the extent to which the family members' interaction and relationships changed during the course of therapy and the present state of their limitations, predicaments, conflicts, crises, and other family troubles.

Recommendation for termination or extension. The therapist's review and evaluation suggests whether or not he feels it is time to conclude therapy. If the family members agree that they achieved their goal as revealed by their interaction and relationships, the therapist covers the other items in the agenda of the concluding appointment. If the family members did not achieve their goal but they are making progress toward it, the therapist invites them to consider continuing therapy for another definite period. He may also explain that they did not achieve their goal because one or more of them opposed or resisted the therapist's efforts. In such a case, he urges them to consider if their goal is in accord with their values and if they want to identify a different goal for further therapy. The therapist should acknowledge his limitations and accept some responsibility for the family members' lack of progress.

The therapist may suggest that the results of the trial period indicate that family members should seek assistance from another therapist in the community. It is probably advisable to send them to the referral service of an appropriate professional association rather than a particular therapist. This is because therapists tend to make referrals to friends or associates whose therapy orientation is similar to their own. Since the therapist's application of the sociocognitive approach was not as helpful as desired, referral to a therapist who shares the same orientation may produce similarly disappointing results.

Maintaining Changes After Therapy Is Concluded

Family members tend to slip back into the pattern of interaction and relationship that existed prior to therapy (Goldstein & Kanfer, 1979). This may occur as a process of erosion in which their new meanings and behavior patterns are slowly ground down by the inertia of the larger community. Or it may happen as a result of sabotage — direct efforts by others to force the family members back into their old ways of behaving, thinking, and feeling (Straus, 1977). This can most easily be understood dramaturgically, in terms of the differences between the therapeutic performance situation and that of the family members' real world context.

During therapy, the therapist as a significant other systematically encourages family members to enact desired behavior, thoughts, and feelings. He helps them to support one another and interact on the basis of contingency and good faith contracts. Their back-home situation becomes a symbolic extension of the therapy setting; a laboratory in which they experiment with and practice new ways of behaving, thinking, and feeling. The therapist's presence remains with them in the looking glass of their imaginations. They perform with the therapist in mind, literally, as their audience.

After termination, they are on their own. Interaction continues in various settings with many different individuals who may not share their values, goals, and interests. These individuals may place contradictory demands on them. They interact with institutions, groups, and individuals who force or seduce them into behaviors, thoughts, and feelings that promote the same personal limitations, predicaments, problems, conflicts, and crises. Consequently, the maintenance and transference of gains made in therapy do not occur automatically. Instead they must be planned and made part of the therapy. The therapist must institute methods to maintain the changes achieved by family members despite the constraints of the larger community.

Home visits. As suggested by clinical sociologists as early as the 1920s (Thomas & Thomas, 1928; Wirth, 1931), the therapist considers and evaluates the home environment because it is the stage on which the family life is acted out. The home setting provides many implicit and explicit cues that promote certain behaviors and directly channel family interaction along particular lines (e.g., the location of the television set may encourage or discourage interaction between children and adults). Furthermore, many intimate interactions occur in the home which family members see as too insignificant to be concerned about or bring to the therapist's attention. However, these play a major role in structuring and maintaining relationships.

Home visits are the way to determine what about the home may make it difficult to maintain gains and cause reversion to the inappropriate behavior, thoughts, and feelings that brought them to therapy. The therapist goes into the home to monitor interaction and make suggestions that are specific to the family setting.

In this way, he may be able to propose changes in the physical organization of the home that will facilitate desired interaction. For example, the television can be moved out of a child's bedroom to promote family interaction in the living area or a child's bed can be relocated to permit the spouses more privacy. The therapist may also propose natural contingencies in the family members' daily routine that serve as ongoing reinforcement for their desired behaviors, thoughts, feelings, and interactions. A photograph taken at a time when spouses were very happy with each other or a copy of their therapy contract can be placed where they will see it repeatedly. At other times, the home visit may uncover the fact that the family's living arrangements effectively bar success in achieving their asserted therapy goal.

Case example: The Matthews-Black-Baptiste menage. Lynette Baptiste's pediatrician called the therapist to inform him about her mother's and grandmother's complaints about her behavior at home and school. He further informed the therapist that she does not have any friends her own age and is enuretic. About a week after the pediatrician's call, Ms. Marie Matthews, who introduced herself as Lynette Baptiste's grandmother, called to set an appointment.

*   *   *

When asked why the child's mother did not call for an appointment, she stated that she is the only person in the household capable of making an appointment. She explained that Lynette is the daughter of Ms. Hilda Matthews Black. Ms. Black is actually the illegitimate daughter of her younger brother and a woman with whom he had a casual relationship and who deserted Hilda shortly after she was born. Marie's brother gave her the child to raise as her own because she was very difficult to rear. She has also had many problems with Hilda, who ran away from home when she was 13 and became pregnant with Lynette at 15.

After Lynette was born, Hilda gave the child to Marie to raise while Hilda continued her irresponsible and disturbing behavior. She was incarcerated in juvenile hall several times, but four or five years ago when she was 20, Hilda had to settle down because of a variety of illnesses. She wanted to take her child with her but Marie refused to give Lynette up because of Hilda's acknowledged laziness, irresponsibility, and drinking. In order to have a home, Hilda moved in with her "mother" Marie. Now Marie, Lynette, Hilda, her husband Willie Black, and their three daughters (all under three years old) live together. Everyone is constantly fighting with everyone else and they have all kinds of trouble. For instance, Ms. Matthews and Willie want to save as much money as they can and therefore continue living together despite the hardship it causes both families. However, Marie wants to put the money aside for Lynette's special education while Willie wants to save it for semi-annual trips to Las Vegas which he takes without family members.

*   *   *

After working with them to reduce the level of immediate conflict, the therapist began to suspect irreconcilable differences in values. He also thought that Lynette could not be adequately helped to overcome her personal limitations within their present living situation. He therefore made a home visit. Based on his observations, the therapist urged the Matthews-Black-Baptiste menage to separate into two different family households. When they did so, he tried to help each family create a home environment wherein the small gains they made would persist and serve as the basis for further gains. In the consultant role of advocate, the therapist also contacted the families' welfare workers and their supervisors. He urged them to give this family the money needed to secure an enuresis training device for Lynette.

Establishing practices. As suggested in the previous chapter, it is useful to train family members with forms of homework that can be converted into ongoing self-management practices. Similarly, family members can be encouraged to establish group practices that support the changes accomplished during therapy. These practices help them to apply coping processes to extend and expand those gains. For example, family members can have a brief silent period before meals in which they hold hands and focus on the benefits and importance of being together as significant others. They might be encouraged to have periodic family meetings. Or spouses might be encouraged to make it a practice to discuss the day's events and settle any disagreements or arguments before going to bed.

The therapist may also introduce the spouses or family members to self-help books of various kinds. Alternatively, he may encourage them to browse through the self-help section of local bookstores and discuss any books that seem particularly interesting. Although they may have been unable to use such materials effectively prior to therapy, the therapy experience has freed creative energies which may enable them to use self-help materials to develop more effective and satisfying family interaction.

Groups and Programs Offering Post-Therapy Assistance

During the concluding appointment, the therapist discusses continuing services and activities that may be helpful or interesting. He may invite them to attend a couples therapy group or a family therapy group which he or his agency sponsors. These groups are composed of spouses or families who can benefit from such participation according to a therapist's evaluation of their situation. Such spouses and family members may have completed a course of therapy and need the continuing reinforcement and validation that a group provides. Others can also benefit from involvement with such groups earlier in the course of therapy. Family members might be invited who are struggling with problems which they despair of overcoming and who need role models who have overcome these problems. Still others could be invited who need peers to point out their inappropriate behavior, meanings, and feelings, and reinforce their desired and desirable behavior, meanings, and feelings.

However, some of these resources are especially appropriate during the post-termination period, including family life enrichment programs such as Marriage Encounter (under either secular or religious auspices). Hurvitz was particularly enthusiastic about the value of peer self-help psychotherapy groups run by the participants without professional leaders — a concept of which he is an acknowledged pioneer (Tennov, 1976).

Senior citizens may be referred to the American Association of Retired Persons and its division Action for Independent Maturity. If spouses divorce, the therapist may refer them to Parents Without Partners or similar groups in their community. If alcoholism played a part in the marital and family problems, the therapist urges continued participation in Alcoholics Anonymous, Alanon, and Alateens (or Narcotics Anonymous for drug abuse problems). The therapist may also introduce the family members to programs that train people in interpersonal communication skills and effective parenting.

Social Support Networks

It is absolutely essential that the therapist recognize the importance of social support to the mental and physical health and well-being of family members (House, Landis & Umberson, 1988; Pilisuk & Parks, 1986). Social support can be defined as

> the sum of the social, emotional and instrumental exchanges [including physical and material assistance as well as information and guidance] with which an individual is involved having the subjective consequence that the individual sees him or herself as an object of continuing value in the eyes of significant others. (Pilisuk & Parks, p. 17)

The therapist should help develop an ongoing social support system that will ratify values and accept and encourage them to be the kind of people with the kind of relationships they desire. Family members should not only be encouraged to provide social support to one another but to invest their time and resources in building a wider support network.

Informal support can be facilitated by encouraging the building up and nurturing of a network of friends, participation in enjoyable activities, and involvement with others who share their values and goals. Thus, the therapist may introduce the family members to community groups in which all the family members can participate. Religious organizations, social action groups, political clubs, home-town societies, fraternal lodges, civic organizations, and veterans or other organizations and their auxiliaries can also serve this purpose.

Depending on their particular needs and personal limitations, family members can be encouraged to join formal support groups such as those mentioned in the previous section. Possibilities range from "twelve step" programs like Alcoholics Anonymous to groups in which parents of handicapped children or individuals with a particular disease can share experiences and discuss resources. Today, there are hundreds of thousands of such groups in the U.S. Information about these can be obtained from the National Self-Help Clearinghouse (33 West 42nd Street, Room 1227, New York City, NY 10036).

Callbacks by the Therapist

The therapist can also help transfer gains into the back-home situation by making periodic telephone calls. These help the family members devise reinforcing contingencies that support desired behavior at home. He asks how they are doing and inquires about their practice of the methods and techniques that have been taught to them. For example, Hurvitz would call to ask how a treatment program is going. He would impress upon parents who wanted their child to behave differently that it is necessary to practice the methods taught to them in the clinic or office to cause and maintain desired changes.

THE THERAPIST'S ACTIVITIES

The sociocognitive therapist's role and responsibility does not end with activities placing him in direct contact with clients. Rather, he engages in a wide variety of educational and preventative activities associated with marriage and family therapy and community life. Although these activities lie outside the tasks of therapy, the sociocognitive therapist cannot and should not make an artificial distinction between the office and the social context of both therapy and the family members whom the therapist serves.

Education and Networking

The therapist's responsibilities include both continuing education and networking on behalf of his clients.

Educational Responsibilities

Improving therapeutic skills and acquiring knowledge about clients enables the therapist to more effectively take the role of family members and act as a significant other. The sociocognitive therapist should engage in an expanded range of learning opportunities. These range from taking continuing education courses and formal training in new methods and techniques to acquiring knowledge about clients' race, sex, social class and ethnic group (see Ho, 1987).

It is especially important to read ethnic and minority group newspapers and journals. This will increase his understanding of these groups, the issues they face, and their terms, symbols, images, or concepts. If there is a large proportion of non-English speakers in the therapist's practice, he should also acquire a working familiarity with the client's language (e.g., Spanish).

Involvement with Community Institutions

Networking both extends that educational activity and provides the therapist with the necessary contacts to improve family members' relationships and functioning within the larger community. The therapist establishes relationships with school administrators, teachers, and Parent-Teacher Association leaders in the community. He does the same with many others: the personnel of churches, synagogues, and mosques; therapists, counselors, social workers with local city, county, and state social agencies; police, court personnel, and probation officers; and others such as board and care home operators and operators of community medical clinics. He should also consider any one else who is concerned with the social and psychological well-being of the community members.

Not only should the therapist get to know the community's resources, but he should become involved with them in developing and expanding community improvement and self-help programs and activities. That is, the sociocognitive therapist should become a community resource him or herself.

Moral and Ethical Concerns

As previously discussed, the sociocognitive therapist is committed to the humanist ethic of non-exploitation and respect for and empowerment of one's clients. This commitment places a responsibility on the therapist to consider the moral and ethical implications of family therapy.

The Therapist-Client Relationship

Because clinical activities can be regarded as experiments with human subjects, all ethical safeguards for experiments with humans should be observed. Certainly, this means that the clinician as ex-

perimenter must not physically or psychologically exploit or oppress people he is attempting to help. The therapy relationship,
where intimate information is discussed in privacy and affective
bonds of transference (or counter-transference) develop, can easily
become eroticized. Not only is it unacceptable for the therapist to
make advances to clients, but if clients of either sex initiate advances, the therapist must control the situation and prevent it from
developing to physical contact.

Additionally, as discussed in the preceding chapters, the sociocognitive therapist follows the principle of minimal intervention.
He minimizes the extent and duration of interventions, the degree of
his authoritarian role, and, most particularly, the changes he demands in lifestyle, relationships, or conduct. It is the client's right
to determine what is acceptable, appropriate, or desirable according
to his or her own beliefs and values. It is the therapist's task to help
family members get on with the business of living in their own
preferred style and manner.

Relationships Between Family Members

The second place for concern is the relationship between spouses
or family members. At times, the therapist is ethically obligated to
point out how one family member's stated desire to achieve his
human potential, self-actualization, personal growth (or whatever
the current buzzword) is an excuse for refusing to meet one's responsibilities to other family members. Each family member should
enhance and assist the other to fulfill himself or herself rather than
attempt to fulfill his own potential at the expense of others. To do
otherwise is, at the very least, irresponsible.

The therapist does not impose normative standards on his clients
except where situations of clear violence, abuse, or exploitation are
involved. It is the therapist's responsibility to be aware of and sensitive to the many legitimate forms marriages and families can take in
contemporary society (Chilman, 1988).

There is always a potential conflict between imposing one's own
moral or ethical code upon the family members and educating them
about the ramifications of their lifestyle and behavior. Thus, while
their values and their values alone should govern their sexual be-

havior, monogamy, dating, and the like, it is also the therapist's responsibility to nonjudgmentally discuss the potential conse- quences of their choices and alternatives. The current HIV (AIDS virus) epidemic, for example, clearly raises the stakes with regard to nonmonogamous behavior whether heterosexual or homosexual.

Overcoming Sexism

The sociocognitive therapist plays an important part in helping men overcome sexism and male chauvinism while helping women to overcome the belief that every male is a sexist and male chauvin- ist. Therapists can be particularly effective in overcoming ingrained definitions of this sort in clients of their same sex. However, by acting in violation of biases widely held by the opposite sex, a male or female therapist can also combat misperceptions held by clients of the opposite sex. Of course, therapists must first overcome their own sexist beliefs. Then, by serving as role models for same-sex clients and by helping each to assume the perspective of the other, the therapist enables family members to learn how the other per- ceives men and women.

The therapist also challenges the assumption that traditional sex roles must and will be continued into the indefinite future. He urges the family members to develop more permissive attitudes toward the husband doing "his wife's work" and the wife doing "her hus- band's work." As in an increasing number of families, the wife may have a more prestigious or higher paying job than the husband. It is particularly important to help overcome the culturally ingrained notion that the husband should be the primary economic supporter and that the wife should accept the husband's authority over eco- nomic matters (Bernard, 1982; Rubin, 1975). It is also important for men to better understand the significance of sexual exploitation and rape for women. They must also recognize that some clichés about women's sexual desires and how to fulfill them that are as- sumed to be humorous are, in fact, demeaning and puerile (Rubin, 1990).

Fostering Effective and Satisfying Family Life

Marital and family problems cannot be considered separately from other problems in the society. The sociological imagination tells us that the family is influenced by institutions, policies, agencies, and social trends over which they have little control. The litany of structural changes, strains, dislocations, and consequent social problems affecting the family is enormous. This is evidenced by even the most cursory look at a newspaper or a walk through virtually any community in this nation.

The sociocognitive therapist is deeply concerned about these issues and works to promote progressive and humanist policy changes to address them. These include, a workable safety net incorporating guarantees of adequate housing, nutrition, and health care for all Americans. The therapist also supports policies fostering equitable compensation for men and women of all races and ethnic groups, jobs and welfare programs that encourage families to remain together and better themselves, improved mass transit, urban renewal, and community development programs. Reduction of barriers to those in nontraditional family relationships (whether heterosexual or homosexual) and fairness and protection to all family members when they break up should also be supported.

Over a decade ago, the Carnegie Council on Children (Keniston, 1977) recognized the importance of "converting commitment into politics." This is even more urgent today after the great reversals of the Reagan era. Therapists must participate in that conversion. As family advocates, they must encourage members to undertake action on their own behalf. Therapists should give information and guidance to political leaders regarding the relationship between family problems and other social problems.

The White Therapist and Minority Families in Need

Some families need help more than others. These tend to be poor families of racial, ethnic, national, and cultural minorities—particularly those families headed by women. Special difficulties are encountered when working with this group which bears much of the deleterious impact of the social changes and dislocations of late 20th century America. Based on Hurvitz's own practice, the examples in this volume have focussed on the case of black welfare mothers, their children, and the husbands or male friends who live with them in the role of spouse.

One difficulty encountered in offering therapy to these families is their lack of complete candor about the family situation. This is primarily because they fear revealing something that will cause their government assistance to be terminated. Although this fear is understandable, it sometimes leads to therapy plans that are impossible to implement. If the therapist inquires why a therapy program did not work, he might be told something which would have signalled that the plan was doomed to fail had it been revealed earlier. Another difficulty is the family members' desperate desire for a rapid and complete change despite their inability to carry out the agreed-upon arrangements because too many factors are beyond their control.

The therapist with a historical and political understanding of the place of blacks and other minorities in American society can be of assistance. Understanding can develop by participation in various community struggles for black equality and liberation. Such evidence of social interest (Adler, 1938) has been found to be positively associated with the client's satisfaction with counseling (Zarski, Sweeney & Barcikowski, 1977). Other participant observation experiences, including actually living in the inner city neighborhood, can help engender necessary understanding of what it means to be a black or minority family member. Sociological and ethnographic discussions of race relations, black and white families, or of other minority populations can be immensely helpful (e.g., Willie, 1981, 1985).

Some white therapists may resist working with black and other minority group members because it does not offer as great an income. There are also special difficulties due to their oppressed status and cultural and, in some cases, language differences. Although the white middle-class therapist is an outsider who has not lived as a black person in our society, this is no reason to withdraw from participation as a therapist with such clients. As an outsider who has not experienced life as a black person but who participates in struggles to change the condition of black and other minority people, he may be as effective as those who are members of the minority community (Hallowitz, 1975; Hurvitz, 1979a).

Accountability and Evaluation Research

One of the most needed but least performed activities of therapists is determining how well they do what they profess to do on behalf of family members. Very few therapists or agencies conduct research about their methods and results.

If the therapist or agency does not obtain feedback from the family members, he does not know whether he is helping them as they desire. If that feedback is not analyzed, evaluated, and used to improve one's practice, the opportunity is lost to learn from experience and enhance the quality of services — let alone share what has been learned with fellow practitioners. It is therefore important for the therapist or agency to conduct research on the effectiveness of his therapy efforts.

Conducting post-therapy evaluation. Information about effectiveness and outcome may be secured by a post-therapy questionnaire or evaluation form. This questionnaire or form can be mailed to the family members after three or six months and then every year after that for two or three years. The family members should have been prepared for these research activities. The therapist should inform them during the opening phase that he will request their participation in a research project when therapy is concluded. This information should be repeated in the final session. A cover letter can be enclosed with the post-therapy evaluation form that explains its purpose and requests the family members to complete it.

Such a questionnaire or form is not typically a scientific instrument. However, the former clients' replies offer the therapist some information about his effectiveness, as imperfect as that information may be. He may learn something from this activity, including how to conduct more effective outcome research and how to better help the family members who come to him for therapy. For this purpose, the therapist may employ objective or open-ended instruments that inquire about family interaction and obtain the perceptions of different family members, such as Hurvitz's Marital Roles Scale Inventory (Hurvitz, 1965).

The Therapist's Social Responsibility

Family therapists made a great step forward when they recognized and acknowledged that each family member must be helped to change in order to enable another family member to change. In the process of helping another family member to change, each must change himself. The family therapy group is a constellation of relationships, all of which change together. This fosters a new perspective for the family members—one which they learn and achieve together.

And yet, even as the therapist helps all the members to change, the family remains in the society of the American Dream. Re-read Chapter One. Consider the effects that striving for the contradictory goals and values of the American Dream have had on you, the members of your family, and the members of families who come to you for help. Consider the competition that fosters aggressive individualism, cheating, the exploitation of others, and the concern that others will cheat and exploit us. Consider the contradictory demands of obeying traditional authority and "looking out for Number One" that lead us to doing one thing while believing and saying another. A pervasive fear of violence and hostility embraces people. It is exacerbated by alarm about nuclear or ecological cataclysm which is reinforced by the dread news and normal irritations of everyday life.

When people have life experiences that disturb their ability to interact effectively and satisfyingly or when they cannot participate in social acts as significant others, they turn to therapists for assistance. The therapist must be aware of and concerned about the values and conditions that our society uses to motivate its members. Therefore, marriage and family problems cannot be seen apart from other problems of the society as a whole. The therapist must participate in preventative programs of education for marriage and similar activities presented earlier in this chapter. He must accept responsibility for fostering programs of social change as an aspect of his situational change activities (Edelman, 1987).

Some may object that this activity is foreign to the therapist's function. Our reply is, "Yes, such an activity has traditionally been foreign to the therapist's function. But must we be beholden to a tradition that has outlived its usefulness?" The therapist must recognize that, while he or she works with one family at a time, the society in which we live is creating families with more problems and more serious problems than he can help in a lifetime. Therapists can justify our one-by-one therapeutic activities only when we recognize and acknowledge that our most intensive therapeutic activity is helping to change the society which creates individuals and families with problems.

Bibliography

Ackerman, N. W. (1958). *The psychodynamics of family life: Diagnosis and treatment of family relationships*. New York: Basic Books.

Adler, A. (1938). *Social interest*. London: Garber & Farber.

Adler, P. A. & Adler, P. (1989). The glorified self: The aggrandizement and the constriction of self. *Social Psychology Quarterly*, *52*, 299-310.

Araoz, D. (1985). *The new hypnosis*. New York: Brunner/Mazel.

Araoz, D. & Negley-Parker, E. (1988). *The new hypnosis in family therapy*. New York: Brunner/Mazel.

Azrin, N. H., Naster, B. J., & Jones, R. (1973). Reciprocity counseling: A rapid learning-based procedure for marital counseling. *Behavior Research and Therapy*, *11*, 365-382.

Balch, R. (1979). Two models of conversion and commitment in a UFO cult. Presented at the annual meeting of the Pacific Sociological Association, Anaheim, CA.

Bandura, A. (1969). *Principles of behavior modification*. New York: Holt, Rinehart & Winston.

Bandura, A. (1986). *The social foundations of thought and action*. Englewood Cliffs, NJ: Prentice-Hall Press.

Barber, T. X. (1979). Training studies to use self-suggestions for personal growth: Methods and word-by-word instructions. *Journal of Suggestive-accelerative Learning and Teaching*, *4*, 111-128.

Barber, T. X. (1988). Foreword to R. Straus, *Strategic self-hypnosis*. (Rev ed). New York: Prentice-Hall Press.

Barber, T. X. (1982). Hypnosis, deep relaxation and active relaxation: Data, theory and clinical applications. In P. Lehrer & R. Woofolk (Eds.), *Clinical guide to stress management*. New York: Guilford.

Barber, T. X. (1983). Hypnosuggestive procedures as catalysts for all psychotherapies. In S. Lynn & J. Garske (Eds.), *Contemporary psychotherapies: Models and methods*. Columbus, OH: Charles Merrill.

Barber, T. X., Spanos, N., & Chaves, J. (1974). *Hypnosis, imagination and human potentialities*. New York: Pergamon.

Bateson, G. (1972). *Steps toward an ecology of mind*. New York: Ballantine.

Bateson, G. (1979). *Mind and nature*. New York: Dutton.

Beck, A. T. (1976). *Cognitive therapy and the emotional disorders*. New York: International Universities Press.

Beck, A. T. (1988). *Love is never enough*. New York: Harper & Row.

Beck, D. F. & Jones, M. A. (1973). *Progress on family problems*. New York: Family Service Association of America.

Bell, R. (1977). *Having it your way: The strategy of settling everyday conflicts*. New York: Norton.

Berger, P. & Luckmann, T. (1966). *The social construction of reality: A treatise in the sociology of knowledge*. Garden City, NY: Anchor.

Bernard, J. (1982). *The female world*. New York: Free Press.

Blau, P. (1964). *Exchange and power in social life*. New York: Wiley.

Blumer, H. (1969). *Symbolic interaction: Perspective and method*. Englewood Cliffs, NJ: Prentice-Hall.

Bowen, M. (1976). Theory in the practice of psychotherapy. In P. Guerin (Ed.), *Family therapy*. New York: Gardner.

Bowers, K. (1983). *Hypnosis for the seriously curious*. New York: Norton.

Burns, D. (1980). *Feeling good: The new mood therapy*. New York: Signet.

Carpenter, F. (1984). *The Skinner primer: Beyond freedom and dignity*. New York: The Free Press.

Charon, J. (1989). *Symbolic interactionism: An introduction, an intepretation, an integration*. (3rd ed.). Englewood Cliffs, NJ: Prentice-Hall.

Chilman, C. (Ed.). (1988). *Variant family forms*. Newbury Park, CA: Sage.

Church, N. (1985). Sociotherapy with married couples: Incorporating dramaturgical and social constructionist elements of marital interaction. *Clinical Sociology Review, 3*, 116-128.

Cohen, H. (1985). Sociology and you: Good living. In R. Straus (Ed.), *Using sociology: An introduction from the clinical perspective*. Bayside, NY: General-Hall.

Cohen, H. (1986). *Connections: Understanding social relationships*. Ames, IA: Iowa State University Press.

Coleman, R. & Rainwater, L., with McClelland, K. A. (1978). *Social standing in America: New dimensions of class*. New York: Basic Books.

Cooley, C. H. (1902). *Human nature and the social order*. New York: Scribner's.

Cooley, C. H. (1908). *Social organization*. New York: Scribner's.

Coser, L. (1956). *The social functions of conflict*. Glencoe, IL: Free Press.

Dawes, R. (1988). *Rational choice in an uncertain world*. New York: Harcourt Brace Jovanovich.

Duhl, B. (1983). *From the inside out and other metaphors: Creative and integrative approaches to training in systems thinking*. New York: Brunner/Mazel.

Edelman, M. (1987). *Families in peril: An agenda for social change*. Cambridge, MA: Harvard University Press.

Edmonston, W. (1981). *Hypnosis and relaxation*. New York: Wiley.

Edmonston, W. (1988). *The induction of hypnosis*. New York: Wiley.

Elkin, F. & Handel, G. (1988). *The child and society*. (5th ed). New York: Random House.

Ellis A. (1974). *Humanistic psychotherapy: The rational-emotional therapy approach*. New York: McGraw-Hill.

Ellis, A. (1984). *Reason and emotion in psychotherapy*. New York: Citadel.

Ellis A. & Grieger, R. (Eds.). (1977). *Handbook of rational-emotional therapy*. New York: Springer.

Eppstein, N., et al. (1988). *Cognitive-behavioral therapy with families*. New York: Brunner/Mazel.

Erickson, M. (1980). *The collected papers of Milton H. Erickson*. E. Rossi (Ed.). New York: Irvington.

Erickson, M., Rossi, E., & Rossi, I. (1976). *Hypnotic realities: The induction of clinical hypnosis and forms of indirect suggestion*. New York: Irvington.

Falloon, I. R. H. (Ed.). (1988). *Handbook of behavioral family therapy*. New York: Guilford.

Festinger, L. (1957). *A theory of cognitive dissonance*. Evanston, IL: Row, Peterson.

Festinger, L. (1964). *Conflict, decision, and dissonance*. Stanford, CA: Stanford University Press.

Fezler, W. (1989). *Creative visualization*. New York: Simon & Schuster.

Fisch, R., Weakland, J., & Segal, L. (1982). *The tactics of change*. San Francisco: Jossey-Bass.

Foley, V. C. (1975). Family therapy with black, disadvantaged families: Some observations on roles, communication, and technique. *Journal of Marriage and Family Counseling, 1*, 29-38.

Freedman J. & Rosenfeld, P. (1983). Clinical sociology: The system as client. Paper presented at the joint meetings of the Eastern Sociological Society and Clinical Sociology Association, Baltimore, MD.

Freeman, M. (1979). Snapshot: Enrico Jones/psychotherapy for blacks by blacks or whites/Washington, DC. *APA Monitor*, November, p. 13.

Fullmer, D. (1975). Comments on Hurvitz: The Miller family: Illustrating the symbolic interactionist approach to family therapy. *The Counseling Psychologist, 5*, 3, 57-109.

Gaines, T. & Stedman, J. M. (1979). Influences of separate interviews on the clinician's evaluative perceptions in family therapy. *Journal of Consulting and Clinical Psychology, 47*, 1138-1139.

Gambrill, E. D. (1977). *Behavior modification: Handbook of assessment, intervention and evaluation*. San Francisco: Jossey-Bass.

Garfinkle, H. (1967). *Studies in ethnomethodology*. Englewood Cliffs, NJ: Prentice-Hall.

Gerth, H. & Mills, C. W. (1946). *From Max Weber: Essays in sociology*. New York: Oxford University Press.

Gibbons, D. (1979). *Applied hypnosis and hyperemperia*. New York: Plenum.

Gilbert, D. & Kahl, J. (1982). *The American class structure: A new synthesis*. Homewood, IL: Dorsey.

Glaser, B. & Strauss, A. (1967). *The discovery of grounded theory*. Chicago: Aldine.

Glassner, B. & Freedman, J. (1979). *Clinical sociology*. New York: Longman.

Goffman, E. (1959). *The presentation of self in everyday life*. Garden City, NY: Doubleday.

Goffman, E. (1961). *Asylums*. Garden City, NY: Anchor.

Goffman, E. (1967). *Interaction ritual*. Garden City, NY: Anchor.

Goldstein, A. P. & Kanfer, F. H. (Eds.). (1979). *Maximizing treatment gains: Transfer enhancement in psychotherapy*. New York: Academic Press.

Goode, W. (1982). *The family*. (2nd ed). Englewood Cliffs, NJ: Prentice-Hall.

Gottman, J. M. (1979). *Marital interaction: Experimental investigations*. New York: Academic Press.

Graziano, A. M. (1971). *Behavior therapy with children*. Chicago: Aldine.

Haley, J. (1981). *Reflections on therapy and other essays*. Chevy Chase, MD: Family Therapy Institute of Washington, DC.

Hall, C. M. (1989). Triadic analysis: A conceptual tool for clinical sociologists. *Clinical Sociology*, 7, 97-110.

Hall, W. (1985). Crime, deviance and the sociological imagination. In R. Straus (Ed.), *Using sociology: An introduction from the clinical perspective*. Bayside, NY: General-Hall.

Hallowitz, D. (1975). Counseling and treatment of the poor black family. *Social Casework*, 56, 8-13.

Handel, W. (1982). *Ethnomethodology: How people make sense*. Englewood Cliffs, NJ: Prentice-Hall.

Hickok, J. E. & Komecheck, M. G. (1974). Behavior modification in marital conflict: A case report. *Family Process*, 13, 111-119.

Ho, M. K. (1987). *Family therapy with ethnic minorities*. Newbury Park, CA: Sage.

Homans, G. C. (1961). *Social behavior: Its elementary forms*. New York: Harcourt, Brace & World.

Horner, B. (1979). Symbolic interactionism and social assessment. *Journal of Sociology and Social Welfare*, 6, 19-33.

House, J., Landis, K., & Umberson, D. (1988). Social relationships and health. *Science, 241*, 540-544.

Howe, L. (1978). Psychomotor: A symbolic interactionist form of socio-physio-psychotherapy. *MSA Newsletter*, Summer.

Hurvitz, N. (1950). The relationship in Jewish center practice. *Jewish Social Service Quarterly, 26*, 450-456.

Hurvitz, N. (1951a). Sources of motivation and achievement in American Jews. *Jewish Social Studies, 23*, 217-234.

Hurvitz, N. (1951b). Understanding the self-hate of Jewish young adults. *Reconstructionist, 18*, 18-24.

Hurvitz, N. (1958). Sources of middle-class values of American Jews. *Social Forces, 37*, 117-123.

Hurvitz, N. (1959a). A scale for the measurement of superordinate-subordinate roles in marriage. *American Catholic Sociological Review, 20*, 234-241.

Hurvitz, N. (1959b). The index of strain as a measure of marital satisfaction. *Sociology and Social Research, 44*, 106-111.

Hurvitz, N. (1959c). The roles of the American wife and mother. *Bulletin of Maternal and Infant Health, 7*(2), 17-19.

Hurvitz, N. (1959d). The significance of discrepancies between the scores of spouses on a marital adjustment scale. *The Deltan, 29*(2), 45-48.

Hurvitz, N. (1960a). The concept of role in family life education. *Forecast for Home Economists, 76*, 14-17.

Hurvitz, N. (1960b). The marital roles scale inventory and the measurement of marital adjustment. *Journal of Clinical Psychology, 16*, 377-380.

Hurvitz, N. (1960c). The measurement of marital strain. *American Journal of Sociology, 65*, 610-615.

Hurvitz, N. (1961a). *Marital roles inventory*. Beverly Hills, CA: Western Psychological Services.

Hurvitz, N. (1961b). The components of marital roles. *Sociology and Social Research, 45*, 301-309.

Hurvitz, N. (1964). Marital strain in the blue-collar family. In A. Shostak & W. Gomberg (Eds.), *Blue collar world: Studies of the American worker*. Englewood Cliffs, NJ: Prentice-Hall.

Hurvitz, N. (1965a). Control roles, marital strain, role deviation, and marital adjustment. *Journal of Marriage and the Family, 27,* 29-31.

Hurvitz, N. (1965b). Marital role strain as a sociological variable. *Family Life Coordinator, 14*(2), 39-42.

Hurvitz, N. (1965c). The marital roles inventory as a counseling instrument. *Journal of Marriage and the Family, 27,* 492-501.

Hurvitz, N. (1967). Marital problems following psychotherapy with one spouse. *Journal of Consulting Psychology, 31,* 38-47.

Hurvitz, N. (1968). How the psychotherapist can assist the attorney in rehabilitating broken marriages. In N. Kohut (Ed.), *Therapeutic family law: A complete guide to marital reconciliations.* Chicago: Family Law Publications.

Hurvitz, N. (1970a). Husbands and wives: Middle-class and working-class. In H. Hughes (Ed.), *Sociological resources for social studies.* Boston: Allyn and Bacon.

Hurvitz, N. (1970b). Interaction hypotheses in marriage counseling. *Family Coordinator, 19,* 64-75.

Hurvitz, N. (1970c). Peer self-help psychotherapy groups and their implications for psychotherapy. *Psychotherapy: Theory, Research and Practice, 7,* 41-49.

Hurvitz, N. (1972a). Symbolic interactionism and behavior modification: A social psychological theory for psychological change. *Abstract Guide of the 20th International Congress of Psychology, Tokyo, Japan,* 658.

Hurvitz, N. (1972b). Symbolic interactionism: A social psychological theory for marriage and family counseling. *Proceedings of the 80th Annual Convention of the American Psychological Association, Washington, DC,* 853-854.

Hurvitz, N. (1973a). Problems, predicaments, and conflicts in marriage and family counseling. Presented at the 35th Annual Convention of the American Association of Marriage and Family Counselors, Palm Springs, CA.

Hurvitz, N. (1973b). Psychotherapy as a means of social control. *Journal of Consulting and Clinical Psychology, 40,* 232-239.

Hurvitz, N. (1973c). Transactional analysis and radical therapy: A critique. *Issues in Radical Therapy, 1,* 21-23.

Hurvitz, N. (1974a). Manifest and latent functions in psychotherapy. *Journal of Consulting and Clinical Psychology, 42,* 301-302.

Hurvitz, N. (1974b). Peer self-help psychotherapy groups: Psychotherapy without psychotherapists. In R. Roman & H. Trice (Eds.), *The sociology of psychotherapy.* New York: Aronson.

Hurvitz, N. (1975). The Miller family: Illustrating the symbolic interactionist approach to family therapy. *The Counseling Psychologist, 5,* 57-109.

Hurvitz, N. (1976). The origins of the peer self-help psychotherapy group movement. *Journal of Applied Behavioral Science, 12,* 283-294.

Hurvitz, N. (1977a). Problems in living and psychotherapy: An alternative view. *The Clinical Psychologist, 31,* 19-21.

Hurvitz, N. (1977b). Similarities and differences betwen conventional and peer self-help psychotherapy groups (PSHGs). In A. Gartner & F. Reissman, *Self-help in the human services.* San Francisco: Jossey-Bass.

Hurvitz, N. (1977c). The status and tasks of radical therapy. *Psychotherapy: Theory, Research and Practice, 14,* 65-73.

Hurvitz, N. (1978a). The mental patients' rights and liberation movement. *ACT/ACTION, 125,* 10-13.

Hurvitz, N. (1978b). "We'd rather do it ourselves!" A people's movement for mental health rejects professional assistance. *Journal of Voluntary Action Research, 6,* 69-72.

Hurvitz, N. (1979a). The sociologist as a marital and family therapist. *American Behavioral Scientist, 22,* 557-576.

Hurvitz, N. (1979b). The radical psychotherapist and the American Dream. *Voices: The Art and Science of Psychotherapy, 14,* 66-75.

Hurvitz, N. (1979c). The significant other in marital and family therapy. *Journal of Sociology and Social Welfare, 6,* 122-143.

Hutter, M. (1985). *The changing family: Comparative perspectives.* (2nd ed). New York: Macmillan.

Jacobsen, E. (1974). *Progressive relaxation.* (3rd rev. ed). Chicago: University of Chicago Press.

Keniston, K., Carnegie Council on Children. (1977). *All our children: The American family under pressure.* New York: Harcourt Brace Jovanovitch.

Knox, D. (1971). *Marriage happiness: A behavioral approach to counseling*. Champaign, IL: Research Press.

Kobasa, S. C. (1981). The hardy personality: Toward a social psychology of stress and health. In J. Suls & G. Sanders (Eds.), *Social psychology of health and illness*. Hillsdale, NJ: Erlbaum.

Kornhauser, W. (1962). Social bases of political commitment. In A. M. Rose (Ed.), *Human behavior and social processes*. Boston: Houghton Mifflin.

Korzybski, A. (1980). *Science and Sanity*. (4th ed). Lakewood, CT: General Semantics Press.

Krause, J. (1986). Symbolic interactionism and interactional family therapy. *Humboldt Journal of Social Relations*, *12*, 2, 48-77.

Kroger, W. (1977). *Clinical and experimental hypnosis*. (2nd ed.). Philadelphia: Lippincott.

Kroger, W. & Fezler, W. (1976). *Hypnosis and behavior modification: Imagery conditioning*. Philadelphia: Lippincott.

Kromboltz, J. D. & Krumboltz, H. B. (1972). *Changing children's behavior*. Englewood Cliffs, NJ: Prentice-Hall.

Lankton, S. & Lankton, M. (1986). *Enchantment and intervention in family therapy: Training in Ericksonian approaches*. New York: Brunner/Mazel.

Lankton, S. & Lankton, M. (1983). *A clinical framework of Ericksonian hypnotherapy*. New York: Brunner/Mazel.

LaRossa, R. (Ed). (1984). Introduction. *Family Case Studies*. New York: Free Press.

Lederer, W. J. & Jackson, D. D. (1968). *The mirages of marriage*. New York: Norton.

Lee, A. M. (1988). *Sociology for people: Toward a caring profession*. Syracuse, NY: Syracuse University Press.

Levant, R. (1984). *Family therapy: A comprehensive overview*. Englewood Cliffs, NJ: Prentice-Hall.

Lipman-Blumen, J. (1984). *Gender roles and power*. Englewood Cliffs, NJ: Prentice-Hall.

Lofland, J. (1976). *Doing social life: The qualitative study of human interaction in natural settings*. New York: Wiley-Interscience.

Lofland, J. (1984). *Analyzing social settings*. Belmont, CA: Wadsworth.

Lofland, J. & Stark, R. (1965). Becoming a world saver: A theory of conversion to a deviant perspective. *American Sociological Review, 30,* 862-75.

McCall, G. & Simmons, J. L. (1978). *Identities and interaction.* (2nd ed.). New York: Free Press.

Maslow, A. (1970). *Motivation and personality.* (Rev ed). New York: Harper & Row.

Mead, G. H. (1934). *Mind, self and society.* Chicago: University of Chicago.

Meichenbaum, D. (1978). *Cognitive-behavior modification: An integrative approach.* New York: Plenum.

Merton, R. K. (1968). *Social theory and social structure.* (Expanded ed.). New York: Free Press.

Mills, C. W. (1940). Situated action and vocabularies of motive. *American Sociological Review, 5,* 904-13.

Mills, C. W. (1956). *The power elite.* New York: Oxford University Press.

Mills, C. W. (1959). *The sociological imagination.* New York: Oxford University Press.

Mills, C. W. (1963). I. L. Horowitz (Ed). *Power, politics and people.* New York: Oxford University Press.

Minuchin, S. (1974). *Families and family therapy.* Cambridge, MA: Harvard University Press.

Moreno, J. (1972 and 1975). *Psychodrama.* (Vol. I, II, & III). Beacon, NY: Beacon.

Moreno, Z. (1975). *A study of psychodramatic techniques.* Beacon, NY: Beacon.

Nadelson, C. C. (1978). Marital therapy. In T. J. Paolino, Jr. & B. S. McCredy (Eds.), *Marriage and marital therapy: Psychoanalytic, behavioral and systems theory perspectives.* New York: Brunner/Mazel.

Neisser, U. (1976). *Cognition and reality: Principles and implications of cognitive psychology.* San Francisco: W. H. Freeman.

Newman, K. S. (1988). *Falling from grace: The experience of downward mobility in the American middle class.* New York: Free Press.

Nye, F. I. (1978). Is choice and exchange theory the key? *Journal of Marriage and the Family, 40,* 219-233.

Parsons, T. (1951). *The social system*. Glencoe, IL: Free Press.

Patterson, G. R. (1975). *Application of social learning to family life*. (Rev. ed.). Champaign, IL: Research Press.

Patterson, G. R. & Reid, J. B. (1970). Reciprocity and coercion: Two facets of social systems. In C. Neuringer & J. L. Michael (Eds.), *Behavior modification in clinical psychology*. New York: Appleton-Century-Crofts.

Pepper, S. (1942). *World hypotheses*. Berkeley, CA: University of California Press.

Pilusuk, M. & Parks, S. H. (1986). *The healing web: Social networks and human survival*. Hanover, NH: University Press of New England.

Reid, W. (1985). *Family problem solving*. New York: Columbia University Press.

Reiss, D. (1981). *The family's construction of reality*. Cambridge, MA: Harvard University Press.

Rice, T. (1985). American public policy formation and implementation. In R. Straus (Ed.), *Using sociology: An introduction from the clinical perspective*. Bayside, NY: General-Hall.

Robinette, P. D. & Harris, R. A. (1989). A conflict resolution model amenable to sociological practice. *Clinical Sociology Review*, 7, 127-140.

Rubin, L. B. (1975). *Worlds of pain: Life in the working-class family*. New York: Basic Books.

Rubin, L. B. (1984). *Intimate strangers*. New York: Harper.

Rubin, L. B. (1990). *Erotic wars: What happened to the sexual revolution?* New York: Farrar, Straus & Giroux.

Ryan, W. (1971). *Blaming the victim*. New York: Pantheon.

Sarbin, T. R. (1977). Contextualism: A world view for modern psychology. In A. Landsfield (Ed.), *1976 Nebraska symposium on motivation*. Lincoln: University of Nebraska Press.

Sarbin, T. R. (1984). The reconstruction of hypnosis. *Annual Review of the International Society for Professional Hypnosis*, 2, 1-27.

Sarbin, T. R. & Coe, W. C. (1972). *Hypnosis: A social-psychological analysis of influence communication*. New York: Holt, Rinehart, & Winston.

Satir, V. (1982). *Conjoint family therapy: A guide to theory and technique*. (3rd rev. ed). Palo Alto, CA: Science & Behavior Books.

Satir, V. (1972). *Peoplemaking*. Palo Alto, CA: Science & Behavior Books.

Schorr, J. E. (Ed.). (1980). *Imagery: Its many dimensions and applications*. New York: Brunner/Mazel.

Seltzer, L. A. (1986). *Paradoxical strategies in psychotherapy*. New York: Wiley.

Shibutani, T. (1954). Reference groups as perspectives. *American Sociological Review*, *60*, 562-569.

Simmel, G. (1964). *The sociology of Georg Simmel*. New York: Free Press.

Siporin, M. (1980a). Ecological systems theory in social work. *Journal of Sociology and Social Welfare*, *7*, 507-32.

Siporin, M. (1980b). Marriage and family therapy in social work. *Social Casework: The Journal of Contemporary Social Work*, *61*, 11-21.

Skinner, B. F. (1965). *Science and human behavior*. New York: Free Press.

Star, A. (1977). *Psychodrama: Rehearsal for living*. Chicago: Nelson-Hall.

Steinmetz, S. K. (1988). *Family and support systems across the lifespan*. New York: Plenum.

Stone, G. (1962). Appearance and the self. In A. M. Rose (Ed.), *Human behavior and social process*. Boston: Houghton Mifflin.

Stone, G. & Farberman, H. (1981). *Social psychology through symbolic interaction*. (2nd ed.). New York: Wiley.

Stover, S. S. (1977). Convergences between symbolic interactionism and systems theory. *Symbolic Interaction*, *1*, 89-103.

Straus, R. A. (1977). The life-change process: Weight loss and other enterprises of personal transformation with particular emphasis on hypnosis, behavior modification and Scientology. (Doctoral dissertation, University of California, Davis). *Dissertation Abstracts*, *30*.

Straus, R. A. (1978). Hypnosis as reality reconstruction. *Pacific Sociogical Review*, *21*, 407-422.

Straus, R. A. (Ed.). (1979a). Clinical sociology, a special issue of the *American Behavioral Scientist*, *22*(4).

Straus, R. A. (1979b). Clinical sociology, an idea whose time has come . . . again. *Sociological Practice*, *3*, 21-42.

Straus, R. A. (1979c). Doing clinical sociology in behavioral counseling: A model weight management program. *Case Analysis*, *1*, 181-201.

Straus, R. A. (1981a). A naturalistic experiment investigating the effects of hypnotic induction on Creative Imagination Scale performance in a clinical setting. *International Journal of Clinical and Experimental Hypnosis*, *XVIII*, 218-224.

Straus, R. A. (1981b). The theoretical frame of symbolic interaction: A contextualist social science. *Symbolic Interaction*, *4*(2), 61-72.

Straus, R. A. (1982). Clinical sociology on the one-to-one level: A social-behavioral approach. *Clinical Sociology Review*, *1*, 59-74.

Straus, R. A. (Ed.). (1985a). *Using sociology: An introduction from the clinical perspective*. Bayside, NY: General-Hall.

Straus, R. A. (1985b). Using social theory to make sense out of life. In R. Straus (Ed.), *Using sociology: An introduction from the clinical perspective*. Bayside, NY: General-Hall.

Straus, R. A. (1986a). Non-coercive persuasion: Theory and practice of strategic reality reconstruction. *Sociological Viewpoints*, *2*, 1-14.

Straus, R. A. (1986b). Simple games for teaching sociological perspectives. *Teaching Sociology*, *14*, 119-28.

Straus, R. A. (1987). The theoretical basis of clinical sociology: Four paradigms. *Clinical Sociology Review*, *5*, 65-82.

Straus, R. A. (1988). *Strategic self-hypnosis*. (Rev. Ed.). New York: Prentice-Hall Press.

Straus, R. A. (1989a). *Creative self-hypnosis*. New York: Prentice-Hall Press.

Straus, R. A. (1989b). Changing the definition of the situation: A theory of sociological interventions. *Sociological Practice*, *7*, 123-135.

Straus, R. & See, P. (1985). The sociology of the individual. In R. Straus (Ed.), *Using sociology: An introduction from the clinical perspective*. Bayside, NY: General-Hall.

Stryker, S. (1968). Identity salience and role performance. *Journal of Marriage and the Family, 30*, 558-64.

Stryker, S. (1980). *Symbolic interactionism.* Menlo Park, CA: Cummings.

Stuart, R. B. (1969). Operant-interpersonal treatment of marital discord. *Journal of Consulting and Clinical Psychology, 33*, 675-682.

Stuart, R. B. (1980). *Helping couples change: A social learning approach to marital therapy.* New York: Guilford.

Sussman, M. B. & Steinmetz, S. K. (1987). *Handbook of marriage and the family.* New York: Plenum.

Tennov, D. (1976). *Psychotherapy: The hazardous cure.* Garden City, NY: Anchor.

Thomas, W. I. & Thomas, D. S. (1928). *The child in America: Behavior problems and programs.* New York: Knopf.

Toby, J. (1983). Crime in the schools. In J. A. Wilson (Ed.), *Crime and public policy.* New Brunswick, NJ: Transaction.

Tugender, H. & Ferinden, W. (1975). *An introduction to hypno-operant therapy.* Orange, NJ: Power.

Turner, J. (1986). *The structure of sociological theory.* (4th ed.). Chicago: Dorsey.

Turner, R. (1976). The real self: From institution to impulse. *American Journal of Sociology, 81*, 986-1016.

Turner, R. (1978). The role and the person. *American Journal of Sociology, 84*, 1-23.

Vail, A. (1978). Factors influencing lower-class Black patients remaining in treatment. *Journal of Consulting and Clinical Psychology, 46*, 341.

Voelkl, G. & Colburn, K. (1984). The clinical sociologist as family therapist: Using the strategic communication approach. *Clinical Sociology Review, 2*, 64-77.

Von Bertalanffy, L. (1968). *General systems theory.* New York: George Braziller.

Weiss, R. L., Hope, H., & Patterson, G. R. (1973). A framework for conceptualizing marital conflict, a technology for altering it, some data for evaluating it. In L. A. Hamerlynck, L. G. Handy & E. J. Mash (Eds.), *Behavior change: Methodology, concepts and practice.* Champaign, IL: Research Press.

Weitzenhoffer, A. M. (1989). *The practice of hypnotism*. New York: Wiley.

Williams, R. (1970). *American society: A sociological interpretation*. (3rd Ed.). New York: Knopf.

Williams, J. M. G. (1984). *The psychological treatment of depression: A guide to the theory and practice of cognitive-behaviour therapy*. New York: Free Press.

Willie, C. (1981). *A new look at black families*. (2nd ed.). Bayside, NY: General-Hall.

Willie, C. (1985). *Black and white families: A study in complementarity*. Bayside, NY: General-Hall.

Willie, C. (1989). *Caste and class controversy: Round two of the Willie/Wilson debate*. (2nd ed.). Bayside, NY: General-Hall.

Wilson, W. J. (1987). *The truly disadvantaged: The inner city, the under-class and public policy*. Chicago: University of Chicago Press.

Wirth, L. (1931). Clinical sociology. *American Journal of Sociology*, *37*, 49-66.

Wirth, L. (1945). The problem of minority groups. In R. Linton, *The science of man in the world crisis*. New York: Columbia University Press.

Wirth, L. (1951). Preface. Karl Mannheim. *Ideology and utopia: An introduction to the sociology of knowledge*. New York: Harcourt Brace.

Yablonsky, L. (1976). *Psychodrama: Resolving emotional problems through role-playing*. New York: Basic Books.

Zaretsky, E. (1976). *Capitalism, the family and personal life*. New York: Harper & Row.

Zarski, J. J., Sweeney, T. J. & Barcikowski, R. S. (1977). Counseling effectiveness as a function of counselor social interest. *Journal of Counseling Psychology*, *24*, 1-5.

Zilbergeld, B. (1984). *Male Sexuality*. New York: Bantam.

Index

Culture
  American Dream and, 19-21
  definition, 18
  familial, 54-55

Decision-making, 136-137
  case examples, 137-143
  definition, 136
Defection, from family, 66
Devil's advocate technique, 175-176
Discrimination, racial, 12-13
Discussion, therapeutic, 34-39
  accounts concept, 37-39,40,41,
    93-97,99
  analytic, 34-35,36
  in cognitive therapy, 172-176
  directed, 35,36
  reflective, 34,36
  two-way, 37
Dissolution, of relationships, 67
Division of labor, sexual, 15
Downward mobility, 18
Dramaturgical interventions, 30-31,
  186-188

Ecological systems perspective, 7
Economy, social structure changes
  and, 17
Ejection, from family, 67
Empowerment, of client, 156-157,
  207
Ethics, of therapist, 207-209
Ethnic consciousness, 13
Ethnicity, 12
Ethnomethodology, 37-39
Exchanges, in social relations, 57

"Face-saving," as bargaining goal,
  148-149
False consciousness, 24
Family
  as co-therapist, 170-171
  gender roles within, 16

hardiness of, 60,61
motives of, 39-40,46
social change and, 18
as social group, 53-80
  conflict within, 64-66,68,76-79
  crisis within, 66-67,68,72-74,
    77-78
  dyad focus, 54
  dynamic aspects, 57-62
  group boundaries, 55
  group structure, 53-54
  as primary group, 55-80
  problems of, 63-64
  problem taxonomy for, 69-80
  as social institution, 24-25
  social status within, 11-12
  therapy involvement, 166-167
Family systems therapy, 6-7
Family therapy
  behaviorist, 57-58
  definition, 4,6
  sociocognitive. *See* sociocognitive
    therapy
Family therapy group, 81-83
Feudal system, 9-10
Four Questions Technique, 50-51,
  84-87,94,104
  bargaining process and, 145
  cognitive therapy and, 172
  family reality evaluation and, 91,
    92
  first appointment and, 102,104
  instrumental hypothesis and, 112
  problem-solving and, 155
  reality reconstruction and, 110
Functionalism, 22-24

Gender differences, 14-15
Gender role, 14-16
Generalized other, 29
Goal(s), 104
  achievement of, 105
  assessment of, 88-91